Oregon State Parks

Travel to all the State Parks in Oregon

This book belongs to _____

Call this number if found _____

My Nature Book Adventures

© 2022 My Nature Book Adventures - All Rights Reserved
www.mynaturebookadventures.com
8th Edition - updated 2022

© 2022 My Nature Book Adventures

All Rights Reserved.

www.mynaturebookadventures.com

ISBN: 978-1-956162-36-3

Designed and printed in the USA.

Copyright © 2022. My Nature Book Adventures, LLC.

This publication is protected under United States and international copyright laws and treaties, and may not be reproduced, publicly displayed, distributed, or derivative works prepared therefrom, without the prior express written permission of My Nature Book Adventures LLC. "My Nature Book Adventures" is a trademark owned by My Nature Book Adventures LLC. All images are used pursuant to license from Adobe Stock and/or Canva, and may not be further used, reproduced, publicly displayed, or distributed without the prior express written permission of the owners of such images.

If you wish to make any use of this publication other than for your own personal use, or to refer to brief excerpts for review purposes, please contact us through the above-referenced website.

Disclaimer

The information in this book is based on the author's opinion, knowledge and experience. The publisher and the author will not be held liable for the use or misuse of the information contained herein.

https://stateparks.oregon.gov

WWW.MYNATUREBOOKADVENTURES.COM

What you will find inside

The **Oregon** Adventure Book is part planner, part journal, and 100% your adventure!

Created to include dedicated space for you to plan your journey and share your experience. Check out each one of the Oregon State Parks and cross them off your MUST DO exploration list. Then look back at the experiences with your family and friends.

Plan your adventures, then share all of the fun!

We have organized each park in alphabetical order, by region, making it a breeze to locate the park you are looking for.

Enjoy all of the natural beauty, unique geological features, and unusual ecosystems the Oregon parks offer us.

Crescent Beach at Ecola State Park, Oregon

Inside your book you will find...

ON THE LEFT SIDE OF EACH 2 PAGE SPREAD, YOU HAVE

A place to plan the details of your trip.

A section for reservation information, including refund policy, reserved dates, address, places to see along the way, places you discovered along the way, and even a place for your confirmation number.

Plus an area to show how far you are traveling.

A fun color-in of the transportation modes you used during your adventures in the park.

A space to attach your favorite postcard, picture, drawing, or ticket stub.

THE RIGHT SIDE INCLUDES PARK INFORMATION AND GIVES YOU A PLACE TO SHARE THE SPECIAL MOMENTS ABOUT YOUR JOURNEY

Park Information

The region the park is located in

The park is close to

Special Moments

Include why you went

Who went with you

When you went

What you did

What you saw

What you learned

An unforgettable moment

A laughable moment

A surprising moment

A unforeseeable moment

Wildlife spotted

Snapped a selfie location

A fun color-in of the weather you experienced during your adventures

Make it all about YOU and your journey!

Also inside is an adventure checklist to make your adventures even more memorable.

We want you to spend every moment of your trip experiencing each and every one of the beautiful Oregon State Parks!

What you will find at the parks

Smith Rock State Park
https://stateparks.oregon.gov

Devil's Punch Bowl State Natural Area

TABLE OF CONTENTS

Central Coast

	Agate Beach State Recreation Site	17
	Alsea Bay Historic Interpretive Center	19
	Beachside State Recreation Site	21
	Beaver Creek State Natural Area	23
	Beverly Beach State Park	25
	Boiler Bay State Scenic Viewpoint	27
	Bolon Island Tideways State Scenic Corridor	29
	Carl G. Washburne Memorial State Park	31
	Darlingtonia State Natural Site	33
	Devils Punch Bowl State Natural Area	35
	Driftwood Beach State Recreation Site	37
	Ellmaker State Wayside	39
	Fogarty Creek State Recreation Area	41
	Gleneden Beach State Recreation Site	43
	Governor Patterson Memorial State Recreation Site	45
	Heceta Head Lighthouse State Scenic Viewpoint	47
	Jessie M. Honeyman Memorial State Park	49
	Lost Creek State Recreation Site	51
	Muriel O. Ponsler Memorial State Scenic Viewpoint	53
	Neptune State Scenic Viewpoint	55
	Ona Beach State Park	57
	Otter Crest State Scenic Viewpoint	59
	Rocky Creek State Scenic Viewpoint	61
	Seal Rock State Recreation Site	63
	Smelt Sands State Recreation Site	65
	South Beach State Park	67
	South Jetty (South Beach)	69
	Stonefield Beach State Recreation Site	71
	Tokatee Klootchman State Natural Site	73
	Umpqua Lighthouse State Park	75
	W. B. Nelson State Recreation Site	77
	Whale Watching Center	79

adventure

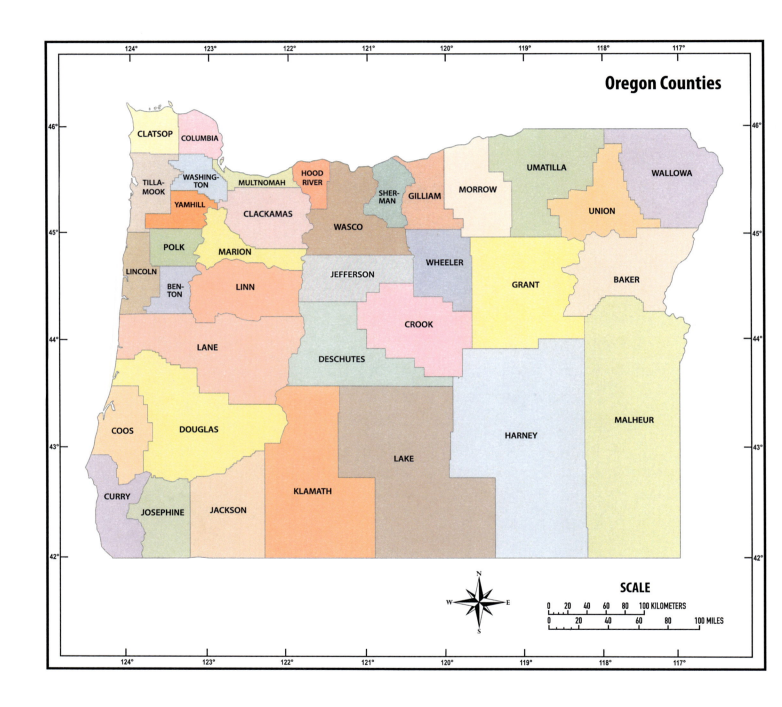

TABLE OF CONTENTS

Yachats Ocean Road State Natural Site	81
Yachats State Recreation Area	83
Yaquina Bay State Recreation Site	85

Central Oregon

Cline Falls State Scenic Viewpoint	87
Cottonwood Canyon State Park	89
Fort Rock Cave (Near Fort Rock State Natural Area)	91
Fort Rock State Natural Area	93
Jasper Point Campground	95
La Pine State Park	97
Ochoco State Scenic Viewpoint	99
Peter Skene Ogden State Scenic Viewpoint	101
Pilot Butte State Scenic Viewpoint	103
Prineville Reservoir State Park	105
Smith Rock State Park	107
The Cove Palisades State Park	109
Tumalo State Park	111

Eastern Oregon

Bates State Park	113
Battle Mountain Forest State Scenic Corridor	115
Blue Mountain Forest State Scenic Corridor	117
Catherine Creek State Park	119
Clyde Holliday State Recreation Site	121
Dyer State Wayside	123
Emigrant Springs State Heritage Area	125
Farewell Bend State Recreation Area	127
Frenchglen Hotel State Heritage Site	129
Hat Rock State Park	131
Hilgard Junction State Recreation Area	133
Iwetemlaykin State Heritage Site	135
Kam Wah Chung State Heritage Site	137
Lake Owyhee State Park	139
Minam State Recreation Area	141

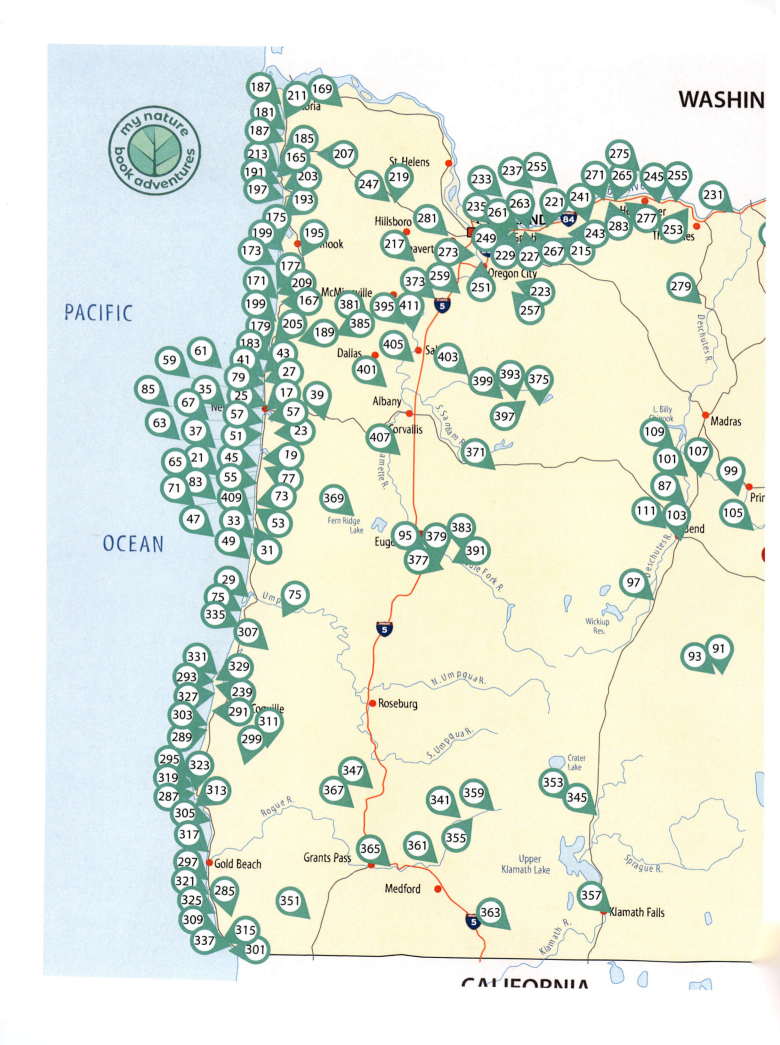

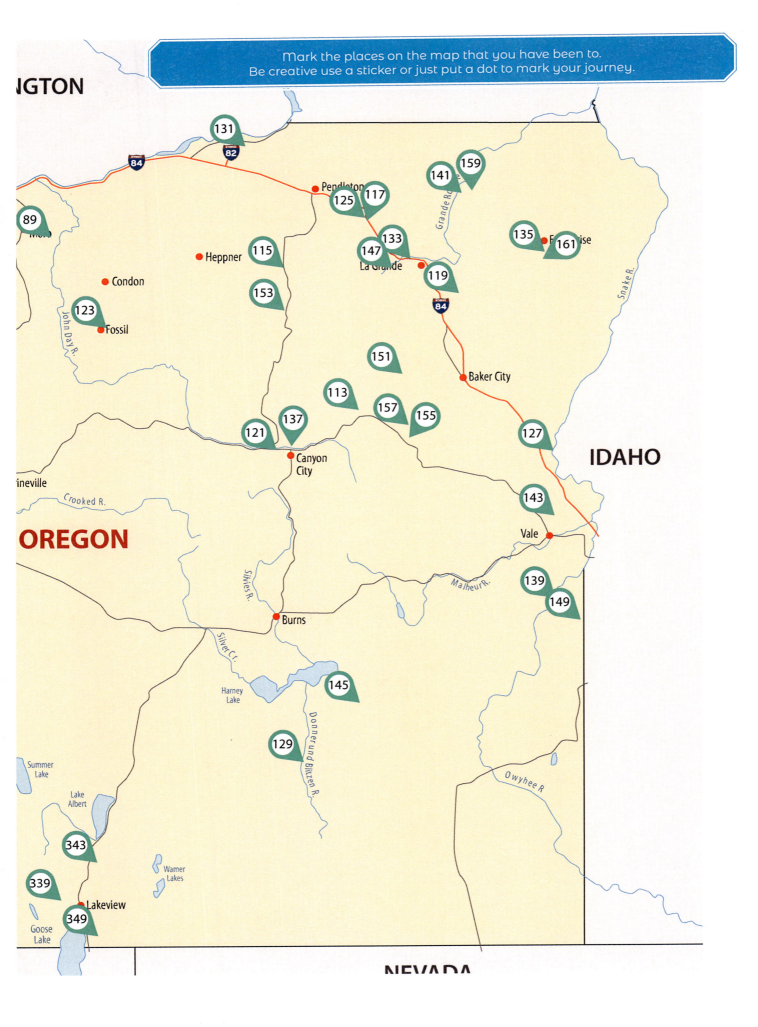

TABLE OF CONTENTS

Ontario State Recreation Site	143
Pete French Round Barn State Heritage Site	145
Red Bridge State Wayside	147
Succor Creek State Natural Area	149
Sumpter Valley Dredge State Heritage Area	151
Ukiah-Dale Forest State Scenic Corridor	153
Unity Forest State Scenic Corridor	155
Unity Lake State Recreation Site	157
Wallowa Lake Highway Forest State Scenic Corridor	159
Wallowa Lake State Recreation Area	161
Wallowa River Rest Area	163

North Coast

Arcadia Beach State Recreation Site	165
Bob Straub State Park	167
Bradley State Scenic Viewpoint	169
Cape Kiwanda State Natural Area	171
Cape Lookout State Park	173
Cape Meares State Scenic Viewpoint	175
Clay Myers State Natural Area at Whalen Island	177
D River State Recreation Site	179
Del Rey Beach State Recreation Site	181
Devils Lake State Recreation Area	183
Ecola State Park	185
Fort Stevens State Park	187
H. B. Van Duzer Forest State Scenic Corridor	189
Hug Point State Recreation Site	191
Manhattan Beach State Recreation Site	193
Munson Creek Falls State Natural Site	195
Nehalem Bay State Park	197
Neskowin Beach State Recreation Site	199
Oceanside Beach State Recreation Site	201
Oswald West State Park	203
Roads End State Recreation Site	205

TABLE OF CONTENTS

Saddle Mountain State Natural Area	207
Sitka Sedge State Natural Area	209
Sunset Beach State Recreation Site	211
Tolovana Beach State Recreation Site	213

Portland/Columbia Gorge

Ainsworth State Park	215
Bald Peak State Scenic Viewpoint	217
Banks-Vernonia State Trail	219
Benson State Recreation Area	221
Bonnie Lure State Recreation Area	223
Bridal Veil Falls State Scenic Viewpoint	225
Crown Point State Scenic Corridor	227
Dabney State Recreation Area	229
Deschutes River State Recreation Area	231
George W. Joseph State Natural Area(accessible from Guy W. Talbot State Park)	233
Government Island State Recreation Area	235
Guy W. Talbot State Park	237
Heritage Landing (Deschutes)	239
Historic Columbia River Highway State Trail	241
John B. Yeon State Scenic Corridor	243
Koberg Beach State Recreation Site	245
L. L. "Stub" Stewart State Park	247
Lewis and Clark State Recreation Site	249
Mary S. Young State Recreation Area	251
Mayer State Park	253
Memaloose State Park	255
Milo McIver State Park	257
Molalla River State Park	259
Portland Women's Forum State Scenic Viewpoint	261
Rooster Rock State Park	263
Seneca Fouts Memorial State Natural Area	265
Shepperd's Dell State Natural Area	267

TABLE OF CONTENTS

	Sheridan State Scenic Corridor	269
	Starvation Creek State Park	271
	Tryon Creek State Natural Area	273
	Viento State Park	275
	Vinzenz Lausmann Memorial State Natural Area	277
	White River Falls State Park	279
	Willamette Stone State Heritage Site	281
	Wygant State Natural Area	283

South Coast

	Alfred A. Loeb State Park	285
	Arizona Beach State Recreation Site	287
	Bandon State Natural Area	289
	Bullards Beach State Park	291
	Cape Arago State Park	293
	Cape Blanco State Park	295
	Cape Sebastian State Scenic Corridor	297
	Coquille Myrtle Grove State Natural Site	299
	Crissey Field State Recreation Site	301
	Face Rock State Scenic Viewpoint	303
	Geisel Monument State Heritage Site	305
	Golden and Silver Falls State Natural Area	307
	Harris Beach State Recreation Area	309
	Hoffman Memorial State Wayside	311
	Humbug Mountain State Park	313
	McVay Rock State Recreation Site	315
	Otter Point State Recreation Site	317
	Paradise Point State Recreation Site	319
	Pistol River State Scenic Viewpoint	321
	Port Orford Heads State Park	323
	Samuel H. Boardman State Scenic Corridor	325
	Seven Devils State Recreation Site	327
	Shore Acres State Park	329
	Sunset Bay State Park	331

TABLE OF CONTENTS

Umpqua State Scenic Corridor	333
William M. Tugman State Park	335
Winchuck State Recreation Site	337

Southern Oregon

Booth State Scenic Corridor	339
Casey State Recreation Site	341
Chandler State Wayside	343
Collier Memorial State Park	345
Golden State Heritage Site	347
Goose Lake State Recreation Area	349
Illinois River Forks State Park	351
Jackson F. Kimball State Recreation Site	353
Joseph H. Stewart State Recreation Area	355
OC&E Woods Line State Trail	357
Prospect State Scenic Viewpoint	359
TouVelle State Recreation Site	361
Tub Springs State Wayside	363
Valley of the Rogue State Recreation Area	365
Wolf Creek Inn State Heritage Site	367

Willamette Valley

Alderwood State Wayside	369
Cascadia State Park	371
Champoeg State Heritage Area	373
Detroit Lake State Recreation Area	375
Dexter State Recreation Site	377
Elijah Bristow State Park	379
Erratic Rock State Natural Site	381
Fall Creek State Recreation Site	383
Fort Yamhill State Heritage Area	385
Holman State Wayside	387
Jasper State Recreation Site	389
Lowell State Recreation Site	391
Maples Rest Area	393
Maud Williamson State Recreation Site	395

What you will find at the parks

The sun sets over the Pacific at Cape Lookout State Park, Oregon
https://stateparks.oregon.gov

Natural Bridge | Samuel H. Boardman State Scenic Corridor

Table of Contents

- Mongold Day-Use Area — 397
- North Santiam State Recreation Area — 399
- Sarah Helmick State Recreation Site — 401
- Silver Falls State Park — 403
- State Capitol State Park — 405
- Thompson's Mills State Heritage Site — 407
- Washburne State Wayside — 409
- Willamette Mission State Park — 411

Lower Soda Creek Falls in Cascadia State Park near Sweet Home, Oregon

What you will find at the parks

Silver Falls State Park
https://stateparks.oregon.gov

Seal Rock Beach on the Oregon Coast

Adventure List

- [ ] Go on a nature scavenger hunt
- [ ] Perfect your bird calls
- [ ] Have a breakfast picnic
- [ ] Go horseback riding
- [ ] Snap a selfie at a park entrance sign
- [ ] Help Someone become a Jr Ranger
- [ ] Go RVing
- [ ] Take a ranger-led tour
- [ ] Splash in a waterfall
- [ ] Stop at scenic overlooks
- [ ] Hunt for fossils
- [ ] Look for EarthCache sites
- [ ] Canoe along a river
- [ ] Go on a photography walk
- [ ] Take a nature hike
- [ ] Hunt for animal tracks
- [ ] Go kayaking
- [ ] Try rock climbing
- [ ] Visit a nature center
- [ ] Watch the sunset
- [ ] Ride a bike
- [ ] Try a night sky program
- [ ] Go geocaching
- [ ] Pitch a tent
- [ ] Photograph wildflowers

- [ ] Cast a fishing line
- [ ] Take a boat cruise across a lake
- [ ] Enjoy a scenic drive
- [ ] Snap lots of photos
- [ ] Smell the fresh air
- [ ] Arrive early for wildlife watching
- [ ] Scramble over rocks
- [ ] Eat a picnic at a scenic spot
- [ ] Go on a night hike
- [ ] Ride a historic train
- [ ] Hike to the top of a mountain
- [ ] Try a cell phone audio tour
- [ ] Enjoy a tidepool walk
- [ ] Go on a full moon ranger hike
- [ ] Go on a cave tour
- [ ] Go stargazing
- [ ] Adhere to Leave No Trace principles
- [ ] Play in the water

Plan Your Trip:

☐ Day Trip ☐ Overnight Stay

Reservations required: ☐ y ☐ n

Date reservations made: _____

Refund Policy: ☐ y ☐ n Site #: _____

Confirmation #: _____

Miles to travel: _____

Time traveling: _____

Dog friendly?: ☐ y ☐ n

Activities Accomplished:

☐ Archery	☐ Fishing	☐ Picnicking	☐ Wildlife Watching
☐ Biking	☐ Hiking	☐ Rock Climbing	☐ _____
☐ Birding	☐ Horseback Riding	☐ Shooting Range	☐ _____
☐ Boating	☐ Hunting	☐ Stargazing	☐ _____
☐ Camping	☐ Off-Roading	☐ Swimming	☐ _____
☐ Caving	☐ Paddle Boarding	☐ Tennis	☐ _____
☐ Geocaching	☐ Photography	☐ Walking	☐ _____

Traveling by: ☐ ☐ ☐ ☐ ☐ ☐ ☐ ☐ ☐ ☐ ☐ ☐

Reservation Information:

Places we discovered along the way

_____

_____

_____

Places to stop and see along the way

_____

_____

_____

Add your favorite ticket stub, postcard, photo, stamp or drawing here

LET NEW ADVENTURES
>> BEGIN →

Agate Beach State Recreation Site

Region: Central Coast - **Close to:** Newport
Recreation Site

Star Rating
☆☆☆☆☆

My favorite thing about this place is... _____

Why I went ... _____

Who I went with ... _____

When I went ... _____

What I did... _____

What I saw... _____

What I learned... _____

An unforgettable moment... _____

A laughable moment... _____

A surprising moment... _____

An unforeseeable moment... _____

Wildlife spotted... _____

Snapped a selfie | Location... _____

Took a park sign photo? - ☐ y ☐ n

The weather was ...

My List
☐ _____
☐ _____
☐ _____
☐ _____
☐ _____
☐ _____
☐ _____
☐ _____
☐ _____
☐ _____
☐ _____
☐ _____
☐ _____
☐ _____
☐ _____
☐ _____
☐ _____
☐ _____

And so the Adventure begins

www.mynaturebookadventures.com

17

| **PLAN YOUR TRIP:** | **RESERVATION INFORMATION:** |

☐ Day Trip ☐ Overnight Stay

Reservations required: ☐y ☐n

Date reservations made: _____

Refund Policy: ☐y ☐n Site #: _____

Confirmation #: _____

Miles to travel: _____

Time traveling: _____

Dog friendly?: ☐y ☐n

PLACES WE DISCOVERED ALONG THE WAY

PLACES TO STOP AND SEE ALONG THE WAY

Activities Accomplished:

☐ Archery ☐ Fishing ☐ Picnicking ☐ Wildlife Watching
☐ Biking ☐ Hiking ☐ Rock Climbing ☐ _____
☐ Birding ☐ Horseback Riding ☐ Shooting Range ☐ _____
☐ Boating ☐ Hunting ☐ Stargazing ☐ _____
☐ Camping ☐ Off-Roading ☐ Swimming ☐ _____
☐ Caving ☐ Paddle Boarding ☐ Tennis ☐ _____
☐ Geocaching ☐ Photography ☐ Walking ☐ _____

Traveling by:

Add your favorite ticket stub, postcard, photo, stamp or drawing here

LET NEW ADVENTURES
>>> BEGIN →

www.mynaturebookadventures.com

18

Alsea Bay Historic Interpretive Center

Region: Central Coast - ***Close to:*** Waldport
Interpretive Center

Star Rating ☆☆☆☆☆

My favorite thing about this place is... _____

Why I went ... _____

Who I went with ... _____

When I went ... _____

What I did... _____

What I saw... _____

What I learned... _____

An unforgettable moment... _____

A laughable moment... _____

A surprising moment... _____

An unforeseeable moment... _____

Wildlife spotted... _____

Snapped a selfie | Location... _____

Took a park sign photo? - ☐ y ☐ n

The weather was ...

My List
☐ _____
☐ _____
☐ _____
☐ _____
☐ _____
☐ _____
☐ _____
☐ _____
☐ _____
☐ _____
☐ _____
☐ _____
☐ _____
☐ _____
☐ _____
☐ _____
☐ _____
☐ _____

And so the Adventure begins

Plan Your Trip:

_____

☐ Day Trip   ☐ Overnight Stay

Reservations required: ☐ y ☐ n

Date reservations made: _____

Refund Policy: ☐ y ☐ n Site #: _____

Confirmation #: _____

Miles to travel: _____

Time traveling: _____

Dog friendly?: ☐ y ☐ n

Activities Accomplished:

☐ Archery	☐ Fishing	☐ Picnicking	☐ Wildlife Watching
☐ Biking	☐ Hiking	☐ Rock Climbing	☐ _____
☐ Birding	☐ Horseback Riding	☐ Shooting Range	☐ _____
☐ Boating	☐ Hunting	☐ Stargazing	☐ _____
☐ Camping	☐ Off-Roading	☐ Swimming	☐ _____
☐ Caving	☐ Paddle Boarding	☐ Tennis	☐ _____
☐ Geocaching	☐ Photography	☐ Walking	☐ _____

Traveling by: ☐ ☐ ☐ ☐ ☐ ☐ ☐ ☐ ☐ ☐ ☐ ☐

Reservation Information:

_____

Places we discovered along the way

_____

Places to stop and see along the way

_____

Add your favorite ticket stub, postcard, photo, stamp or drawing here

LET NEW ADVENTURES
»» BEGIN →

Beachside State Recreation Site

Region: Central Coast - **Close to:** Waldport
Recreation Site

Star Rating ☆☆☆☆☆

My favorite thing about this place is... _____

Why I went ... _____

Who I went with ... _____

When I went ... _____

What I did... _____

What I saw... _____

What I learned... _____

An unforgettable moment... _____

A laughable moment... _____

A surprising moment... _____

An unforeseeable moment... _____

Wildlife spotted... _____

Snapped a selfie | Location... _____

Took a park sign photo? - ☐ y ☐ n

The weather was ...

My List
☐ _____
☐ _____
☐ _____
☐ _____
☐ _____
☐ _____
☐ _____
☐ _____
☐ _____
☐ _____
☐ _____
☐ _____
☐ _____
☐ _____
☐ _____
☐ _____
☐ _____
☐ _____

And so the Adventure begins

Plan Your Trip:

☐ Day Trip   ☐ Overnight Stay

Reservations required: ☐ y ☐ n

Date reservations made: _____

Refund Policy: ☐ y ☐ n Site #: _____

Confirmation #: _____

Miles to travel: _____

Time traveling: _____

Dog friendly?: ☐ y ☐ n

Activities Accomplished:

- ☐ Archery
- ☐ Biking
- ☐ Birding
- ☐ Boating
- ☐ Camping
- ☐ Caving
- ☐ Geocaching

- ☐ Fishing
- ☐ Hiking
- ☐ Horseback Riding
- ☐ Hunting
- ☐ Off-Roading
- ☐ Paddle Boarding
- ☐ Photography

- ☐ Picnicking
- ☐ Rock Climbing
- ☐ Shooting Range
- ☐ Stargazing
- ☐ Swimming
- ☐ Tennis
- ☐ Walking

- ☐ Wildlife Watching
- ☐ _____
- ☐ _____
- ☐ _____
- ☐ _____
- ☐ _____
- ☐ _____

Traveling by: ☐ car ☐ truck ☐ SUV ☐ van ☐ airplane ☐ trolley ☐ bicycle ☐ bus ☐ train ☐ helicopter ☐ motorcycle ☐ boat

Reservation Information:

Places we discovered along the way

Places to stop and see along the way

Add your favorite ticket stub, postcard, photo, stamp or drawing here

LET NEW ADVENTURES
»» BEGIN →

BEAVER CREEK STATE NATURAL AREA

Region: Central Coast - **Close to:** Newport

State Park

Star Rating ☆☆☆☆☆

My favorite thing about this place is... _____

Why I went ... _____

Who I went with ... _____

When I went ... _____

What I did... _____

What I saw... _____

What I learned... _____

An unforgettable moment... _____

A laughable moment... _____

A surprising moment... _____

An unforeseeable moment... _____

Wildlife spotted... _____

Snapped a selfie | Location... _____

Took a park sign photo? - ☐ y ☐ n

The weather was ...

My List
☐ _____
☐ _____
☐ _____
☐ _____
☐ _____
☐ _____
☐ _____
☐ _____
☐ _____
☐ _____
☐ _____
☐ _____
☐ _____
☐ _____
☐ _____
☐ _____
☐ _____

And so the Adventure begins

Plan Your Trip:

☐ Day Trip ☐ Overnight Stay

Reservations required: ☐ y ☐ n

Date reservations made: _____

Refund Policy: ☐ y ☐ n Site #: _____

Confirmation #: _____

Miles to travel: _____

Time traveling: _____

Dog friendly?: ☐ y ☐ n

Activities Accomplished:

- ☐ Archery
- ☐ Biking
- ☐ Birding
- ☐ Boating
- ☐ Camping
- ☐ Caving
- ☐ Geocaching
- ☐ Fishing
- ☐ Hiking
- ☐ Horseback Riding
- ☐ Hunting
- ☐ Off-Roading
- ☐ Paddle Boarding
- ☐ Photography
- ☐ Picnicking
- ☐ Rock Climbing
- ☐ Shooting Range
- ☐ Stargazing
- ☐ Swimming
- ☐ Tennis
- ☐ Walking
- ☐ Wildlife Watching
- ☐ _____
- ☐ _____
- ☐ _____
- ☐ _____
- ☐ _____
- ☐ _____

Traveling by:

Reservation Information:

Places we discovered along the way

Places to stop and see along the way

Add your favorite ticket stub, postcard, photo, stamp or drawing here

LET NEW ADVENTURES
»› BEGIN →

www.mynaturebookadventures.com

Beverly Beach State Park

Region: Central Coast - **Close to:** Newport
State Park

Star Rating
☆☆☆☆☆

My favorite thing about this place is... _____

Why I went ... _____

Who I went with ... _____

When I went ... _____

What I did... _____

What I saw... _____

What I learned... _____

An unforgettable moment... _____

A laughable moment... _____

A surprising moment... _____

An unforeseeable moment... _____

Wildlife spotted... _____

Snapped a selfie | Location... _____

Took a park sign photo? - ☐ y ☐ n

The weather was ... ☐ ☐ ☐ ☐ ☐ ☐ ☐

My List
☐ _____
☐ _____
☐ _____
☐ _____
☐ _____
☐ _____
☐ _____
☐ _____
☐ _____
☐ _____
☐ _____
☐ _____
☐ _____
☐ _____
☐ _____
☐ _____
☐ _____
☐ _____

And so the Adventure begins

www.mynaturebookadventures.com

25

Plan Your Trip:

☐ Day Trip   ☐ Overnight Stay

Reservations required: ☐ y ☐ n

Date reservations made: _____

Refund Policy: ☐ y ☐ n Site #: _____

Confirmation #: _____

Miles to travel: _____

Time traveling: _____

Dog friendly?: ☐ y ☐ n

Activities Accomplished:

☐ Archery	☐ Fishing	☐ Picnicking	☐ Wildlife Watching
☐ Biking	☐ Hiking	☐ Rock Climbing	☐ _____
☐ Birding	☐ Horseback Riding	☐ Shooting Range	☐ _____
☐ Boating	☐ Hunting	☐ Stargazing	☐ _____
☐ Camping	☐ Off-Roading	☐ Swimming	☐ _____
☐ Caving	☐ Paddle Boarding	☐ Tennis	☐ _____
☐ Geocaching	☐ Photography	☐ Walking	☐ _____

Traveling by:

☐ car ☐ truck ☐ SUV ☐ van ☐ airplane ☐ trolley ☐ bicycle ☐ bus ☐ train ☐ helicopter ☐ motorcycle ☐ boat

Add your favorite ticket stub, postcard, photo, stamp or drawing here

LET NEW ADVENTURES
» BEGIN →

Reservation Information:

_____

Places we discovered along the way

_____
_____

Places to stop and see along the way

_____
_____

www.mynaturebookadventures.com

Boiler Bay State Scenic Viewpoint

Region: Central Coast - **Close to:** Depoe Bay

Scenic Viewpoint

Star Rating
☆☆☆☆☆

My favorite thing about this place is...

Why I went ...

Who I went with ...

When I went ...

What I did...

What I saw...

What I learned...

An unforgettable moment...

A laughable moment...

A surprising moment...

An unforeseeable moment...

Wildlife spotted...

Snapped a selfie | Location...

Took a park sign photo? - ☐ y ☐ n

The weather was ...

My List
☐
☐
☐
☐
☐
☐
☐
☐
☐
☐
☐
☐
☐
☐
☐
☐
☐
☐

And so the Adventure begins

www.mynaturebookadventures.com

Plan Your Trip:

☐ Day Trip ☐ Overnight Stay

Reservations required: ☐ y ☐ n

Date reservations made: _____

Refund Policy: ☐ y ☐ n Site #: _____

Confirmation #: _____

Miles to travel: _____

Time traveling: _____

Dog friendly?: ☐ y ☐ n

Activities Accomplished:

☐ Archery	☐ Fishing	☐ Picnicking	☐ Wildlife Watching
☐ Biking	☐ Hiking	☐ Rock Climbing	☐ _____
☐ Birding	☐ Horseback Riding	☐ Shooting Range	☐ _____
☐ Boating	☐ Hunting	☐ Stargazing	☐ _____
☐ Camping	☐ Off-Roading	☐ Swimming	☐ _____
☐ Caving	☐ Paddle Boarding	☐ Tennis	☐ _____
☐ Geocaching	☐ Photography	☐ Walking	☐ _____

Traveling by:

Reservation Information:

Places we discovered along the way

Places to stop and see along the way

Add your favorite ticket stub, postcard, photo, stamp or drawing here

LET NEW ADVENTURES
»» BEGIN →

www.mynaturebookadventures.com

Bolon Island Tideways State Scenic Corridor

Region: Central Coast - *Close to:* Reedsport
Scenic Corridor

Star Rating
☆☆☆☆☆

My favorite thing about this place is...

Why I went ...

Who I went with ...

When I went ...

What I did...

What I saw...

What I learned...

An unforgettable moment...

A laughable moment...

A surprising moment...

An unforeseeable moment...

Wildlife spotted...

Snapped a selfie | Location...

Took a park sign photo? - ☐ y ☐ n

The weather was ...

My List

And so the Adventure begins

www.mynaturebookadventures.com

Plan Your Trip:

☐ Day Trip ☐ Overnight Stay

Reservations required: ☐ y ☐ n

Date reservations made: _____

Refund Policy: ☐ y ☐ n Site #: _____

Confirmation #: _____

Miles to travel: _____

Time traveling: _____

Dog friendly?: ☐ y ☐ n

Activities Accomplished:

- ☐ Archery
- ☐ Biking
- ☐ Birding
- ☐ Boating
- ☐ Camping
- ☐ Caving
- ☐ Geocaching
- ☐ Fishing
- ☐ Hiking
- ☐ Horseback Riding
- ☐ Hunting
- ☐ Off-Roading
- ☐ Paddle Boarding
- ☐ Photography
- ☐ Picnicking
- ☐ Rock Climbing
- ☐ Shooting Range
- ☐ Stargazing
- ☐ Swimming
- ☐ Tennis
- ☐ Walking
- ☐ Wildlife Watching
- ☐ _____
- ☐ _____
- ☐ _____
- ☐ _____
- ☐ _____
- ☐ _____

Traveling by: ☐ ☐ ☐ ☐ ☐ ☐ ☐ ☐ ☐ ☐ ☐ ☐

Reservation information:

Places we discovered along the way

Places to stop and see along the way

Add your favorite ticket stub, postcard, photo, stamp or drawing here

LET NEW ADVENTURES ›› BEGIN →

www.mynaturebookadventures.com

Carl G. Washburne Memorial State Park

Region: Central Coast - ***Close to:*** Florence
State Park

Star Rating
☆☆☆☆☆

My favorite thing about this place is... _____

Why I went ... _____

Who I went with ... _____

When I went ... _____

What I did... _____

What I saw... _____

What I learned... _____

An unforgettable moment... _____

A laughable moment... _____

A surprising moment... _____

An unforeseeable moment... _____

Wildlife spotted... _____

Snapped a selfie | Location... _____

Took a park sign photo? - ☐ y ☐ n

The weather was ...

My List
☐ _____
☐ _____
☐ _____
☐ _____
☐ _____
☐ _____
☐ _____
☐ _____
☐ _____
☐ _____
☐ _____
☐ _____
☐ _____
☐ _____
☐ _____
☐ _____

And so the Adventure begins

Plan Your Trip:

☐ Day Trip ☐ Overnight Stay

Reservations required: ☐ y ☐ n

Date reservations made: _____

Refund Policy: ☐ y ☐ n Site #: _____

Confirmation #: _____

Miles to travel: _____

Time traveling: _____

Dog friendly?: ☐ y ☐ n

Activities Accomplished:

- ☐ Archery
- ☐ Biking
- ☐ Birding
- ☐ Boating
- ☐ Camping
- ☐ Caving
- ☐ Geocaching

- ☐ Fishing
- ☐ Hiking
- ☐ Horseback Riding
- ☐ Hunting
- ☐ Off-Roading
- ☐ Paddle Boarding
- ☐ Photography

- ☐ Picnicking
- ☐ Rock Climbing
- ☐ Shooting Range
- ☐ Stargazing
- ☐ Swimming
- ☐ Tennis
- ☐ Walking

- ☐ Wildlife Watching
- ☐ _____
- ☐ _____
- ☐ _____
- ☐ _____
- ☐ _____
- ☐ _____

Traveling by: ☐ car ☐ truck ☐ SUV ☐ van ☐ airplane ☐ trolley ☐ bike ☐ bus ☐ train ☐ helicopter ☐ motorcycle ☐ boat

Reservation Information:

_____

Places we discovered along the way

_____
_____
_____

Places to stop and see along the way

_____
_____
_____

Add your favorite ticket stub, postcard, photo, stamp or drawing here

LET NEW ADVENTURES ≫ BEGIN →

Darlingtonia State Natural Site

Region: Central Coast - **Close to:** Florence

Natural Site

Star Rating ☆☆☆☆☆

My favorite thing about this place is... _____

Why I went ... _____

Who I went with ... _____

When I went ... _____

What I did... _____

What I saw... _____

What I learned... _____

An unforgettable moment... _____

A laughable moment... _____

A surprising moment... _____

An unforeseeable moment... _____

Wildlife spotted... _____

Snapped a selfie | Location... _____

Took a park sign photo? - ☐ y ☐ n

The weather was ...

My List
☐ _____

And so the Adventure begins

Plan Your Trip:

☐ Day Trip   ☐ Overnight Stay

Reservations required: ☐ y ☐ n

Date reservations made: _____

Refund Policy: ☐ y ☐ n Site #: _____

Confirmation #: _____

Miles to travel: _____

Time traveling: _____

Dog friendly?: ☐ y ☐ n

Activities Accomplished:

- ☐ Archery
- ☐ Biking
- ☐ Birding
- ☐ Boating
- ☐ Camping
- ☐ Caving
- ☐ Geocaching
- ☐ Fishing
- ☐ Hiking
- ☐ Horseback Riding
- ☐ Hunting
- ☐ Off-Roading
- ☐ Paddle Boarding
- ☐ Photography
- ☐ Picnicking
- ☐ Rock Climbing
- ☐ Shooting Range
- ☐ Stargazing
- ☐ Swimming
- ☐ Tennis
- ☐ Walking
- ☐ Wildlife Watching
- ☐ _____
- ☐ _____
- ☐ _____
- ☐ _____
- ☐ _____
- ☐ _____

Traveling by:

Reservation Information:

Places we discovered along the way

Places to stop and see along the way

Add your favorite ticket stub, postcard, photo, stamp or drawing here

LET NEW ADVENTURES ›› BEGIN →

34

www.mynaturebookadventures.com

Devils Punch Bowl State Natural Area

Region: Central Coast - *Close to:* Newport

Natural Area

Star Rating
☆☆☆☆☆

My favorite thing about this place is... _____

Why I went ... _____

Who I went with ... _____

When I went ... _____

What I did... _____

What I saw... _____

What I learned... _____

An unforgettable moment... _____

A laughable moment... _____

A surprising moment... _____

An unforeseeable moment... _____

Wildlife spotted... _____

Snapped a selfie | Location... _____

Took a park sign photo? - ☐ y ☐ n

The weather was ...

My List
☐ _____
☐ _____
☐ _____
☐ _____
☐ _____
☐ _____
☐ _____
☐ _____
☐ _____
☐ _____
☐ _____
☐ _____
☐ _____
☐ _____
☐ _____
☐ _____
☐ _____
☐ _____

And so the Adventure begins

www.mynaturebookadventures.com

Plan Your Trip:

☐ Day Trip ☐ Overnight Stay

Reservations required: ☐ y ☐ n

Date reservations made: _____

Refund Policy: ☐ y ☐ n Site #: _____

Confirmation #: _____

Miles to travel: _____

Time traveling: _____

Dog friendly?: ☐ y ☐ n

Activities Accomplished:

- ☐ Archery
- ☐ Biking
- ☐ Birding
- ☐ Boating
- ☐ Camping
- ☐ Caving
- ☐ Geocaching

- ☐ Fishing
- ☐ Hiking
- ☐ Horseback Riding
- ☐ Hunting
- ☐ Off-Roading
- ☐ Paddle Boarding
- ☐ Photography

- ☐ Picnicking
- ☐ Rock Climbing
- ☐ Shooting Range
- ☐ Stargazing
- ☐ Swimming
- ☐ Tennis
- ☐ Walking

- ☐ Wildlife Watching
- ☐ _____
- ☐ _____
- ☐ _____
- ☐ _____
- ☐ _____
- ☐ _____

Traveling by:

Reservation Information:

Places we discovered along the way

Places to stop and see along the way

Add your favorite ticket stub, postcard, photo, stamp or drawing here

LET NEW ADVENTURES ≫ BEGIN →

www.mynaturebookadventures.com

Driftwood Beach State Recreation Site

Region: Central Coast - *Close to:* Waldport
Recreation Site

Star Rating
☆☆☆☆☆

My favorite thing about this place is... _____

Why I went ... _____

Who I went with ... _____

When I went ... _____

What I did... _____

What I saw... _____

What I learned... _____

An unforgettable moment... _____

A laughable moment... _____

A surprising moment... _____

An unforeseeable moment... _____

Wildlife spotted... _____

Snapped a selfie | Location... _____

Took a park sign photo? - ☐ y ☐ n

The weather was ...

My List
☐ _____
☐ _____
☐ _____
☐ _____
☐ _____
☐ _____
☐ _____
☐ _____
☐ _____
☐ _____
☐ _____
☐ _____
☐ _____
☐ _____
☐ _____
☐ _____
☐ _____
☐ _____

And so the Adventure begins

Plan Your Trip:

_____

☐ Day Trip ☐ Overnight Stay

Reservations required: ☐ y ☐ n

Date reservations made: _____

Refund Policy: ☐ y ☐ n Site #: _____

Confirmation #: _____

Miles to travel: _____

Time traveling: _____

Dog friendly?: ☐ y ☐ n

Activities Accomplished:

☐ Archery	☐ Fishing	☐ Picnicking	☐ Wildlife Watching
☐ Biking	☐ Hiking	☐ Rock Climbing	☐ _____
☐ Birding	☐ Horseback Riding	☐ Shooting Range	☐ _____
☐ Boating	☐ Hunting	☐ Stargazing	☐ _____
☐ Camping	☐ Off-Roading	☐ Swimming	☐ _____
☐ Caving	☐ Paddle Boarding	☐ Tennis	☐ _____
☐ Geocaching	☐ Photography	☐ Walking	☐ _____

Traveling by:

☐ ☐ ☐ ☐ ☐ ☐ ☐ ☐ ☐ ☐ ☐ ☐

Reservation Information:

_____
_____

Places we discovered along the way

_____
_____
_____

Places to stop and see along the way

_____
_____

Add your favorite ticket stub, postcard, photo, stamp or drawing here

LET NEW ADVENTURES
»» BEGIN →

Ellmaker State Wayside

Region: Central Coast - **Close to:** Newport

Wayside

Star Rating
☆☆☆☆☆

My favorite thing about this place is... _____

Why I went ... _____

Who I went with ... _____

When I went ... _____

What I did... _____

What I saw... _____

What I learned... _____

An unforgettable moment... _____

A laughable moment... _____

A surprising moment... _____

An unforeseeable moment... _____

Wildlife spotted... _____

Snapped a selfie | Location... _____

Took a park sign photo? - ☐ y ☐ n

The weather was ...

My List
☐ _____
☐ _____
☐ _____
☐ _____
☐ _____
☐ _____
☐ _____
☐ _____
☐ _____
☐ _____
☐ _____
☐ _____
☐ _____
☐ _____
☐ _____

And so the Adventure begins

www.mynaturebookadventures.com

39

Plan Your Trip:

☐ Day Trip ☐ Overnight Stay

Reservations required: ☐ y ☐ n

Date reservations made: _____

Refund Policy: ☐ y ☐ n Site #: _____

Confirmation #: _____

Miles to travel: _____

Time traveling: _____

Dog friendly?: ☐ y ☐ n

Activities Accomplished:

☐ Archery	☐ Fishing	☐ Picnicking	☐ Wildlife Watching
☐ Biking	☐ Hiking	☐ Rock Climbing	☐ _____
☐ Birding	☐ Horseback Riding	☐ Shooting Range	☐ _____
☐ Boating	☐ Hunting	☐ Stargazing	☐ _____
☐ Camping	☐ Off-Roading	☐ Swimming	☐ _____
☐ Caving	☐ Paddle Boarding	☐ Tennis	☐ _____
☐ Geocaching	☐ Photography	☐ Walking	☐ _____

Traveling by:

Reservation Information:

_____

Places we discovered along the way

_____
_____

Places to stop and see along the way

_____
_____

Add your favorite ticket stub, postcard, photo, stamp or drawing here

LET NEW ADVENTURES
»» BEGIN →

www.mynaturebookadventures.com

Fogarty Creek State Recreation Area

Region: Central Coast - ***Close to:*** Depoe Bay

Recreation Area

Star Rating
☆☆☆☆☆

My favorite thing about this place is... _____

Why I went ... _____

Who I went with ... _____

When I went ... _____

What I did... _____

What I saw... _____

What I learned... _____

An unforgettable moment... _____

A laughable moment... _____

A surprising moment... _____

An unforeseeable moment... _____

Wildlife spotted... _____

Snapped a selfie | Location... _____

Took a park sign photo? - ☐ y ☐ n

The weather was ...

My List
☐ _____
☐ _____
☐ _____
☐ _____
☐ _____
☐ _____
☐ _____
☐ _____
☐ _____
☐ _____
☐ _____
☐ _____
☐ _____
☐ _____
☐ _____
☐ _____
☐ _____
☐ _____
☐ _____

And so the Adventure begins

Plan Your Trip:

_____

☐ Day Trip   ☐ Overnight Stay

Reservations required: ☐ y ☐ n

Date reservations made: _____

Refund Policy: ☐ y ☐ n Site #: _____

Confirmation #: _____

Miles to travel: _____

Time traveling: _____

Dog friendly?: ☐ y ☐ n

Activities Accomplished:

☐ Archery	☐ Fishing	☐ Picnicking	☐ Wildlife Watching
☐ Biking	☐ Hiking	☐ Rock Climbing	☐ _____
☐ Birding	☐ Horseback Riding	☐ Shooting Range	☐ _____
☐ Boating	☐ Hunting	☐ Stargazing	☐ _____
☐ Camping	☐ Off-Roading	☐ Swimming	☐ _____
☐ Caving	☐ Paddle Boarding	☐ Tennis	☐ _____
☐ Geocaching	☐ Photography	☐ Walking	☐ _____

Traveling by:

☐ car ☐ truck ☐ SUV ☐ van ☐ airplane ☐ trolley ☐ bicycle ☐ bus ☐ train ☐ helicopter ☐ motorcycle ☐ boat

Reservation Information:

_____
_____

Places we discovered along the way

_____
_____
_____

Places to stop and see along the way

_____
_____
_____

Add your favorite ticket stub, postcard, photo, stamp or drawing here

LET NEW ADVENTURES
»> BEGIN →

Gleneden Beach State Recreation Site

Region: Central Coast - *Close to:* Lincoln City

Recreation Area

Star Rating
☆☆☆☆☆

My favorite thing about this place is... _____

Why I went ... _____

Who I went with ... _____

When I went ... _____

What I did... _____

What I saw... _____

What I learned... _____

An unforgettable moment... _____

A laughable moment... _____

A surprising moment... _____

An unforeseeable moment... _____

Wildlife spotted... _____

Snapped a selfie | Location... _____

Took a park sign photo? - ☐ y ☐ n

The weather was ...

My List

And so the Adventure begins

www.mynaturebookadventures.com

43

Plan Your Trip:

☐ Day Trip   ☐ Overnight Stay

Reservations required: ☐ y ☐ n

Date reservations made: _____

Refund Policy: ☐ y ☐ n Site #: _____

Confirmation #: _____

Miles to travel: _____

Time traveling: _____

Dog friendly?: ☐ y ☐ n

Activities Accomplished:

- ☐ Archery
- ☐ Biking
- ☐ Birding
- ☐ Boating
- ☐ Camping
- ☐ Caving
- ☐ Geocaching
- ☐ Fishing
- ☐ Hiking
- ☐ Horseback Riding
- ☐ Hunting
- ☐ Off-Roading
- ☐ Paddle Boarding
- ☐ Photography
- ☐ Picnicking
- ☐ Rock Climbing
- ☐ Shooting Range
- ☐ Stargazing
- ☐ Swimming
- ☐ Tennis
- ☐ Walking
- ☐ Wildlife Watching
- ☐ _____
- ☐ _____
- ☐ _____
- ☐ _____
- ☐ _____
- ☐ _____

Traveling by:

Reservation Information:

Places we discovered along the way

Places to stop and see along the way

Add your favorite ticket stub, postcard, photo, stamp or drawing here

LET NEW ADVENTURES
>> BEGIN →

www.mynaturebookadventures.com

Governor Patterson Memorial State Recreation Site

Region: Central Coast - ***Close to:*** Waldport

Recreation Site

Star Rating
☆☆☆☆☆

My favorite thing about this place is... _____

Why I went ... _____

Who I went with ... _____

When I went ... _____

What I did... _____

What I saw... _____

What I learned... _____

An unforgettable moment... _____

A laughable moment... _____

A surprising moment... _____

An unforeseeable moment... _____

Wildlife spotted... _____

Snapped a selfie | Location... _____

Took a park sign photo? - ☐ y ☐ n

The weather was ...

My List
☐ _____
☐ _____
☐ _____
☐ _____
☐ _____
☐ _____
☐ _____
☐ _____
☐ _____
☐ _____
☐ _____
☐ _____
☐ _____
☐ _____
☐ _____
☐ _____
☐ _____
☐ _____

And so the Adventure begins

Plan Your Trip:

☐ Day Trip ☐ Overnight Stay

Reservations required: ☐ y ☐ n

Date reservations made: _____

Refund Policy: ☐ y ☐ n Site #: _____

Confirmation #: _____

Miles to travel: _____

Time traveling: _____

Dog friendly?: ☐ y ☐ n

Activities Accomplished:

☐ Archery
☐ Biking
☐ Birding
☐ Boating
☐ Camping
☐ Caving
☐ Geocaching

☐ Fishing
☐ Hiking
☐ Horseback Riding
☐ Hunting
☐ Off-Roading
☐ Paddle Boarding
☐ Photography

☐ Picnicking
☐ Rock Climbing
☐ Shooting Range
☐ Stargazing
☐ Swimming
☐ Tennis
☐ Walking

☐ Wildlife Watching
☐ _____
☐ _____
☐ _____
☐ _____
☐ _____
☐ _____

Traveling by:

Reservation Information:

Places we discovered along the way

Places to stop and see along the way

Add your favorite ticket stub, postcard, photo, stamp or drawing here

LET NEW ADVENTURES
»> BEGIN →

www.mynaturebookadventures.com

Heceta Head Lighthouse State Scenic Viewpoint

Region: Central Coast - **Close to:** Florence
Scenic Viewpoint

Star Rating
☆☆☆☆☆

My favorite thing about this place is...
Why I went ...
Who I went with ...
When I went ...
What I did...
What I saw...

What I learned...

An unforgettable moment...

A laughable moment...

A surprising moment...

An unforeseeable moment...

Wildlife spotted...

Snapped a selfie | Location...

Took a park sign photo? - ☐ y ☐ n

The weather was ...

My List
☐ ___
☐ ___
☐ ___
☐ ___
☐ ___
☐ ___
☐ ___
☐ ___
☐ ___
☐ ___
☐ ___
☐ ___
☐ ___
☐ ___
☐ ___
☐ ___
☐ ___
☐ ___

And so the Adventure begins

www.mynaturebookadventures.com

Plan Your Trip:

☐ Day Trip   ☐ Overnight Stay

Reservations required: ☐ y ☐ n

Date reservations made: _____

Refund Policy: ☐ y ☐ n Site #: _____

Confirmation #: _____

Miles to travel: _____

Time traveling: _____

Dog friendly?: ☐ y ☐ n

Activities Accomplished:

- ☐ Archery
- ☐ Biking
- ☐ Birding
- ☐ Boating
- ☐ Camping
- ☐ Caving
- ☐ Geocaching

- ☐ Fishing
- ☐ Hiking
- ☐ Horseback Riding
- ☐ Hunting
- ☐ Off-Roading
- ☐ Paddle Boarding
- ☐ Photography

- ☐ Picnicking
- ☐ Rock Climbing
- ☐ Shooting Range
- ☐ Stargazing
- ☐ Swimming
- ☐ Tennis
- ☐ Walking

- ☐ Wildlife Watching
- ☐ _____
- ☐ _____
- ☐ _____
- ☐ _____
- ☐ _____
- ☐ _____

Traveling by:

Reservation Information:

Places we discovered along the way

Places to stop and see along the way

Add your favorite ticket stub, postcard, photo, stamp or drawing here

LET NEW ADVENTURES ≫ BEGIN →

48

www.mynaturebookadventures.com

Jessie M. Honeyman Memorial State Park

Region: Central Coast - **Close to:** Florence
State Park

Star Rating
☆☆☆☆☆

My favorite thing about this place is... _____

Why I went ... _____

Who I went with ... _____

When I went ... _____

What I did... _____

What I saw... _____

What I learned... _____

An unforgettable moment... _____

A laughable moment... _____

A surprising moment... _____

An unforeseeable moment... _____

Wildlife spotted... _____

Snapped a selfie | Location... _____

Took a park sign photo? - ☐ y ☐ n

The weather was ...

My List
☐ _____
☐ _____
☐ _____
☐ _____
☐ _____
☐ _____
☐ _____
☐ _____
☐ _____
☐ _____
☐ _____
☐ _____
☐ _____
☐ _____
☐ _____
☐ _____
☐ _____
☐ _____

And so the Adventure begins

www.mynaturebookadventures.com

Plan Your Trip:

☐ Day Trip ☐ Overnight Stay

Reservations required: ☐ y ☐ n

Date reservations made: _____

Refund Policy: ☐ y ☐ n Site #: _____

Confirmation #: _____

Miles to travel: _____

Time traveling: _____

Dog friendly?: ☐ y ☐ n

Activities Accomplished:

- ☐ Archery
- ☐ Biking
- ☐ Birding
- ☐ Boating
- ☐ Camping
- ☐ Caving
- ☐ Geocaching

- ☐ Fishing
- ☐ Hiking
- ☐ Horseback Riding
- ☐ Hunting
- ☐ Off-Roading
- ☐ Paddle Boarding
- ☐ Photography

- ☐ Picnicking
- ☐ Rock Climbing
- ☐ Shooting Range
- ☐ Stargazing
- ☐ Swimming
- ☐ Tennis
- ☐ Walking

- ☐ Wildlife Watching
- ☐ _____
- ☐ _____
- ☐ _____
- ☐ _____
- ☐ _____
- ☐ _____

Traveling by:

☐ ☐ ☐ ☐ ☐ ☐ ☐ ☐ ☐ ☐ ☐ ☐

Reservation information:

Places we discovered along the way

Places to stop and see along the way

Add your favorite ticket stub, postcard, photo, stamp or drawing here

LET NEW ADVENTURES
» BEGIN →

www.mynaturebookadventures.com

LOST CREEK STATE RECREATION SITE

Region: Central Coast - **Close to:** Newport

Recreation Site

Star Rating
☆☆☆☆☆

My favorite thing about this place is... _____

Why I went ... _____

Who I went with ... _____

When I went ... _____

What I did... _____

What I saw... _____

What I learned... _____

An unforgettable moment... _____

A laughable moment... _____

A surprising moment... _____

An unforeseeable moment... _____

Wildlife spotted... _____

Snapped a selfie | Location... _____

Took a park sign photo? - ☐ y ☐ n

The weather was ...

My List
☐ _____
☐ _____
☐ _____
☐ _____
☐ _____
☐ _____
☐ _____
☐ _____
☐ _____
☐ _____
☐ _____
☐ _____
☐ _____
☐ _____
☐ _____
☐ _____

And so the Adventure begins

www.mynaturebookadventures.com

Plan Your Trip:

☐ Day Trip ☐ Overnight Stay

Reservations required: ☐ y ☐ n

Date reservations made: _____

Refund Policy: ☐ y ☐ n Site #: _____

Confirmation #: _____

Miles to travel: _____

Time traveling: _____

Dog friendly?: ☐ y ☐ n

Activities Accomplished:

- ☐ Archery
- ☐ Biking
- ☐ Birding
- ☐ Boating
- ☐ Camping
- ☐ Caving
- ☐ Geocaching
- ☐ Fishing
- ☐ Hiking
- ☐ Horseback Riding
- ☐ Hunting
- ☐ Off-Roading
- ☐ Paddle Boarding
- ☐ Photography
- ☐ Picnicking
- ☐ Rock Climbing
- ☐ Shooting Range
- ☐ Stargazing
- ☐ Swimming
- ☐ Tennis
- ☐ Walking
- ☐ Wildlife Watching
- ☐ _____
- ☐ _____
- ☐ _____
- ☐ _____
- ☐ _____
- ☐ _____

Traveling by: ☐ car ☐ truck ☐ SUV ☐ van ☐ plane ☐ trolley ☐ bike ☐ bus ☐ train ☐ helicopter ☐ motorcycle ☐ boat

Reservation Information:

_____

Places we discovered along the way
_____
_____
_____

Places to stop and see along the way
_____
_____
_____

Add your favorite ticket stub, postcard, photo, stamp or drawing here

LET NEW ADVENTURES ≫ BEGIN →

www.mynaturebookadventures.com

Muriel O. Ponsler Memorial State Scenic Viewpoint

Region: Central Coast - **Close to:** Florence

Scenic Viewpoint

Star Rating
☆☆☆☆☆

My favorite thing about this place is... _____

Why I went ... _____

Who I went with ... _____

When I went ... _____

What I did... _____

What I saw... _____

What I learned... _____

An unforgettable moment... _____

A laughable moment... _____

A surprising moment... _____

An unforeseeable moment... _____

Wildlife spotted... _____

Snapped a selfie | Location... _____

Took a park sign photo? - ☐ y ☐ n

The weather was ...

My List
☐ _____
☐ _____
☐ _____
☐ _____
☐ _____
☐ _____
☐ _____
☐ _____
☐ _____
☐ _____
☐ _____
☐ _____
☐ _____
☐ _____
☐ _____
☐ _____

And so the Adventure begins

www.mynaturebookadventures.com

Plan Your Trip:

_____

☐ Day Trip ☐ Overnight Stay

Reservations required: ☐ y ☐ n

Date reservations made: _____

Refund Policy: ☐ y ☐ n Site #: _____

Confirmation #: _____

Miles to travel: _____

Time traveling: _____

Dog friendly?: ☐ y ☐ n

Activities Accomplished:

☐ Archery	☐ Fishing	☐ Picnicking	☐ Wildlife Watching
☐ Biking	☐ Hiking	☐ Rock Climbing	☐ _____
☐ Birding	☐ Horseback Riding	☐ Shooting Range	☐ _____
☐ Boating	☐ Hunting	☐ Stargazing	☐ _____
☐ Camping	☐ Off-Roading	☐ Swimming	☐ _____
☐ Caving	☐ Paddle Boarding	☐ Tennis	☐ _____
☐ Geocaching	☐ Photography	☐ Walking	☐ _____

Traveling by:

☐ car ☐ truck ☐ SUV ☐ van ☐ plane ☐ trolley ☐ bicycle ☐ bus ☐ train ☐ helicopter ☐ motorcycle ☐ boat

Reservation Information:

_____

Places we discovered along the way

_____
_____
_____

Places to stop and see along the way

_____
_____
_____

Add your favorite ticket stub, postcard, photo, stamp or drawing here

LET NEW ADVENTURES
»» BEGIN →

www.mynaturebookadventures.com

54

Neptune State Scenic Viewpoint

Region: Central Coast - **Close to:** Yachats
Scenic Viewpoint

Star Rating
☆☆☆☆☆

My favorite thing about this place is... _____

Why I went ... _____

Who I went with ... _____

When I went ... _____

What I did... _____

What I saw... _____

What I learned... _____

An unforgettable moment... _____

A laughable moment... _____

A surprising moment... _____

An unforeseeable moment... _____

Wildlife spotted... _____

Snapped a selfie | Location... _____

Took a park sign photo? - ☐ y ☐ n

The weather was ...

My List
☐ _____
☐ _____
☐ _____
☐ _____
☐ _____
☐ _____
☐ _____
☐ _____
☐ _____
☐ _____
☐ _____
☐ _____
☐ _____
☐ _____
☐ _____
☐ _____
☐ _____
☐ _____

And so the Adventure begins

Plan Your Trip:

☐ Day Trip ☐ Overnight Stay

Reservations required: ☐ y ☐ n

Date reservations made: _____

Refund Policy: ☐ y ☐ n Site #: _____

Confirmation #: _____

Miles to travel: _____

Time traveling: _____

Dog friendly?: ☐ y ☐ n

Activities Accomplished:

- ☐ Archery
- ☐ Biking
- ☐ Birding
- ☐ Boating
- ☐ Camping
- ☐ Caving
- ☐ Geocaching
- ☐ Fishing
- ☐ Hiking
- ☐ Horseback Riding
- ☐ Hunting
- ☐ Off-Roading
- ☐ Paddle Boarding
- ☐ Photography
- ☐ Picnicking
- ☐ Rock Climbing
- ☐ Shooting Range
- ☐ Stargazing
- ☐ Swimming
- ☐ Tennis
- ☐ Walking
- ☐ Wildlife Watching
- ☐ _____
- ☐ _____
- ☐ _____
- ☐ _____
- ☐ _____
- ☐ _____

Traveling by:

Reservation Information:

Places we discovered along the way

Places to stop and see along the way

Add your favorite ticket stub, postcard, photo, stamp or drawing here

LET NEW ADVENTURES ≫ BEGIN →

www.mynaturebookadventures.com

ONA BEACH STATE PARK

Region: Central Coast - **Close to:** Newport
State Park

Star Rating ☆☆☆☆☆

My favorite thing about this place is...
Why I went ...
Who I went with ...
When I went ...
What I did...
What I saw...
What I learned...
An unforgettable moment...
A laughable moment...
A surprising moment...
An unforeseeable moment...
Wildlife spotted...
Snapped a selfie | Location...
Took a park sign photo? - ☐ y ☐ n

My List
☐ ___
☐ ___
☐ ___
☐ ___
☐ ___
☐ ___
☐ ___
☐ ___
☐ ___
☐ ___
☐ ___
☐ ___
☐ ___
☐ ___
☐ ___
☐ ___
☐ ___
☐ ___

And so the Adventure begins

The weather was ...

www.mynaturebookadventures.com

Plan Your Trip:

☐ Day Trip ☐ Overnight Stay

Reservations required: ☐ y ☐ n
Date reservations made: _____
Refund Policy: ☐ y ☐ n Site #: _____
Confirmation #: _____
Miles to travel: _____
Time traveling: _____
Dog friendly?: ☐ y ☐ n

Activities Accomplished:

☐ Archery	☐ Fishing	☐ Picnicking	☐ Wildlife Watching
☐ Biking	☐ Hiking	☐ Rock Climbing	☐ _____
☐ Birding	☐ Horseback Riding	☐ Shooting Range	☐ _____
☐ Boating	☐ Hunting	☐ Stargazing	☐ _____
☐ Camping	☐ Off-Roading	☐ Swimming	☐ _____
☐ Caving	☐ Paddle Boarding	☐ Tennis	☐ _____
☐ Geocaching	☐ Photography	☐ Walking	☐ _____

Traveling by:
☐ ☐ ☐ ☐ ☐ ☐ ☐ ☐ ☐ ☐ ☐ ☐

Reservation Information:

_____
_____

Places we discovered along the way
_____
_____
_____

Places to stop and see along the way
_____
_____
_____

Add your favorite ticket stub, postcard, photo, stamp or drawing here

LET NEW ADVENTURES ≫ BEGIN →

www.mynaturebookadventures.com

Otter Crest State Scenic Viewpoint

Region: Central Coast - **Close to:** Newport

Scenic Viewpoint

Star Rating ☆☆☆☆☆

My favorite thing about this place is...

Why I went ...

Who I went with ...

When I went ...

What I did...

What I saw...

What I learned...

An unforgettable moment...

A laughable moment...

A surprising moment...

An unforeseeable moment...

Wildlife spotted...

Snapped a selfie | Location...

Took a park sign photo? - ☐ y ☐ n

The weather was ...

My List
☐ ___
☐ ___
☐ ___
☐ ___
☐ ___
☐ ___
☐ ___
☐ ___
☐ ___
☐ ___
☐ ___
☐ ___
☐ ___
☐ ___
☐ ___
☐ ___
☐ ___
☐ ___

And so the Adventure begins

Plan Your Trip:

_____

☐ Day Trip ☐ Overnight Stay

Reservations required: ☐ y ☐ n

Date reservations made: _____

Refund Policy: ☐ y ☐ n Site #: _____

Confirmation #: _____

Miles to travel: _____

Time traveling: _____

Dog friendly?: ☐ y ☐ n

Activities Accomplished:

☐ Archery	☐ Fishing	☐ Picnicking	☐ Wildlife Watching
☐ Biking	☐ Hiking	☐ Rock Climbing	☐ _____
☐ Birding	☐ Horseback Riding	☐ Shooting Range	☐ _____
☐ Boating	☐ Hunting	☐ Stargazing	☐ _____
☐ Camping	☐ Off-Roading	☐ Swimming	☐ _____
☐ Caving	☐ Paddle Boarding	☐ Tennis	☐ _____
☐ Geocaching	☐ Photography	☐ Walking	☐ _____

Traveling by:

☐ ☐ ☐ ☐ ☐ ☐ ☐ ☐ ☐ ☐ ☐ ☐

Reservation information:

_____
_____

Places we discovered along the way

_____
_____
_____

Places to stop and see along the way

_____
_____
_____

Add your favorite ticket stub, postcard, photo, stamp or drawing here

LET NEW ADVENTURES
»» BEGIN →

Rocky Creek State Scenic Viewpoint

Region: Central Coast - **Close to:** Depoe Bay
Scenic Viewpoint

Star Rating ☆☆☆☆☆

My favorite thing about this place is...

Why I went ...

Who I went with ...

When I went ...

What I did...

What I saw...

What I learned...

An unforgettable moment...

A laughable moment...

A surprising moment...

An unforeseeable moment...

Wildlife spotted...

Snapped a selfie | Location...

Took a park sign photo? - ☐ y ☐ n

The weather was ...

My List

And so the Adventure begins

Plan Your Trip:

_____

☐ Day Trip ☐ Overnight Stay

Reservations required: ☐ y ☐ n

Date reservations made: _____

Refund Policy: ☐ y ☐ n Site #: _____

Confirmation #: _____

Miles to travel: _____

Time traveling: _____

Dog friendly?: ☐ y ☐ n

Activities Accomplished:

☐ Archery	☐ Fishing	☐ Picnicking	☐ Wildlife Watching
☐ Biking	☐ Hiking	☐ Rock Climbing	☐ _____
☐ Birding	☐ Horseback Riding	☐ Shooting Range	☐ _____
☐ Boating	☐ Hunting	☐ Stargazing	☐ _____
☐ Camping	☐ Off-Roading	☐ Swimming	☐ _____
☐ Caving	☐ Paddle Boarding	☐ Tennis	☐ _____
☐ Geocaching	☐ Photography	☐ Walking	☐ _____

Traveling by:

☐ ☐ ☐ ☐ ☐ ☐ ☐ ☐ ☐ ☐ ☐ ☐

Reservation Information:

_____

_____

Places we discovered along the way

_____

_____

_____

Places to stop and see along the way

_____

_____

_____

Add your favorite ticket stub, postcard, photo, stamp or drawing here

LET NEW ADVENTURES
»» BEGIN →

Seal Rock State Recreation Site

Region: Central Coast - **Close to:** Newport
Recreation Site

Star Rating
☆☆☆☆☆

My favorite thing about this place is... _____

Why I went ... _____

Who I went with ... _____

When I went ... _____

What I did... _____

What I saw... _____

What I learned... _____

An unforgettable moment... _____

A laughable moment... _____

A surprising moment... _____

An unforeseeable moment... _____

Wildlife spotted... _____

Snapped a selfie | Location... _____

Took a park sign photo? - ☐ y ☐ n

The weather was ...

My List
☐ _____
☐ _____
☐ _____
☐ _____
☐ _____
☐ _____
☐ _____
☐ _____
☐ _____
☐ _____
☐ _____
☐ _____
☐ _____
☐ _____
☐ _____
☐ _____
☐ _____

And so the Adventure begins

www.mynaturebookadventures.com

Plan Your Trip:

_____

☐ Day Trip ☐ Overnight Stay

Reservations required: ☐ y ☐ n

Date reservations made: _____

Refund Policy: ☐ y ☐ n Site #: _____

Confirmation #: _____

Miles to travel: _____

Time traveling: _____

Dog friendly?: ☐ y ☐ n

Activities Accomplished:

☐ Archery	☐ Fishing	☐ Picnicking	☐ Wildlife Watching
☐ Biking	☐ Hiking	☐ Rock Climbing	☐ _____
☐ Birding	☐ Horseback Riding	☐ Shooting Range	☐ _____
☐ Boating	☐ Hunting	☐ Stargazing	☐ _____
☐ Camping	☐ Off-Roading	☐ Swimming	☐ _____
☐ Caving	☐ Paddle Boarding	☐ Tennis	☐ _____
☐ Geocaching	☐ Photography	☐ Walking	☐ _____

Traveling by:

☐ ☐ ☐ ☐ ☐ ☐ ☐ ☐ ☐ ☐ ☐ ☐

Reservation Information:

_____
_____

Places we discovered along the way

_____
_____
_____

Places to stop and see along the way

_____
_____
_____

Add your favorite ticket stub, postcard, photo, stamp or drawing here

LET NEW ADVENTURES ≫ BEGIN →

Smelt Sands State Recreation Site

Region: Central Coast - **Close to:** Yachats

Recreation Site

Star Rating ☆☆☆☆☆

My favorite thing about this place is... _____

Why I went ... _____

Who I went with ... _____

When I went ... _____

What I did... _____

What I saw... _____

What I learned... _____

An unforgettable moment... _____

A laughable moment... _____

A surprising moment... _____

An unforeseeable moment... _____

Wildlife spotted... _____

Snapped a selfie | Location... _____

Took a park sign photo? - ☐ y ☐ n

The weather was ...

My List
☐ _____
☐ _____
☐ _____
☐ _____
☐ _____
☐ _____
☐ _____
☐ _____
☐ _____
☐ _____
☐ _____
☐ _____
☐ _____
☐ _____
☐ _____
☐ _____
☐ _____

And so the Adventure begins

Plan Your Trip:

☐ Day Trip ☐ Overnight Stay

Reservations required: ☐ y ☐ n

Date reservations made: _____

Refund Policy: ☐ y ☐ n Site #: _____

Confirmation #: _____

Miles to travel: _____

Time traveling: _____

Dog friendly?: ☐ y ☐ n

Activities Accomplished:

☐ Archery	☐ Fishing	☐ Picnicking	☐ Wildlife Watching
☐ Biking	☐ Hiking	☐ Rock Climbing	☐ _____
☐ Birding	☐ Horseback Riding	☐ Shooting Range	☐ _____
☐ Boating	☐ Hunting	☐ Stargazing	☐ _____
☐ Camping	☐ Off-Roading	☐ Swimming	☐ _____
☐ Caving	☐ Paddle Boarding	☐ Tennis	☐ _____
☐ Geocaching	☐ Photography	☐ Walking	☐ _____

Traveling by:

☐ ☐ ☐ ☐ ☐ ☐ ☐ ☐ ☐ ☐ ☐ ☐

Reservation Information:

Places we discovered along the way

Places to stop and see along the way

Add your favorite ticket stub, postcard, photo, stamp or drawing here

LET NEW ADVENTURES
» BEGIN →

South Beach State Park

Region: Central Coast - **Close to:** Newport

State Park

Star Rating
☆☆☆☆☆

My favorite thing about this place is... _____

Why I went ... _____

Who I went with ... _____

When I went ... _____

What I did... _____

What I saw... _____

What I learned... _____

An unforgettable moment... _____

A laughable moment... _____

A surprising moment... _____

An unforeseeable moment... _____

Wildlife spotted... _____

Snapped a selfie | Location... _____

Took a park sign photo? - ☐ y ☐ n

The weather was ...

My List
☐ _____
☐ _____
☐ _____
☐ _____
☐ _____
☐ _____
☐ _____
☐ _____
☐ _____
☐ _____
☐ _____
☐ _____
☐ _____
☐ _____
☐ _____
☐ _____
☐ _____

And so the Adventure begins

www.mynaturebookadventures.com

Plan Your Trip:

☐ Day Trip   ☐ Overnight Stay

Reservations required: ☐y ☐n

Date reservations made: _____

Refund Policy: ☐y ☐n Site #: _____

Confirmation #: _____

Miles to travel: _____

Time traveling: _____

Dog friendly?: ☐y ☐n

Activities Accomplished:

☐ Archery
☐ Biking
☐ Birding
☐ Boating
☐ Camping
☐ Caving
☐ Geocaching

☐ Fishing
☐ Hiking
☐ Horseback Riding
☐ Hunting
☐ Off-Roading
☐ Paddle Boarding
☐ Photography

☐ Picnicking
☐ Rock Climbing
☐ Shooting Range
☐ Stargazing
☐ Swimming
☐ Tennis
☐ Walking

☐ Wildlife Watching
☐ _____
☐ _____
☐ _____
☐ _____
☐ _____
☐ _____

Traveling by:

☐ ☐ ☐ ☐ ☐ ☐ ☐ ☐ ☐ ☐ ☐ ☐

Reservation Information:

_____
_____
_____

Places we discovered along the way
_____
_____
_____

Places to stop and see along the way
_____
_____
_____

Add your favorite ticket stub, postcard, photo, stamp or drawing here

LET NEW ADVENTURES ≫ BEGIN →

South Jetty (South Beach)

Region: Central Coast - **Close to:** Newport
Beach access (adjacent to South Beach State Park)

Star Rating
☆☆☆☆☆

My favorite thing about this place is...

Why I went ...

Who I went with ...

When I went ...

What I did...

What I saw...

What I learned...

An unforgettable moment...

A laughable moment...

A surprising moment...

An unforeseeable moment...

Wildlife spotted...

Snapped a selfie | Location...

Took a park sign photo? - ☐ y ☐ n

The weather was ... ☐ ☐ ☐ ☐ ☐ ☐ ☐

My List
☐ ___
☐ ___
☐ ___
☐ ___
☐ ___
☐ ___
☐ ___
☐ ___
☐ ___
☐ ___
☐ ___
☐ ___
☐ ___
☐ ___
☐ ___
☐ ___
☐ ___
☐ ___

And so the Adventure begins

www.mynaturebookadventures.com

Plan Your Trip:

☐ Day Trip ☐ Overnight Stay

Reservations required: ☐ y ☐ n

Date reservations made: _____

Refund Policy: ☐ y ☐ n Site #: _____

Confirmation #: _____

Miles to travel: _____

Time traveling: _____

Dog friendly?: ☐ y ☐ n

Activities Accomplished:

☐ Archery	☐ Fishing	☐ Picnicking	☐ Wildlife Watching
☐ Biking	☐ Hiking	☐ Rock Climbing	☐ _____
☐ Birding	☐ Horseback Riding	☐ Shooting Range	☐ _____
☐ Boating	☐ Hunting	☐ Stargazing	☐ _____
☐ Camping	☐ Off-Roading	☐ Swimming	☐ _____
☐ Caving	☐ Paddle Boarding	☐ Tennis	☐ _____
☐ Geocaching	☐ Photography	☐ Walking	☐ _____

Traveling by:

Reservation Information:

_____

Places we discovered along the way

_____
_____
_____

Places to stop and see along the way

_____
_____
_____

Add your favorite ticket stub, postcard, photo, stamp or drawing here

LET NEW ADVENTURES
›› BEGIN →

www.mynaturebookadventures.com

Stonefield Beach State Recreation Site

Region: Central Coast - **Close to:** Yachats
Recreation Site

Star Rating
☆☆☆☆☆

My favorite thing about this place is... _____

Why I went ... _____

Who I went with ... _____

When I went ... _____

What I did... _____

What I saw... _____

What I learned... _____

An unforgettable moment... _____

A laughable moment... _____

A surprising moment... _____

An unforeseeable moment... _____

Wildlife spotted... _____

Snapped a selfie | Location... _____

Took a park sign photo? - ☐ y ☐ n

The weather was ...

My List
☐ _____
☐ _____
☐ _____
☐ _____
☐ _____
☐ _____
☐ _____
☐ _____
☐ _____
☐ _____
☐ _____
☐ _____
☐ _____
☐ _____
☐ _____
☐ _____
☐ _____

And so the Adventure begins

www.mynaturebookadventures.com

Plan Your Trip:

☐ Day Trip ☐ Overnight Stay

Reservations required: ☐ y ☐ n

Date reservations made: _____

Refund Policy: ☐ y ☐ n Site #: _____

Confirmation #: _____

Miles to travel: _____

Time traveling: _____

Dog friendly?: ☐ y ☐ n

Activities Accomplished:

- ☐ Archery
- ☐ Biking
- ☐ Birding
- ☐ Boating
- ☐ Camping
- ☐ Caving
- ☐ Geocaching

- ☐ Fishing
- ☐ Hiking
- ☐ Horseback Riding
- ☐ Hunting
- ☐ Off-Roading
- ☐ Paddle Boarding
- ☐ Photography

- ☐ Picnicking
- ☐ Rock Climbing
- ☐ Shooting Range
- ☐ Stargazing
- ☐ Swimming
- ☐ Tennis
- ☐ Walking

- ☐ Wildlife Watching
- ☐ _____
- ☐ _____
- ☐ _____
- ☐ _____
- ☐ _____
- ☐ _____

Traveling by:

Reservation Information:

Places we discovered along the way

Places to stop and see along the way

Add your favorite ticket stub, postcard, photo, stamp or drawing here

LET NEW ADVENTURES ≫ BEGIN →

72

www.mynaturebookadventures.com

Tokatee Klootchman State Natural Site

Region: Central Coast - **Close to:** Florence
Natural Site

Star Rating
☆☆☆☆☆

My favorite thing about this place is...
Why I went ...
Who I went with ...
When I went ...
What I did...
What I saw...

What I learned...

An unforgettable moment...

A laughable moment...

A surprising moment...

An unforeseeable moment...

Wildlife spotted...
Snapped a selfie | Location...
Took a park sign photo? - ☐ y ☐ n

The weather was ...

My List
☐ _____
☐ _____
☐ _____
☐ _____
☐ _____
☐ _____
☐ _____
☐ _____
☐ _____
☐ _____
☐ _____
☐ _____
☐ _____
☐ _____
☐ _____
☐ _____
☐ _____
☐ _____
☐ _____
☐ _____

And so the Adventure begins

www.mynaturebookadventures.com

Plan Your Trip:

_____

☐ Day Trip ☐ Overnight Stay

Reservations required: ☐ y ☐ n

Date reservations made: _____

Refund Policy: ☐ y ☐ n Site #: _____

Confirmation #: _____

Miles to travel: _____

Time traveling: _____

Dog friendly?: ☐ y ☐ n

Activities Accomplished:

☐ Archery	☐ Fishing	☐ Picnicking	☐ Wildlife Watching
☐ Biking	☐ Hiking	☐ Rock Climbing	☐ _____
☐ Birding	☐ Horseback Riding	☐ Shooting Range	☐ _____
☐ Boating	☐ Hunting	☐ Stargazing	☐ _____
☐ Camping	☐ Off-Roading	☐ Swimming	☐ _____
☐ Caving	☐ Paddle Boarding	☐ Tennis	☐ _____
☐ Geocaching	☐ Photography	☐ Walking	☐ _____

Traveling by:

☐ ☐ ☐ ☐ ☐ ☐ ☐ ☐ ☐ ☐ ☐ ☐

Reservation Information:

_____
_____

Places we discovered along the way

_____
_____
_____

Places to stop and see along the way

_____
_____
_____

Add your favorite ticket stub, postcard, photo, stamp or drawing here

LET NEW ADVENTURES
»› BEGIN →

www.mynaturebookadventures.com

Umpqua Lighthouse State Park

Region: Central Coast - **Close to:** Reedsport

State Park

Star Rating

My favorite thing about this place is... _____

Why I went ... _____

Who I went with ... _____

When I went ... _____

What I did... _____

What I saw... _____

What I learned... _____

An unforgettable moment... _____

A laughable moment... _____

A surprising moment... _____

An unforeseeable moment... _____

Wildlife spotted... _____

Snapped a selfie | Location... _____

Took a park sign photo? - ☐ y ☐ n

The weather was ...

My List

And so the Adventure begins

www.mynaturebookadventures.com

75

Plan Your Trip:

☐ Day Trip ☐ Overnight Stay

Reservations required: ☐ y ☐ n

Date reservations made: _____

Refund Policy: ☐ y ☐ n Site #: _____

Confirmation #: _____

Miles to travel: _____

Time traveling: _____

Dog friendly?: ☐ y ☐ n

Activities Accomplished:

☐ Archery	☐ Fishing	☐ Picnicking	☐ Wildlife Watching
☐ Biking	☐ Hiking	☐ Rock Climbing	☐ _____
☐ Birding	☐ Horseback Riding	☐ Shooting Range	☐ _____
☐ Boating	☐ Hunting	☐ Stargazing	☐ _____
☐ Camping	☐ Off-Roading	☐ Swimming	☐ _____
☐ Caving	☐ Paddle Boarding	☐ Tennis	☐ _____
☐ Geocaching	☐ Photography	☐ Walking	☐ _____

Traveling by:

Reservation Information:

_____

Places we discovered along the way

_____
_____
_____

Places to stop and see along the way

_____
_____
_____

Add your favorite ticket stub, postcard, photo, stamp or drawing here

LET NEW ADVENTURES ›› BEGIN →

W. B. Nelson State Recreation Site

Region: Central Coast - **Close to:** Waldport
Recreation Site

Star Rating

My favorite thing about this place is... _____

Why I went ... _____

Who I went with ... _____

When I went ... _____

What I did... _____

What I saw... _____

What I learned... _____

My List

An unforgettable moment... _____

A laughable moment... _____

A surprising moment... _____

An unforeseeable moment... _____

And so the Adventure begins

Wildlife spotted... _____

Snapped a selfie | Location... _____

Took a park sign photo? - ☐ y ☐ n

The weather was ...

Plan Your Trip:

_____

☐ Day Trip ☐ Overnight Stay

Reservations required: ☐ y ☐ n

Date reservations made: _____

Refund Policy: ☐ y ☐ n Site #: _____

Confirmation #: _____

Miles to travel: _____

Time traveling: _____

Dog friendly?: ☐ y ☐ n

Activities Accomplished:

☐ Archery	☐ Fishing	☐ Picnicking	☐ Wildlife Watching
☐ Biking	☐ Hiking	☐ Rock Climbing	☐ _____
☐ Birding	☐ Horseback Riding	☐ Shooting Range	☐ _____
☐ Boating	☐ Hunting	☐ Stargazing	☐ _____
☐ Camping	☐ Off-Roading	☐ Swimming	☐ _____
☐ Caving	☐ Paddle Boarding	☐ Tennis	☐ _____
☐ Geocaching	☐ Photography	☐ Walking	☐ _____

Traveling by:

Reservation Information:

_____

Places we discovered along the way

_____
_____
_____

Places to stop and see along the way

_____
_____
_____

Add your favorite ticket stub, postcard, photo, stamp or drawing here

LET NEW ADVENTURES
»› BEGIN →

www.mynaturebookadventures.com

Whale Watching Center

Region: Central Coast - **Close to:** Depoe Bay
Guided ocean viewpoint

Star Rating
☆☆☆☆☆

My favorite thing about this place is...

Why I went ...

Who I went with ...

When I went ...

What I did...

What I saw...

What I learned...

An unforgettable moment...

A laughable moment...

A surprising moment...

An unforeseeable moment...

Wildlife spotted...

Snapped a selfie | Location...

Took a park sign photo? - ☐ y ☐ n

The weather was ...

My List

And so the Adventure begins

Plan Your Trip:

☐ Day Trip ☐ Overnight Stay

Reservations required: ☐ y ☐ n

Date reservations made: _____

Refund Policy: ☐ y ☐ n Site #: _____

Confirmation #: _____

Miles to travel: _____

Time traveling: _____

Dog friendly?: ☐ y ☐ n

Activities Accomplished:

☐ Archery	☐ Fishing	☐ Picnicking	☐ Wildlife Watching
☐ Biking	☐ Hiking	☐ Rock Climbing	☐ _____
☐ Birding	☐ Horseback Riding	☐ Shooting Range	☐ _____
☐ Boating	☐ Hunting	☐ Stargazing	☐ _____
☐ Camping	☐ Off-Roading	☐ Swimming	☐ _____
☐ Caving	☐ Paddle Boarding	☐ Tennis	☐ _____
☐ Geocaching	☐ Photography	☐ Walking	☐ _____

Traveling by:

☐ ☐ ☐ ☐ ☐ ☐ ☐ ☐ ☐ ☐ ☐ ☐

Add your favorite ticket stub, postcard, photo, stamp or drawing here

LET NEW ADVENTURES
»› BEGIN →

Reservation Information:

Places we discovered along the way

_____
_____
_____

Places to stop and see along the way

_____
_____
_____

Yachats Ocean Road State Natural Site

Region: Central Coast - **Close to:** Yachats
Natural Site

Star Rating
☆☆☆☆☆

My favorite thing about this place is… _____

Why I went … _____

Who I went with … _____

When I went … _____

What I did… _____

What I saw… _____

What I learned… _____

An unforgettable moment… _____

A laughable moment… _____

A surprising moment… _____

An unforeseeable moment… _____

Wildlife spotted… _____

Snapped a selfie | Location… _____

Took a park sign photo? - ☐ y ☐ n

The weather was …

My List
☐ _____
☐ _____
☐ _____
☐ _____
☐ _____
☐ _____
☐ _____
☐ _____
☐ _____
☐ _____
☐ _____
☐ _____
☐ _____
☐ _____
☐ _____

And so the Adventure begins

Plan Your Trip:

☐ Day Trip ☐ Overnight Stay

Reservations required: ☐ y ☐ n

Date reservations made: _____

Refund Policy: ☐ y ☐ n Site #: _____

Confirmation #: _____

Miles to travel: _____

Time traveling: _____

Dog friendly?: ☐ y ☐ n

Activities Accomplished:

- ☐ Archery
- ☐ Biking
- ☐ Birding
- ☐ Boating
- ☐ Camping
- ☐ Caving
- ☐ Geocaching

- ☐ Fishing
- ☐ Hiking
- ☐ Horseback Riding
- ☐ Hunting
- ☐ Off-Roading
- ☐ Paddle Boarding
- ☐ Photography

- ☐ Picnicking
- ☐ Rock Climbing
- ☐ Shooting Range
- ☐ Stargazing
- ☐ Swimming
- ☐ Tennis
- ☐ Walking

- ☐ Wildlife Watching
- ☐ _____
- ☐ _____
- ☐ _____
- ☐ _____
- ☐ _____
- ☐ _____

Traveling by: ☐ ☐ ☐ ☐ ☐ ☐ ☐ ☐ ☐ ☐ ☐ ☐

Reservation Information:

Places we discovered along the way

_____

Places to stop and see along the way

_____

Add your favorite ticket stub, postcard, photo, stamp or drawing here

LET NEW ADVENTURES ›› BEGIN →

www.mynaturebookadventures.com

Yachats State Recreation Area

Region: Central Coast - **Close to:** Yachats
Recreation Area

Star Rating
☆☆☆☆☆

My favorite thing about this place is...

Why I went ...

Who I went with ...

When I went ...

What I did...

What I saw...

What I learned...

An unforgettable moment...

A laughable moment...

A surprising moment...

An unforeseeable moment...

Wildlife spotted...

Snapped a selfie | Location...

Took a park sign photo? - ☐ y ☐ n

My List
☐ ____
☐ ____
☐ ____
☐ ____
☐ ____
☐ ____
☐ ____
☐ ____
☐ ____
☐ ____
☐ ____
☐ ____
☐ ____
☐ ____
☐ ____
☐ ____
☐ ____
☐ ____

And so the Adventure begins

The weather was ...

www.mynaturebookadventures.com

Plan Your Trip:

☐ Day Trip ☐ Overnight Stay

Reservations required: ☐ y ☐ n

Date reservations made: _____

Refund Policy: ☐ y ☐ n Site #: _____

Confirmation #: _____

Miles to travel: _____

Time traveling: _____

Dog friendly?: ☐ y ☐ n

Activities Accomplished:

- ☐ Archery
- ☐ Biking
- ☐ Birding
- ☐ Boating
- ☐ Camping
- ☐ Caving
- ☐ Geocaching
- ☐ Fishing
- ☐ Hiking
- ☐ Horseback Riding
- ☐ Hunting
- ☐ Off-Roading
- ☐ Paddle Boarding
- ☐ Photography
- ☐ Picnicking
- ☐ Rock Climbing
- ☐ Shooting Range
- ☐ Stargazing
- ☐ Swimming
- ☐ Tennis
- ☐ Walking
- ☐ Wildlife Watching
- ☐ _____
- ☐ _____
- ☐ _____
- ☐ _____
- ☐ _____
- ☐ _____

Traveling by: ☐ ☐ ☐ ☐ ☐ ☐ ☐ ☐ ☐ ☐ ☐ ☐

Reservation Information:

Places we discovered along the way

Places to stop and see along the way

Add your favorite ticket stub, postcard, photo, stamp or drawing here

LET NEW ADVENTURES ≫ BEGIN →

www.mynaturebookadventures.com

Yaquina Bay State Recreation Site

Region: Central Coast - **Close to:** Newport

Recreation Site

Star Rating ☆☆☆☆☆

My favorite thing about this place is... _____

Why I went ... _____

Who I went with ... _____

When I went ... _____

What I did... _____

What I saw... _____

What I learned... _____

An unforgettable moment... _____

A laughable moment... _____

A surprising moment... _____

An unforeseeable moment... _____

Wildlife spotted... _____

Snapped a selfie | Location... _____

Took a park sign photo? - ☐ y ☐ n

The weather was ...

My List
- ☐ ____
- ☐ ____
- ☐ ____
- ☐ ____
- ☐ ____
- ☐ ____
- ☐ ____
- ☐ ____
- ☐ ____
- ☐ ____
- ☐ ____
- ☐ ____
- ☐ ____
- ☐ ____
- ☐ ____
- ☐ ____
- ☐ ____

And so the Adventure begins

www.mynaturebookadventures.com

Plan Your Trip:

☐ Day Trip ☐ Overnight Stay

Reservations required: ☐ y ☐ n

Date reservations made: _____

Refund Policy: ☐ y ☐ n Site #: _____

Confirmation #: _____

Miles to travel: _____

Time traveling: _____

Dog friendly?: ☐ y ☐ n

Activities Accomplished:

☐ Archery   ☐ Fishing   ☐ Picnicking   ☐ Wildlife Watching
☐ Biking   ☐ Hiking   ☐ Rock Climbing   ☐ _____
☐ Birding   ☐ Horseback Riding   ☐ Shooting Range   ☐ _____
☐ Boating   ☐ Hunting   ☐ Stargazing   ☐ _____
☐ Camping   ☐ Off-Roading   ☐ Swimming   ☐ _____
☐ Caving   ☐ Paddle Boarding   ☐ Tennis   ☐ _____
☐ Geocaching   ☐ Photography   ☐ Walking   ☐ _____

Traveling by:
☐ car ☐ truck ☐ SUV ☐ van ☐ plane ☐ trolley ☐ bicycle ☐ bus ☐ train ☐ helicopter ☐ motorcycle ☐ boat

Reservation Information:

_____
_____

Places we discovered along the way

_____
_____
_____

Places to stop and see along the way

_____
_____
_____

Add your favorite ticket stub, postcard, photo, stamp or drawing here

LET NEW ADVENTURES
»› BEGIN →

Cline Falls State Scenic Viewpoint

Region: Central Oregon - **Close to:** Redmond
Scenic Viewpoint

Star Rating
☆☆☆☆☆

My favorite thing about this place is... _____
Why I went ... _____
Who I went with ... _____
When I went ... _____
What I did... _____
What I saw... _____

What I learned... _____

An unforgettable moment... _____

A laughable moment... _____

A surprising moment... _____

An unforeseeable moment... _____

Wildlife spotted... _____

My List
☐ _____
☐ _____
☐ _____
☐ _____
☐ _____
☐ _____
☐ _____
☐ _____
☐ _____
☐ _____
☐ _____
☐ _____
☐ _____
☐ _____
☐ _____
☐ _____
☐ _____

And so the Adventure begins

📷 Snapped a selfie | Location... _____
📷 Took a park sign photo? - ☐ y ☐ n
The weather was ... ☐ ☐ ☐ ☐ ☐ ☐ ☐

www.mynaturebookadventures.com

Plan Your Trip:

☐ Day Trip ☐ Overnight Stay

Reservations required: ☐y ☐n

Date reservations made: _____

Refund Policy: ☐y ☐n Site #: _____

Confirmation #: _____

Miles to travel: _____

Time traveling: _____

Dog friendly?: ☐y ☐n

Activities Accomplished:

- ☐ Archery
- ☐ Biking
- ☐ Birding
- ☐ Boating
- ☐ Camping
- ☐ Caving
- ☐ Geocaching
- ☐ Fishing
- ☐ Hiking
- ☐ Horseback Riding
- ☐ Hunting
- ☐ Off-Roading
- ☐ Paddle Boarding
- ☐ Photography
- ☐ Picnicking
- ☐ Rock Climbing
- ☐ Shooting Range
- ☐ Stargazing
- ☐ Swimming
- ☐ Tennis
- ☐ Walking
- ☐ Wildlife Watching
- ☐ _____
- ☐ _____
- ☐ _____
- ☐ _____
- ☐ _____
- ☐ _____

Traveling by:

Reservation Information:

Places we discovered along the way

Places to stop and see along the way

Add your favorite ticket stub, postcard, photo, stamp or drawing here

LET NEW ADVENTURES
»› BEGIN →

www.mynaturebookadventures.com

Cottonwood Canyon State Park

Region: Central Oregon - **Close to:** Moro

State Park

Star Rating ☆☆☆☆☆

My favorite thing about this place is... _____

Why I went ... _____

Who I went with ... _____

When I went ... _____

What I did... _____

What I saw... _____

What I learned... _____

An unforgettable moment... _____

A laughable moment... _____

A surprising moment... _____

An unforeseeable moment... _____

Wildlife spotted... _____

Snapped a selfie | Location... _____

Took a park sign photo? - ☐ y ☐ n

The weather was ...

My List
☐ _____
☐ _____
☐ _____
☐ _____
☐ _____
☐ _____
☐ _____
☐ _____
☐ _____
☐ _____
☐ _____
☐ _____
☐ _____
☐ _____
☐ _____
☐ _____

And so the Adventure begins

Plan Your Trip:

☐ Day Trip ☐ Overnight Stay

Reservations required: ☐ y ☐ n

Date reservations made: _____

Refund Policy: ☐ y ☐ n Site #: _____

Confirmation #: _____

Miles to travel: _____

Time traveling: _____

Dog friendly?: ☐ y ☐ n

Activities Accomplished:

☐ Archery	☐ Fishing	☐ Picnicking	☐ Wildlife Watching
☐ Biking	☐ Hiking	☐ Rock Climbing	☐ _____
☐ Birding	☐ Horseback Riding	☐ Shooting Range	☐ _____
☐ Boating	☐ Hunting	☐ Stargazing	☐ _____
☐ Camping	☐ Off-Roading	☐ Swimming	☐ _____
☐ Caving	☐ Paddle Boarding	☐ Tennis	☐ _____
☐ Geocaching	☐ Photography	☐ Walking	☐ _____

Traveling by:

☐ car ☐ truck ☐ SUV ☐ van ☐ plane ☐ trolley ☐ bicycle ☐ bus ☐ train ☐ helicopter ☐ motorcycle ☐ boat

Reservation Information:

Places we discovered along the way

Places to stop and see along the way

Add your favorite ticket stub, postcard, photo, stamp or drawing here

LET NEW ADVENTURES
»› BEGIN →

Fort Rock Cave (Near Fort Rock State Natural Area)

Region: Central Oregon - **Close to:** Fort Rock
National Historic Landmark

Star Rating
☆☆☆☆☆

My favorite thing about this place is... _____

Why I went ... _____

Who I went with ... _____

When I went ... _____

What I did... _____

What I saw... _____

What I learned... _____

An unforgettable moment... _____

A laughable moment... _____

A surprising moment... _____

An unforeseeable moment... _____

Wildlife spotted... _____

Snapped a selfie | Location... _____

Took a park sign photo? - ☐ y ☐ n

The weather was ...

My List
☐ _____
☐ _____
☐ _____
☐ _____
☐ _____
☐ _____
☐ _____
☐ _____
☐ _____
☐ _____
☐ _____
☐ _____
☐ _____
☐ _____
☐ _____
☐ _____
☐ _____

And so the Adventure begins

www.mynaturebookadventures.com

Plan Your Trip:

_____

☐ Day Trip   ☐ Overnight Stay

Reservations required: ☐ y ☐ n

Date reservations made: _____

Refund Policy: ☐ y ☐ n Site #: _____

Confirmation #: _____

Miles to travel: _____

Time traveling: _____

Dog friendly?: ☐ y ☐ n

Activities Accomplished:

☐ Archery	☐ Fishing	☐ Picnicking	☐ Wildlife Watching
☐ Biking	☐ Hiking	☐ Rock Climbing	☐ _____
☐ Birding	☐ Horseback Riding	☐ Shooting Range	☐ _____
☐ Boating	☐ Hunting	☐ Stargazing	☐ _____
☐ Camping	☐ Off-Roading	☐ Swimming	☐ _____
☐ Caving	☐ Paddle Boarding	☐ Tennis	☐ _____
☐ Geocaching	☐ Photography	☐ Walking	☐ _____

Traveling by:

☐ ☐ ☐ ☐ ☐ ☐ ☐ ☐ ☐ ☐ ☐ ☐ ☐

Reservation Information:

_____

Places we discovered along the way

_____
_____
_____

Places to stop and see along the way

_____
_____
_____

Add your favorite ticket stub, postcard, photo, stamp or drawing here

LET NEW ADVENTURES ≫ BEGIN →

Fort Rock State Natural Area

Region: Central Oregon - **Close to:** Fort Rock

Natural Area

Star Rating
☆☆☆☆☆

My favorite thing about this place is... _____

Why I went ... _____

Who I went with ... _____

When I went ... _____

What I did... _____

What I saw... _____

What I learned... _____

An unforgettable moment... _____

A laughable moment... _____

A surprising moment... _____

An unforeseeable moment... _____

Wildlife spotted... _____

Snapped a selfie | Location... _____

Took a park sign photo? - ☐ y ☐ n

The weather was ...

My List
☐ _____
☐ _____
☐ _____
☐ _____
☐ _____
☐ _____
☐ _____
☐ _____
☐ _____
☐ _____
☐ _____
☐ _____
☐ _____
☐ _____
☐ _____
☐ _____

And so the Adventure begins

Plan Your Trip:

☐ Day Trip ☐ Overnight Stay

Reservations required: ☐ y ☐ n

Date reservations made: _____

Refund Policy: ☐ y ☐ n Site #: _____

Confirmation #: _____

Miles to travel: _____

Time traveling: _____

Dog friendly?: ☐ y ☐ n

Reservation information:

Places we discovered along the way

_____
_____

Places to stop and see along the way

_____
_____

Activities Accomplished:

- ☐ Archery
- ☐ Biking
- ☐ Birding
- ☐ Boating
- ☐ Camping
- ☐ Caving
- ☐ Geocaching

- ☐ Fishing
- ☐ Hiking
- ☐ Horseback Riding
- ☐ Hunting
- ☐ Off-Roading
- ☐ Paddle Boarding
- ☐ Photography

- ☐ Picnicking
- ☐ Rock Climbing
- ☐ Shooting Range
- ☐ Stargazing
- ☐ Swimming
- ☐ Tennis
- ☐ Walking

- ☐ Wildlife Watching
- ☐ _____
- ☐ _____
- ☐ _____
- ☐ _____
- ☐ _____
- ☐ _____

Traveling by:

Add your favorite ticket stub, postcard, photo, stamp or drawing here

LET NEW ADVENTURES ≫ BEGIN →

Jasper Point Campground

Region: Central Oregon - **Close to:** Prineville
Campground

Star Rating
☆☆☆☆☆

My favorite thing about this place is... _____

Why I went ... _____

Who I went with ... _____

When I went ... _____

What I did... _____

What I saw... _____

What I learned... _____

An unforgettable moment... _____

A laughable moment... _____

A surprising moment... _____

An unforeseeable moment... _____

Wildlife spotted... _____

Snapped a selfie | Location... _____

Took a park sign photo? - ☐ y ☐ n

The weather was ...

My List
☐ _____
☐ _____
☐ _____
☐ _____
☐ _____
☐ _____
☐ _____
☐ _____
☐ _____
☐ _____
☐ _____
☐ _____
☐ _____
☐ _____
☐ _____
☐ _____

And so the Adventure begins

www.mynaturebookadventures.com

Plan Your Trip:

☐ Day Trip   ☐ Overnight Stay

Reservations required: ☐ y ☐ n

Date reservations made: _____

Refund Policy: ☐ y ☐ n   Site #: _____

Confirmation #: _____

Miles to travel: _____

Time traveling: _____

Dog friendly?: ☐ y ☐ n

Activities Accomplished:

- ☐ Archery
- ☐ Biking
- ☐ Birding
- ☐ Boating
- ☐ Camping
- ☐ Caving
- ☐ Geocaching

- ☐ Fishing
- ☐ Hiking
- ☐ Horseback Riding
- ☐ Hunting
- ☐ Off-Roading
- ☐ Paddle Boarding
- ☐ Photography

- ☐ Picnicking
- ☐ Rock Climbing
- ☐ Shooting Range
- ☐ Stargazing
- ☐ Swimming
- ☐ Tennis
- ☐ Walking

- ☐ Wildlife Watching
- ☐ _____
- ☐ _____
- ☐ _____
- ☐ _____
- ☐ _____
- ☐ _____

Traveling by:

☐ car ☐ truck ☐ SUV ☐ van ☐ airplane ☐ trolley ☐ bicycle ☐ bus ☐ train ☐ helicopter ☐ motorcycle ☐ boat

Reservation Information:

Places we discovered along the way

_____
_____
_____

Places to stop and see along the way

_____
_____
_____

Add your favorite ticket stub, postcard, photo, stamp or drawing here

LET NEW ADVENTURES ≫ BEGIN →

La Pine State Park

Region: Central Oregon - **Close to:** La Pine

State Park

Star Rating
☆☆☆☆☆

My favorite thing about this place is... _____

Why I went ... _____

Who I went with ... _____

When I went ... _____

What I did... _____

What I saw... _____

What I learned... _____

An unforgettable moment... _____

A laughable moment... _____

A surprising moment... _____

An unforeseeable moment... _____

Wildlife spotted... _____

Snapped a selfie | Location... _____

Took a park sign photo? - ☐ y ☐ n

The weather was ...

My List
☐ _____
☐ _____
☐ _____
☐ _____
☐ _____
☐ _____
☐ _____
☐ _____
☐ _____
☐ _____
☐ _____
☐ _____
☐ _____
☐ _____
☐ _____
☐ _____
☐ _____

And so the Adventure begins

Plan Your Trip:

_____

☐ Day Trip ☐ Overnight Stay

Reservations required: ☐ y ☐ n

Date reservations made: _____

Refund Policy: ☐ y ☐ n Site #: _____

Confirmation #: _____

Miles to travel: _____

Time traveling: _____

Dog friendly?: ☐ y ☐ n

Reservation Information:

_____
_____

Places we discovered along the way

_____
_____
_____

Places to stop and see along the way

_____
_____
_____

Activities Accomplished:

☐ Archery	☐ Fishing	☐ Picnicking	☐ Wildlife Watching
☐ Biking	☐ Hiking	☐ Rock Climbing	☐ _____
☐ Birding	☐ Horseback Riding	☐ Shooting Range	☐ _____
☐ Boating	☐ Hunting	☐ Stargazing	☐ _____
☐ Camping	☐ Off-Roading	☐ Swimming	☐ _____
☐ Caving	☐ Paddle Boarding	☐ Tennis	☐ _____
☐ Geocaching	☐ Photography	☐ Walking	☐ _____

Traveling by: 🚗 🛻 🚙 🚐 ✈️ 🚊 🚲 🚌 🚂 🚁 🏍️ 🛥️

Add your favorite ticket stub, postcard, photo, stamp or drawing here

LET NEW ADVENTURES ≫ BEGIN →

OCHOCO STATE SCENIC VIEWPOINT

Region: Central Oregon - **Close to:** Prineville

Scenic Viewpoint

Star Rating ☆☆☆☆☆

My favorite thing about this place is... _____

Why I went ... _____

Who I went with ... _____

When I went ... _____

What I did... _____

What I saw... _____

What I learned... _____

An unforgettable moment... _____

A laughable moment... _____

A surprising moment... _____

An unforeseeable moment... _____

Wildlife spotted... _____

Snapped a selfie | Location... _____

Took a park sign photo? - ☐ y ☐ n

The weather was ...

My List
☐ _____
☐ _____
☐ _____
☐ _____
☐ _____
☐ _____
☐ _____
☐ _____
☐ _____
☐ _____
☐ _____
☐ _____
☐ _____
☐ _____
☐ _____
☐ _____

And so the Adventure begins

www.mynaturebookadventures.com

Plan Your Trip:

☐ Day Trip ☐ Overnight Stay

Reservations required: ☐ y ☐ n

Date reservations made: _____

Refund Policy: ☐ y ☐ n Site #: _____

Confirmation #: _____

Miles to travel: _____

Time traveling: _____

Dog friendly?: ☐ y ☐ n

Activities Accomplished:

- ☐ Archery
- ☐ Biking
- ☐ Birding
- ☐ Boating
- ☐ Camping
- ☐ Caving
- ☐ Geocaching
- ☐ Fishing
- ☐ Hiking
- ☐ Horseback Riding
- ☐ Hunting
- ☐ Off-Roading
- ☐ Paddle Boarding
- ☐ Photography
- ☐ Picnicking
- ☐ Rock Climbing
- ☐ Shooting Range
- ☐ Stargazing
- ☐ Swimming
- ☐ Tennis
- ☐ Walking
- ☐ Wildlife Watching
- ☐ _____
- ☐ _____
- ☐ _____
- ☐ _____
- ☐ _____
- ☐ _____

Traveling by:

Reservation Information:

Places we discovered along the way

_____
_____
_____

Places to stop and see along the way

_____
_____
_____

Add your favorite ticket stub, postcard, photo, stamp or drawing here

LET NEW ADVENTURES
»› BEGIN →

Peter Skene Ogden State Scenic Viewpoint

Region: Central Oregon - *Close to:* Redmond
Scenic Viewpoint

Star Rating
☆☆☆☆☆

My favorite thing about this place is... _____

Why I went ... _____

Who I went with ... _____

When I went ... _____

What I did... _____

What I saw... _____

What I learned... _____

An unforgettable moment... _____

A laughable moment... _____

A surprising moment... _____

An unforeseeable moment... _____

Wildlife spotted... _____

Snapped a selfie | Location... _____

Took a park sign photo? - ☐ y ☐ n

The weather was ...

My List
☐ _____
☐ _____
☐ _____
☐ _____
☐ _____
☐ _____
☐ _____
☐ _____
☐ _____
☐ _____
☐ _____
☐ _____
☐ _____
☐ _____
☐ _____

AND SO the Adventure begins

Plan Your Trip:

_____

☐ Day Trip   ☐ Overnight Stay

Reservations required: ☐ y ☐ n

Date reservations made: _____

Refund Policy: ☐ y ☐ n Site #: _____

Confirmation #: _____

Miles to travel: _____

Time traveling: _____

Dog friendly?: ☐ y ☐ n

Activities Accomplished:

☐ Archery	☐ Fishing	☐ Picnicking	☐ Wildlife Watching
☐ Biking	☐ Hiking	☐ Rock Climbing	☐ _____
☐ Birding	☐ Horseback Riding	☐ Shooting Range	☐ _____
☐ Boating	☐ Hunting	☐ Stargazing	☐ _____
☐ Camping	☐ Off-Roading	☐ Swimming	☐ _____
☐ Caving	☐ Paddle Boarding	☐ Tenn's	☐ _____
☐ Geocaching	☐ Photography	☐ Walking	☐ _____

Traveling by:

☐ ☐ ☐ ☐ ☐ ☐ ☐ ☐ ☐ ☐ ☐ ☐

Reservation Information:

_____

Places we discovered along the way

_____
_____
_____

Places to stop and see along the way

_____
_____
_____

Add your favorite ticket stub, postcard, photo, stamp or drawing here

LET NEW ADVENTURES
» BEGIN →

Pilot Butte State Scenic Viewpoint

Region: Central Oregon - **Close to:** Bend

Scenic Viewpoint

Star Rating

My favorite thing about this place is...

Why I went ...

Who I went with ...

When I went ...

What I did...

What I saw...

What I learned...

An unforgettable moment...

A laughable moment...

A surprising moment...

An unforeseeable moment...

Wildlife spotted...

Snapped a selfie | Location...

Took a park sign photo? - ☐ y ☐ n

The weather was ...

My List

www.mynaturebookadventures.com

103

Plan Your Trip:

☐ Day Trip ☐ Overnight Stay

Reservations required: ☐y ☐n

Date reservations made: _____

Refund Policy: ☐y ☐n Site #: _____

Confirmation #: _____

Miles to travel: _____

Time traveling: _____

Dog friendly?: ☐y ☐n

Reservation Information:

_____

Places we discovered along the way

_____

_____

Places to stop and see along the way

_____

_____

Activities Accomplished:

- ☐ Archery
- ☐ Biking
- ☐ Birding
- ☐ Boating
- ☐ Camping
- ☐ Caving
- ☐ Geocaching

- ☐ Fishing
- ☐ Hiking
- ☐ Horseback Riding
- ☐ Hunting
- ☐ Off-Roading
- ☐ Paddle Boarding
- ☐ Photography

- ☐ Picnicking
- ☐ Rock Climbing
- ☐ Shooting Range
- ☐ Stargazing
- ☐ Swimming
- ☐ Tennis
- ☐ Walking

- ☐ Wildlife Watching
- ☐ _____
- ☐ _____
- ☐ _____
- ☐ _____
- ☐ _____
- ☐ _____

Traveling by: ☐ ☐ ☐ ☐ ☐ ☐ ☐ ☐ ☐ ☐ ☐ ☐

Add your favorite ticket stub, postcard, photo, stamp or drawing here

LET NEW ADVENTURES BEGIN →

Prineville Reservoir State Park

Region: Central Oregon - **Close to:** Prineville

State Park

Star Rating

My favorite thing about this place is... _____

Why I went ... _____

Who I went with ... _____

When I went ... _____

What I did... _____

What I saw... _____

What I learned... _____

An unforgettable moment... _____

A laughable moment... _____

A surprising moment... _____

An unforeseeable moment... _____

Wildlife spotted... _____

Snapped a selfie | Location... _____

Took a park sign photo? - ☐ y ☐ n

The weather was ...

My List

And so the Adventure begins

Plan Your Trip:

☐ Day Trip ☐ Overnight Stay

Reservations required: ☐ y ☐ n

Date reservations made: _____

Refund Policy: ☐ y ☐ n Site #: _____

Confirmation #: _____

Miles to travel: _____

Time traveling: _____

Dog friendly?: ☐ y ☐ n

Activities Accomplished:

- ☐ Archery
- ☐ Biking
- ☐ Birding
- ☐ Boating
- ☐ Camping
- ☐ Caving
- ☐ Geocaching

- ☐ Fishing
- ☐ Hiking
- ☐ Horseback Riding
- ☐ Hunting
- ☐ Off-Roading
- ☐ Paddle Boarding
- ☐ Photography

- ☐ Picnicking
- ☐ Rock Climbing
- ☐ Shooting Range
- ☐ Stargazing
- ☐ Swimming
- ☐ Tennis
- ☐ Walking

- ☐ Wildlife Watching
- ☐ _____
- ☐ _____
- ☐ _____
- ☐ _____
- ☐ _____
- ☐ _____

Traveling by:

☐ ☐ ☐ ☐ ☐ ☐ ☐ ☐ ☐ ☐ ☐ ☐

Reservation Information:

Places we discovered along the way

Places to stop and see along the way

Add your favorite ticket stub, postcard, photo, stamp or drawing here

LET NEW ADVENTURES ≫ BEGIN →

Smith Rock State Park

Region: Central Oregon - **Close to:** Redmond
State Park

Star Rating
☆☆☆☆☆

My favorite thing about this place is...
Why I went ...
Who I went with ...
When I went ...
What I did...
What I saw...

What I learned...

An unforgettable moment...

A laughable moment...

A surprising moment...

An unforeseeable moment...

Wildlife spotted...

Snapped a selfie | Location...
Took a park sign photo? - ☐ y ☐ n

My List
☐ _____
☐ _____
☐ _____
☐ _____
☐ _____
☐ _____
☐ _____
☐ _____
☐ _____
☐ _____
☐ _____
☐ _____
☐ _____
☐ _____
☐ _____
☐ _____
☐ _____

And so the Adventure begins

The weather was ... ☐ ☐ ☐ ☐ ☐ ☐ ☐

www.mynaturebookadventures.com

Plan Your Trip:

☐ Day Trip ☐ Overnight Stay

Reservations required: ☐ y ☐ n
Date reservations made: _____
Refund Policy: ☐ y ☐ n Site #: _____
Confirmation #: _____
Miles to travel: _____
Time traveling: _____
Dog friendly?: ☐ y ☐ n

Activities Accomplished:

☐ Archery	☐ Fishing	☐ Picnicking	☐ Wildlife Watching
☐ Biking	☐ Hiking	☐ Rock Climbing	☐ _____
☐ Birding	☐ Horseback Riding	☐ Shooting Range	☐ _____
☐ Boating	☐ Hunting	☐ Stargazing	☐ _____
☐ Camping	☐ Off-Roading	☐ Swimming	☐ _____
☐ Caving	☐ Paddle Boarding	☐ Tennis	☐ _____
☐ Geocaching	☐ Photography	☐ Walking	☐ _____

Traveling by:

☐ car ☐ truck ☐ SUV ☐ van ☐ airplane ☐ bus ☐ bicycle ☐ bus ☐ train ☐ helicopter ☐ motorcycle ☐ boat

Reservation Information:

Places we discovered along the way

Places to stop and see along the way

Add your favorite ticket stub, postcard, photo, stamp or drawing here

LET NEW ADVENTURES
»» BEGIN →

108 www.mynaturebookadventures.com

The Cove Palisades State Park

Region: Central Oregon - *Close to:* Madras

State Park

Star Rating ☆☆☆☆☆

My favorite thing about this place is... _____

Why I went ... _____

Who I went with ... _____

When I went ... _____

What I did... _____

What I saw... _____

What I learned... _____

An unforgettable moment... _____

A laughable moment... _____

A surprising moment... _____

An unforeseeable moment... _____

Wildlife spotted... _____

Snapped a selfie | Location... _____

Took a park sign photo? - ☐y ☐n

The weather was ...

My List
☐ _____
☐ _____
☐ _____
☐ _____
☐ _____
☐ _____
☐ _____
☐ _____
☐ _____
☐ _____
☐ _____
☐ _____
☐ _____
☐ _____
☐ _____
☐ _____
☐ _____

And so the Adventure begins

Plan Your Trip:

☐ Day Trip ☐ Overnight Stay

Reservations required: ☐ y ☐ n
Date reservations made: _____
Refund Policy: ☐ y ☐ n Site #: _____
Confirmation #: _____
Miles to travel: _____
Time traveling: _____
Dog friendly?: ☐ y ☐ n

Activities Accomplished:

☐ Archery	☐ Fishing	☐ Picnicking	☐ Wildlife Watching
☐ Biking	☐ Hiking	☐ Rock Climbing	☐ _____
☐ Birding	☐ Horseback Riding	☐ Shooting Range	☐ _____
☐ Boating	☐ Hunting	☐ Stargazing	☐ _____
☐ Camping	☐ Off-Roading	☐ Swimming	☐ _____
☐ Caving	☐ Paddle Boarding	☐ Tenn's	☐ _____
☐ Geocaching	☐ Photography	☐ Walking	☐ _____

Traveling by:

Reservation Information:

Places we discovered along the way

Places to stop and see along the way

Add your favorite ticket stub, postcard, photo, stamp or drawing here

LET NEW ADVENTURES
»» BEGIN →

www.mynaturebookadventures.com

Tumalo State Park

Region: Central Oregon - **Close to:** Bend

State Park

Star Rating
☆☆☆☆☆

My favorite thing about this place is... _____

Why I went ... _____

Who I went with ... _____

When I went ... _____

What I did... _____

What I saw... _____

What I learned... _____

An unforgettable moment... _____

A laughable moment... _____

A surprising moment... _____

An unforeseeable moment... _____

Wildlife spotted... _____

Snapped a selfie | Location... _____

Took a park sign photo? - ☐ y ☐ n

The weather was ...

My List
☐ _____
☐ _____
☐ _____
☐ _____
☐ _____
☐ _____
☐ _____
☐ _____
☐ _____
☐ _____
☐ _____
☐ _____
☐ _____
☐ _____
☐ _____
☐ _____
☐ _____
☐ _____

And so the Adventure begins

www.mynaturebookadventures.com

Plan Your Trip:

☐ Day Trip ☐ Overnight Stay

Reservations required: ☐ y ☐ n

Date reservations made: _____

Refund Policy: ☐ y ☐ n Site #: _____

Confirmation #: _____

Miles to travel: _____

Time traveling: _____

Dog friendly?: ☐ y ☐ n

Activities Accomplished:

- ☐ Archery
- ☐ Biking
- ☐ Birding
- ☐ Boating
- ☐ Camping
- ☐ Caving
- ☐ Geocaching
- ☐ Fishing
- ☐ Hiking
- ☐ Horseback Riding
- ☐ Hunting
- ☐ Off-Roading
- ☐ Paddle Boarding
- ☐ Photography
- ☐ Picnicking
- ☐ Rock Climbing
- ☐ Shooting Range
- ☐ Stargazing
- ☐ Swimming
- ☐ Tenn s
- ☐ Walking
- ☐ Wildlife Watching
- ☐ _____
- ☐ _____
- ☐ _____
- ☐ _____
- ☐ _____
- ☐ _____

Traveling by:

☐ ☐ ☐ ☐ ☐ ☐ ☐ ☐ ☐ ☐ ☐ ☐ ☐

Reservation Information:

Places we discovered along the way

_____
_____
_____

Places to stop and see along the way

_____
_____
_____

Add your favorite ticket stub, postcard, photo, stamp or drawing here

LET NEW ADVENTURES
»› BEGIN →

www.mynaturebookadventures.com

Bates State Park

Region: Eastern Oregon - **Close to:** Prairie City
State Park

Star Rating
☆☆☆☆☆

My favorite thing about this place is...
Why I went ...
Who I went with ...
When I went ...
What I did...
What I saw...

What I learned...

An unforgettable moment...

A laughable moment...

A surprising moment...

An unforeseeable moment...

Wildlife spotted...

Snapped a selfie | Location...

Took a park sign photo? - ☐y ☐n

The weather was ...

My List

And so the Adventure begins

Plan Your Trip:

☐ Day Trip ☐ Overnight Stay

Reservations required: ☐ y ☐ n

Date reservations made: _____

Refund Policy: ☐ y ☐ n Site #: _____

Confirmation #: _____

Miles to travel: _____

Time traveling: _____

Dog friendly?: ☐ y ☐ n

Activities Accomplished:

☐ Archery
☐ Biking
☐ Birding
☐ Boating
☐ Camping
☐ Caving
☐ Geocaching

☐ Fishing
☐ Hiking
☐ Horseback Riding
☐ Hunting
☐ Off-Roading
☐ Paddle Boarding
☐ Photography

☐ Picnicking
☐ Rock Climbing
☐ Shooting Range
☐ Stargazing
☐ Swimming
☐ Tennis
☐ Walking

☐ Wildlife Watching
☐ _____
☐ _____
☐ _____
☐ _____
☐ _____
☐ _____

Traveling by:
☐ car ☐ truck ☐ SUV ☐ van ☐ plane ☐ trolley ☐ bicycle ☐ bus ☐ train ☐ helicopter ☐ motorcycle ☐ boat

Reservation Information:

_____
_____

Places we discovered along the way
_____
_____
_____

Places to stop and see along the way
_____
_____
_____

Add your favorite ticket stub, postcard, photo, stamp or drawing here

LET NEW ADVENTURES
»» BEGIN →

Battle Mountain Forest State Scenic Corridor

Region: Eastern Oregon - **Close to:** Ukiah

Scenic Corridor

Star Rating ☆☆☆☆☆

My favorite thing about this place is... _____
Why I went ... _____
Who I went with ... _____
When I went ... _____
What I did... _____
What I saw... _____

What I learned... _____

An unforgettable moment... _____

A laughable moment... _____

A surprising moment... _____

An unforeseeable moment... _____

Wildlife spotted... _____

Snapped a selfie | Location... _____
Took a park sign photo? - ☐ y ☐ n

The weather was ...

My List
☐ _____ (×20)

And so the Adventure begins

www.mynaturebookadventures.com
115

Plan Your Trip:

☐ Day Trip ☐ Overnight Stay

Reservations required: ☐ y ☐ n

Date reservations made: _____

Refund Policy: ☐ y ☐ n Site #: _____

Confirmation #: _____

Miles to travel: _____

Time traveling: _____

Dog friendly?: ☐ y ☐ n

Activities Accomplished:

- ☐ Archery
- ☐ Biking
- ☐ Birding
- ☐ Boating
- ☐ Camping
- ☐ Caving
- ☐ Geocaching
- ☐ Fishing
- ☐ Hiking
- ☐ Horseback Riding
- ☐ Hunting
- ☐ Off-Roading
- ☐ Paddle Boarding
- ☐ Photography
- ☐ Picnicking
- ☐ Rock Climbing
- ☐ Shooting Range
- ☐ Stargazing
- ☐ Swimming
- ☐ Tenn's
- ☐ Walking
- ☐ Wildlife Watching
- ☐ _____
- ☐ _____
- ☐ _____
- ☐ _____
- ☐ _____
- ☐ _____

Traveling by:

Reservation Information:

Places we discovered along the way

Places to stop and see along the way

Add your favorite ticket stub, postcard, photo, stamp or drawing here

LET NEW ADVENTURES
≫ BEGIN →

Blue Mountain Forest State Scenic Corridor

Region: Eastern Oregon - **Close to:** La Grande
Scenic Corridor

Star Rating
☆☆☆☆☆

My favorite thing about this place is... _____

Why I went ... _____

Who I went with ... _____

When I went ... _____

What I did... _____

What I saw... _____

What I learned... _____

An unforgettable moment... _____

A laughable moment... _____

A surprising moment... _____

An unforeseeable moment... _____

Wildlife spotted... _____

Snapped a selfie | Location... _____

Took a park sign photo? - ☐ y ☐ n

The weather was ...

My List
☐ _____
☐ _____
☐ _____
☐ _____
☐ _____
☐ _____
☐ _____
☐ _____
☐ _____
☐ _____
☐ _____
☐ _____
☐ _____
☐ _____
☐ _____
☐ _____
☐ _____

And so the Adventure begins

www.mynaturebookadventures.com

Plan Your Trip:

☐ Day Trip ☐ Overnight Stay

Reservations required: ☐ y ☐ n

Date reservations made: _____

Refund Policy: ☐ y ☐ n Site #: _____

Confirmation #: _____

Miles to travel: _____

Time traveling: _____

Dog friendly?: ☐ y ☐ n

Activities Accomplished:

☐ Archery	☐ Fishing	☐ Picnicking	☐ Wildlife Watching
☐ Biking	☐ Hiking	☐ Rock Climbing	☐ _____
☐ Birding	☐ Horseback Riding	☐ Shooting Range	☐ _____
☐ Boating	☐ Hunting	☐ Stargazing	☐ _____
☐ Camping	☐ Off-Roading	☐ Swimming	☐ _____
☐ Caving	☐ Paddle Boarding	☐ Tenn's	☐ _____
☐ Geocaching	☐ Photography	☐ Walking	☐ _____

Traveling by:

☐ car ☐ truck ☐ SUV ☐ van ☐ airplane ☐ trolley ☐ bicycle ☐ bus ☐ train ☐ helicopter ☐ motorcycle ☐ boat

Reservation Information:

_____
_____

Places we discovered along the way

_____
_____
_____

Places to stop and see along the way

_____
_____
_____

Add your favorite ticket stub, postcard, photo, stamp or drawing here

LET NEW ADVENTURES ›› BEGIN →

Catherine Creek State Park

Region: Eastern Oregon - **Close to:** Union

State Park

Star Rating
☆☆☆☆☆

My favorite thing about this place is...

Why I went ...

Who I went with ...

When I went ...

What I did...

What I saw...

What I learned...

An unforgettable moment...

A laughable moment...

A surprising moment...

An unforeseeable moment...

Wildlife spotted...

Snapped a selfie | Location...

Took a park sign photo? - ☐ y ☐ n

The weather was ...

My List

And so the Adventure begins

www.mynaturebookadventures.com

119

Plan Your Trip:

☐ Day Trip   ☐ Overnight Stay

Reservations required: ☐ y ☐ n

Date reservations made: _____

Refund Policy: ☐ y ☐ n   Site #: _____

Confirmation #: _____

Miles to travel: _____

Time traveling: _____

Dog friendly?: ☐ y ☐ n

Activities Accomplished:

- ☐ Archery
- ☐ Biking
- ☐ Birding
- ☐ Boating
- ☐ Camping
- ☐ Caving
- ☐ Geocaching

- ☐ Fishing
- ☐ Hiking
- ☐ Horseback Riding
- ☐ Hunting
- ☐ Off-Roading
- ☐ Paddle Boarding
- ☐ Photography

- ☐ Picnicking
- ☐ Rock Climbing
- ☐ Shooting Range
- ☐ Stargazing
- ☐ Swimming
- ☐ Tennis
- ☐ Walking

- ☐ Wildlife Watching
- ☐ _____
- ☐ _____
- ☐ _____
- ☐ _____
- ☐ _____
- ☐ _____

Traveling by:

Reservation Information:

Places we discovered along the way

Places to stop and see along the way

Add your favorite ticket stub, postcard, photo, stamp or drawing here

LET NEW ADVENTURES BEGIN →

120   www.mynaturebookadventures.com

Clyde Holliday State Recreation Site

Region: Eastern Oregon - **Close to:** John Day
Recreation Site

Star Rating
☆☆☆☆☆

My favorite thing about this place is... _____

Why I went ... _____

Who I went with ... _____

When I went ... _____

What I did... _____

What I saw... _____

What I learned... _____

An unforgettable moment... _____

A laughable moment... _____

A surprising moment... _____

An unforeseeable moment... _____

Wildlife spotted... _____

Snapped a selfie | Location... _____

Took a park sign photo? - ☐ y ☐ n

The weather was ...

My List
☐ _____
☐ _____
☐ _____
☐ _____
☐ _____
☐ _____
☐ _____
☐ _____
☐ _____
☐ _____
☐ _____
☐ _____
☐ _____
☐ _____
☐ _____
☐ _____
☐ _____
☐ _____

And so the Adventure begins

www.mynaturebookadventures.com

121

Plan Your Trip:

☐ Day Trip   ☐ Overnight Stay

Reservations required: ☐ y ☐ n

Date reservations made: _____

Refund Policy: ☐ y ☐ n   Site #: _____

Confirmation #: _____

Miles to travel: _____

Time traveling: _____

Dog friendly?: ☐ y ☐ n

Activities Accomplished:

☐ Archery	☐ Fishing	☐ Picnicking	☐ Wildlife Watching
☐ Biking	☐ Hiking	☐ Rock Climbing	☐ _____
☐ Birding	☐ Horseback Riding	☐ Shooting Range	☐ _____
☐ Boating	☐ Hunting	☐ Stargazing	☐ _____
☐ Camping	☐ Off-Roading	☐ Swimming	☐ _____
☐ Caving	☐ Paddle Boarding	☐ Tennis	☐ _____
☐ Geocaching	☐ Photography	☐ Walking	☐ _____

Reservation Information:

Places we discovered along the way

Places to stop and see along the way

Traveling by:

Add your favorite ticket stub, postcard, photo, stamp or drawing here

LET NEW ADVENTURES ≫ BEGIN →

Dyer State Wayside

Region: Eastern Oregon - **Close to:** Condon

Wayside

Star Rating ☆☆☆☆☆

My favorite thing about this place is...

Why I went ...

Who I went with ...

When I went ...

What I did...

What I saw...

What I learned...

An unforgettable moment...

A laughable moment...

A surprising moment...

An unforeseeable moment...

Wildlife spotted...

Snapped a selfie | Location...

Took a park sign photo? - ☐ y ☐ n

The weather was ...

My List
☐ ___
☐ ___
☐ ___
☐ ___
☐ ___
☐ ___
☐ ___
☐ ___
☐ ___
☐ ___
☐ ___
☐ ___
☐ ___
☐ ___
☐ ___
☐ ___
☐ ___
☐ ___

And so the Adventure begins

Plan Your Trip:

☐ Day Trip   ☐ Overnight Stay

Reservations required: ☐ y ☐ n

Date reservations made: _____

Refund Policy: ☐ y ☐ n   Site #: _____

Confirmation #: _____

Miles to travel: _____

Time traveling: _____

Dog friendly?: ☐ y ☐ n

Activities Accomplished:

- ☐ Archery
- ☐ Biking
- ☐ Birding
- ☐ Boating
- ☐ Camping
- ☐ Caving
- ☐ Geocaching
- ☐ Fishing
- ☐ Hiking
- ☐ Horseback Riding
- ☐ Hunting
- ☐ Off-Roading
- ☐ Paddle Boarding
- ☐ Photography
- ☐ Picnicking
- ☐ Rock Climbing
- ☐ Shooting Range
- ☐ Stargazing
- ☐ Swimming
- ☐ Tennis
- ☐ Walking
- ☐ Wildlife Watching
- ☐ _____
- ☐ _____
- ☐ _____
- ☐ _____
- ☐ _____
- ☐ _____

Traveling by:

Reservation Information:

Places we discovered along the way

Places to stop and see along the way

Add your favorite ticket stub, postcard, photo, stamp or drawing here

LET NEW ADVENTURES
»» BEGIN →

www.mynaturebookadventures.com

Emigrant Springs State Heritage Area

Region: Eastern Oregon - **Close to:** Pendleton

Heritage Area

Star Rating ☆☆☆☆☆

My favorite thing about this place is... _____

Why I went ... _____

Who I went with ... _____

When I went ... _____

What I did... _____

What I saw... _____

What I learned... _____

An unforgettable moment... _____

A laughable moment... _____

A surprising moment... _____

An unforeseeable moment... _____

Wildlife spotted... _____

Snapped a selfie | Location... _____

Took a park sign photo? - ☐ y ☐ n

The weather was ...

My List
☐ _____
☐ _____
☐ _____
☐ _____
☐ _____
☐ _____
☐ _____
☐ _____
☐ _____
☐ _____
☐ _____
☐ _____
☐ _____
☐ _____
☐ _____
☐ _____
☐ _____

And so the Adventure begins

Plan Your Trip:

_____

☐ Day Trip   ☐ Overnight Stay

Reservations required: ☐ y ☐ n

Date reservations made: _____

Refund Policy: ☐ y ☐ n Site #: _____

Confirmation #: _____

Miles to travel: _____

Time traveling: _____

Dog friendly?: ☐ y ☐ n

Activities Accomplished:

☐ Archery	☐ Fishing	☐ Picnicking	☐ Wildlife Watching
☐ Biking	☐ Hiking	☐ Rock Climbing	☐ _____
☐ Birding	☐ Horseback Riding	☐ Shooting Range	☐ _____
☐ Boating	☐ Hunting	☐ Stargazing	☐ _____
☐ Camping	☐ Off-Roading	☐ Swimming	☐ _____
☐ Caving	☐ Paddle Boarding	☐ Tennis	☐ _____
☐ Geocaching	☐ Photography	☐ Walking	☐ _____

Traveling by:
☐ ☐ ☐ ☐ ☐ ☐ ☐ ☐ ☐ ☐ ☐ ☐

Reservation Information:

_____

Places we discovered along the way

_____
_____
_____

Places to stop and see along the way

_____
_____
_____

Add your favorite ticket stub, postcard, photo, stamp or drawing here

LET NEW ADVENTURES ≫ BEGIN →

126 www.mynaturebookadventures.com

Farewell Bend State Recreation Area

Region: Eastern Oregon - ***Close to:*** Ontario
Recreation Area

Star Rating
☆☆☆☆☆

My favorite thing about this place is... _____

Why I went ... _____

Who I went with ... _____

When I went ... _____

What I did... _____

What I saw... _____

What I learned... _____

An unforgettable moment... _____

A laughable moment... _____

A surprising moment... _____

An unforeseeable moment... _____

Wildlife spotted... _____

Snapped a selfie | Location... _____

Took a park sign photo? - ☐ y ☐ n

The weather was ... ☐ ☐ ☐ ☐ ☐ ☐ ☐

My List
☐ _____
☐ _____
☐ _____
☐ _____
☐ _____
☐ _____
☐ _____
☐ _____
☐ _____
☐ _____
☐ _____
☐ _____
☐ _____
☐ _____
☐ _____
☐ _____

And so the Adventure begins

www.mynaturebookadventures.com

Plan Your Trip:

☐ Day Trip ☐ Overnight Stay

Reservations required: ☐ y ☐ n

Date reservations made: _____

Refund Policy: ☐ y ☐ n Site #: _____

Confirmation #: _____

Miles to travel: _____

Time traveling: _____

Dog friendly?: ☐ y ☐ n

Activities Accomplished:

☐ Archery	☐ Fishing	☐ Picnicking	☐ Wildlife Watching
☐ Biking	☐ Hiking	☐ Rock Climbing	☐ _____
☐ Birding	☐ Horseback Riding	☐ Shooting Range	☐ _____
☐ Boating	☐ Hunting	☐ Stargazing	☐ _____
☐ Camping	☐ Off-Roading	☐ Swimming	☐ _____
☐ Caving	☐ Paddle Boarding	☐ Tennis	☐ _____
☐ Geocaching	☐ Photography	☐ Walking	☐ _____

Traveling by:

Reservation Information:

_____

Places we discovered along the way
_____
_____
_____

Places to stop and see along the way
_____
_____
_____

Add your favorite ticket stub, postcard, photo, stamp or drawing here

LET NEW ADVENTURES BEGIN →

128

www.mynaturebookadventures.com

Frenchglen Hotel State Heritage Site

Region: Eastern Oregon - **Close to:** Burns
Heritage Site

Star Rating

My favorite thing about this place is...

Why I went ...

Who I went with ...

When I went ...

What I did...

What I saw...

What I learned...

An unforgettable moment...

A laughable moment...

A surprising moment...

An unforeseeable moment...

Wildlife spotted...

Snapped a selfie | Location...

Took a park sign photo? - ☐ y ☐ n

The weather was ...

My List

And so the Adventure begins

Plan Your Trip:

☐ Day Trip ☐ Overnight Stay

Reservations required: ☐ y ☐ n

Date reservations made: _____

Refund Policy: ☐ y ☐ n Site #: _____

Confirmation #: _____

Miles to travel: _____

Time traveling: _____

Dog friendly?: ☐ y ☐ n

Activities Accomplished:

- ☐ Archery
- ☐ Biking
- ☐ Birding
- ☐ Boating
- ☐ Camping
- ☐ Caving
- ☐ Geocaching
- ☐ Fishing
- ☐ Hiking
- ☐ Horseback Riding
- ☐ Hunting
- ☐ Off-Roading
- ☐ Paddle Boarding
- ☐ Photography
- ☐ Picnicking
- ☐ Rock Climbing
- ☐ Shooting Range
- ☐ Stargazing
- ☐ Swimming
- ☐ Tennis
- ☐ Walking
- ☐ Wildlife Watching
- ☐ _____
- ☐ _____
- ☐ _____
- ☐ _____
- ☐ _____
- ☐ _____

Traveling by: ☐ ☐ ☐ ☐ ☐ ☐ ☐ ☐ ☐ ☐ ☐ ☐

Reservation Information:

Places we discovered along the way

Places to stop and see along the way

Add your favorite ticket stub, postcard, photo, stamp or drawing here

LET NEW ADVENTURES
>>> BEGIN →

Hat Rock State Park

Region: Eastern Oregon - **Close to:** Umatilla
State Park

Star Rating
☆☆☆☆☆

My favorite thing about this place is... _____

Why I went ... _____

Who I went with ... _____

When I went ... _____

What I did... _____

What I saw... _____

What I learned... _____

An unforgettable moment... _____

A laughable moment... _____

A surprising moment... _____

An unforeseeable moment... _____

Wildlife spotted... _____

Snapped a selfie | Location... _____

Took a park sign photo? - ☐ y ☐ n

The weather was ...

My List
☐ _____
☐ _____
☐ _____
☐ _____
☐ _____
☐ _____
☐ _____
☐ _____
☐ _____
☐ _____
☐ _____
☐ _____
☐ _____
☐ _____
☐ _____
☐ _____
☐ _____

And so the Adventure begins

www.mynaturebookadventures.com

131

Plan Your Trip:

☐ Day Trip   ☐ Overnight Stay

Reservations required: ☐ y ☐ n

Date reservations made: _____

Refund Policy: ☐ y ☐ n Site #: _____

Confirmation #: _____

Miles to travel: _____

Time traveling: _____

Dog friendly?: ☐ y ☐ n

Activities Accomplished:

☐ Archery	☐ Fishing	☐ Picnicking	☐ Wildlife Watching
☐ Biking	☐ Hiking	☐ Rock Climbing	☐ _____
☐ Birding	☐ Horseback Riding	☐ Shooting Range	☐ _____
☐ Boating	☐ Hunting	☐ Stargazing	☐ _____
☐ Camping	☐ Off-Roading	☐ Swimming	☐ _____
☐ Caving	☐ Paddle Boarding	☐ Tennis	☐ _____
☐ Geocaching	☐ Photography	☐ Walking	☐ _____

Traveling by:

Reservation Information:

Places we discovered along the way

Places to stop and see along the way

Add your favorite ticket stub, postcard, photo, stamp or drawing here

LET NEW ADVENTURES ›› BEGIN →

Hilgard Junction State Recreation Area

Region: Eastern Oregon - *Close to:* La Grande
Recreation Area

Star Rating
☆☆☆☆☆

My favorite thing about this place is...

Why I went ...

Who I went with ...

When I went ...

What I did...

What I saw...

What I learned...

An unforgettable moment...

A laughable moment...

A surprising moment...

An unforeseeable moment...

Wildlife spotted...

Snapped a selfie | Location...

Took a park sign photo? - ☐ y ☐ n

The weather was ...

My List
☐ ___
☐ ___
☐ ___
☐ ___
☐ ___
☐ ___
☐ ___
☐ ___
☐ ___
☐ ___
☐ ___
☐ ___
☐ ___
☐ ___
☐ ___
☐ ___
☐ ___
☐ ___

And so the Adventure begins

Plan Your Trip:

_____

☐ Day Trip ☐ Overnight Stay

Reservations required: ☐ y ☐ n

Date reservations made: _____

Refund Policy: ☐ y ☐ n Site #: _____

Confirmation #: _____

Miles to travel: _____

Time traveling: _____

Dog friendly?: ☐ y ☐ n

Activities Accomplished:

☐ Archery	☐ Fishing	☐ Picnicking	☐ Wildlife Watching
☐ Biking	☐ Hiking	☐ Rock Climbing	☐ _____
☐ Birding	☐ Horseback Riding	☐ Shooting Range	☐ _____
☐ Boating	☐ Hunting	☐ Stargazing	☐ _____
☐ Camping	☐ Off-Roading	☐ Swimming	☐ _____
☐ Caving	☐ Paddle Boarding	☐ Tennis	☐ _____
☐ Geocaching	☐ Photography	☐ Walking	☐ _____

Traveling by:

☐ ☐ ☐ ☐ ☐ ☐ ☐ ☐ ☐ ☐ ☐ ☐

Reservation Information:

_____
_____

Places we discovered along the way

_____
_____
_____

Places to stop and see along the way

_____
_____

Add your favorite ticket stub, postcard, photo, stamp or drawing here

LET NEW ADVENTURES
>>> BEGIN →

Iwetemlaykin State Heritage Site

Region: Eastern Oregon - **Close to:** Joseph

Heritage Site

Star Rating ☆☆☆☆☆

My favorite thing about this place is... _____

Why I went ... _____

Who I went with ... _____

When I went ... _____

What I did... _____

What I saw... _____

What I learned... _____

An unforgettable moment... _____

A laughable moment... _____

A surprising moment... _____

An unforeseeable moment... _____

Wildlife spotted... _____

Snapped a selfie | Location... _____

Took a park sign photo? - ☐ y ☐ n

The weather was ...

My List
☐ _____
☐ _____
☐ _____
☐ _____
☐ _____
☐ _____
☐ _____
☐ _____
☐ _____
☐ _____
☐ _____
☐ _____
☐ _____
☐ _____

And so the Adventure begins

www.mynaturebookadventures.com

Plan Your Trip:

☐ Day Trip ☐ Overnight Stay

Reservations required: ☐ y ☐ n

Date reservations made: _____

Refund Policy: ☐ y ☐ n   Site #: _____

Confirmation #: _____

Miles to travel: _____

Time traveling: _____

Dog friendly?: ☐ y ☐ n

Activities Accomplished:

☐ Archery	☐ Fishing	☐ Picnicking	☐ Wildlife Watching
☐ Biking	☐ Hiking	☐ Rock Climbing	☐ _____
☐ Birding	☐ Horseback Riding	☐ Shooting Range	☐ _____
☐ Boating	☐ Hunting	☐ Stargazing	☐ _____
☐ Camping	☐ Off-Roading	☐ Swimming	☐ _____
☐ Caving	☐ Paddle Boarding	☐ Tennis	☐ _____
☐ Geocaching	☐ Photography	☐ Walking	☐ _____

Traveling by:
☐ ☐ ☐ ☐ ☐ ☐ ☐ ☐ ☐ ☐ ☐ ☐

Reservation Information:

Places we discovered along the way

_____
_____
_____

Places to stop and see along the way

_____
_____
_____

Add your favorite ticket stub, postcard, photo, stamp or drawing here

LET NEW ADVENTURES ≫ BEGIN →

136

www.mynaturebookadventures.com

Kam Wah Chung State Heritage Site

Region: Eastern Oregon - **Close to:** John Day
Heritage Site

Star Rating
☆☆☆☆☆

My favorite thing about this place is... _____

Why I went ... _____

Who I went with ... _____

When I went ... _____

What I did... _____

What I saw... _____

What I learned... _____

An unforgettable moment... _____

A laughable moment... _____

A surprising moment... _____

An unforeseeable moment... _____

Wildlife spotted... _____

Snapped a selfie | Location... _____

Took a park sign photo? - ☐ y ☐ n

The weather was ...

My List
☐ _____
☐ _____
☐ _____
☐ _____
☐ _____
☐ _____
☐ _____
☐ _____
☐ _____
☐ _____
☐ _____
☐ _____
☐ _____
☐ _____
☐ _____
☐ _____
☐ _____
☐ _____
☐ _____
☐ _____

And so the Adventure begins

Plan Your Trip:

☐ Day Trip ☐ Overnight Stay

Reservations required: ☐ y ☐ n

Date reservations made: _____

Refund Policy: ☐ y ☐ n Site #: _____

Confirmation #: _____

Miles to travel: _____

Time traveling: _____

Dog friendly?: ☐ y ☐ n

Activities Accomplished:

- ☐ Archery
- ☐ Biking
- ☐ Birding
- ☐ Boating
- ☐ Camping
- ☐ Caving
- ☐ Geocaching

- ☐ Fishing
- ☐ Hiking
- ☐ Horseback Riding
- ☐ Hunting
- ☐ Off-Roading
- ☐ Paddle Boarding
- ☐ Photography

- ☐ Picnicking
- ☐ Rock Climbing
- ☐ Shooting Range
- ☐ Stargazing
- ☐ Swimming
- ☐ Tennis
- ☐ Walking

- ☐ Wildlife Watching
- ☐ _____
- ☐ _____
- ☐ _____
- ☐ _____
- ☐ _____
- ☐ _____

Traveling by:

Reservation Information:

Places we discovered along the way

Places to stop and see along the way

Add your favorite ticket stub, postcard, photo, stamp or drawing here

LET NEW ADVENTURES
≫ BEGIN →

www.mynaturebookadventures.com

Lake Owyhee State Park

Region: Eastern Oregon - **Close to:** Nyssa

State Park

Star Rating
☆☆☆☆☆

My favorite thing about this place is...

Why I went ...

Who I went with ...

When I went ...

What I did...

What I saw...

What I learned...

An unforgettable moment...

A laughable moment...

A surprising moment...

An unforeseeable moment...

Wildlife spotted...

My List

And so the Adventure begins

Snapped a selfie | Location...

Took a park sign photo? - ☐ y ☐ n

The weather was ...

Plan Your Trip:

☐ Day Trip   ☐ Overnight Stay

Reservations required: ☐ y ☐ n

Date reservations made: _____

Refund Policy: ☐ y ☐ n Site #: _____

Confirmation #: _____

Miles to travel: _____

Time traveling: _____

Dog friendly?: ☐ y ☐ n

Activities Accomplished:

- ☐ Archery
- ☐ Biking
- ☐ Birding
- ☐ Boating
- ☐ Camping
- ☐ Caving
- ☐ Geocaching

- ☐ Fishing
- ☐ Hiking
- ☐ Horseback Riding
- ☐ Hunting
- ☐ Off-Roading
- ☐ Paddle Boarding
- ☐ Photography

- ☐ Picnicking
- ☐ Rock Climbing
- ☐ Shooting Range
- ☐ Stargazing
- ☐ Swimming
- ☐ Tennis
- ☐ Walking

- ☐ Wildlife Watching
- ☐ _____
- ☐ _____
- ☐ _____
- ☐ _____
- ☐ _____
- ☐ _____

Traveling by:

Reservation Information:

Places we discovered along the way

Places to stop and see along the way

Add your favorite ticket stub, postcard, photo, stamp or drawing here

LET NEW ADVENTURES ≫ BEGIN →

Minam State Recreation Area

Region: Eastern Oregon - **Close to:** Elgin

Recreation Area

Star Rating
☆☆☆☆☆

My favorite thing about this place is... _____

Why I went ... _____

Who I went with ... _____

When I went ... _____

What I did... _____

What I saw... _____

What I learned... _____

An unforgettable moment... _____

A laughable moment... _____

A surprising moment... _____

An unforeseeable moment... _____

Wildlife spotted... _____

Snapped a selfie | Location... _____

Took a park sign photo? - ☐ y ☐ n

The weather was ...

My List
☐ _____
☐ _____
☐ _____
☐ _____
☐ _____
☐ _____
☐ _____
☐ _____
☐ _____
☐ _____
☐ _____
☐ _____
☐ _____
☐ _____
☐ _____
☐ _____
☐ _____
☐ _____
☐ _____
☐ _____

And so the Adventure begins

Plan Your Trip:

☐ Day Trip   ☐ Overnight Stay

Reservations required: ☐ y ☐ n

Date reservations made: _____

Refund Policy: ☐ y ☐ n Site #: _____

Confirmation #: _____

Miles to travel: _____

Time traveling: _____

Dog friendly?: ☐ y ☐ n

Activities Accomplished:

☐ Archery
☐ Biking
☐ Birding
☐ Boating
☐ Camping
☐ Caving
☐ Geocaching

☐ Fishing
☐ Hiking
☐ Horseback Riding
☐ Hunting
☐ Off-Roading
☐ Paddle Boarding
☐ Photography

☐ Picnicking
☐ Rock Climbing
☐ Shooting Range
☐ Stargazing
☐ Swimming
☐ Tennis
☐ Walking

☐ Wildlife Watching
☐ _____
☐ _____
☐ _____
☐ _____
☐ _____
☐ _____

Traveling by:

Reservation Information:

Places we discovered along the way

Places to stop and see along the way

Add your favorite ticket stub, postcard, photo, stamp or drawing here

LET NEW ADVENTURES ≫ BEGIN →

www.mynaturebookadventures.com

Ontario State Recreation Site

Region: Eastern Oregon - **Close to:** Ontario

Recreation Site

Star Rating
☆☆☆☆☆

My favorite thing about this place is...

Why I went ...

Who I went with ...

When I went ...

What I did...

What I saw...

What I learned...

An unforgettable moment...

A laughable moment...

A surprising moment...

An unforeseeable moment...

Wildlife spotted...

Snapped a selfie | Location...

Took a park sign photo? - ☐ y ☐ n

The weather was ...

My List
☐
☐
☐
☐
☐
☐
☐
☐
☐
☐
☐
☐
☐
☐
☐
☐
☐

And so the Adventure begins

www.mynaturebookadventures.com

143

Plan Your Trip:

☐ Day Trip ☐ Overnight Stay

Reservations required: ☐ y ☐ n
Date reservations made: _____
Refund Policy: ☐ y ☐ n Site #: _____
Confirmation #: _____
Miles to travel: _____
Time traveling: _____
Dog friendly?: ☐ y ☐ n

Activities Accomplished:

- ☐ Archery
- ☐ Biking
- ☐ Birding
- ☐ Boating
- ☐ Camping
- ☐ Caving
- ☐ Geocaching
- ☐ Fishing
- ☐ Hiking
- ☐ Horseback Riding
- ☐ Hunting
- ☐ Off-Roading
- ☐ Paddle Boarding
- ☐ Photography
- ☐ Picnicking
- ☐ Rock Climbing
- ☐ Shooting Range
- ☐ Stargazing
- ☐ Swimming
- ☐ Tennis
- ☐ Walking
- ☐ Wildlife Watching
- ☐ _____
- ☐ _____
- ☐ _____
- ☐ _____
- ☐ _____
- ☐ _____

Traveling by: ☐ ☐ ☐ ☐ ☐ ☐ ☐ ☐ ☐ ☐ ☐ ☐

Reservation Information:

Places we discovered along the way

Places to stop and see along the way

Add your favorite ticket stub, postcard, photo, stamp or drawing here

LET NEW ADVENTURES ›› BEGIN →

Pete French Round Barn State Heritage Site

Region: Eastern Oregon - **Close to:** New Princeton
Heritage Site

Star Rating
☆☆☆☆☆

My favorite thing about this place is…

Why I went …

Who I went with …

When I went …

What I did…

What I saw…

What I learned…

An unforgettable moment…

A laughable moment…

A surprising moment…

An unforeseeable moment…

Wildlife spotted…

Snapped a selfie | Location…

Took a park sign photo? - ☐ y ☐ n

The weather was …

My List

And so the Adventure begins

www.mynaturebookadventures.com

145

Plan Your Trip:

☐ Day Trip   ☐ Overnight Stay

Reservations required: ☐ y ☐ n

Date reservations made: _____

Refund Policy: ☐ y ☐ n Site #: _____

Confirmation #: _____

Miles to travel: _____

Time traveling: _____

Dog friendly?: ☐ y ☐ n

Activities Accomplished:

- ☐ Archery
- ☐ Biking
- ☐ Birding
- ☐ Boating
- ☐ Camping
- ☐ Caving
- ☐ Geocaching

- ☐ Fishing
- ☐ Hiking
- ☐ Horseback Riding
- ☐ Hunting
- ☐ Off-Roading
- ☐ Paddle Boarding
- ☐ Photography

- ☐ Picnicking
- ☐ Rock Climbing
- ☐ Shooting Range
- ☐ Stargazing
- ☐ Swimming
- ☐ Tennis
- ☐ Walking

- ☐ Wildlife Watching
- ☐ _____
- ☐ _____
- ☐ _____
- ☐ _____
- ☐ _____
- ☐ _____

Traveling by:

Reservation Information:

Places we discovered along the way

Places to stop and see along the way

Add your favorite ticket stub, postcard, photo, stamp or drawing here

LET NEW ADVENTURES ≫ BEGIN →

Red Bridge State Wayside

Region: Eastern Oregon - **Close to:** La Grande

Wayside

Star Rating ☆☆☆☆☆

My favorite thing about this place is... _____

Why I went ... _____

Who I went with ... _____

When I went ... _____

What I did... _____

What I saw... _____

What I learned... _____

An unforgettable moment... _____

A laughable moment... _____

A surprising moment... _____

An unforeseeable moment... _____

Wildlife spotted... _____

Snapped a selfie | Location... _____

Took a park sign photo? - ☐ y ☐ n

The weather was ...

My List
☐ _____
☐ _____
☐ _____
☐ _____
☐ _____
☐ _____
☐ _____
☐ _____
☐ _____
☐ _____
☐ _____
☐ _____
☐ _____
☐ _____
☐ _____

And so the Adventure begins

Plan Your Trip:

☐ Day Trip ☐ Overnight Stay

Reservations required: ☐ y ☐ n

Date reservations made: _____

Refund Policy: ☐ y ☐ n Site #: _____

Confirmation #: _____

Miles to travel: _____

Time traveling: _____

Dog friendly?: ☐ y ☐ n

Activities Accomplished:

☐ Archery	☐ Fishing	☐ Picnicking	☐ Wildlife Watching
☐ Biking	☐ Hiking	☐ Rock Climbing	☐ _____
☐ Birding	☐ Horseback Riding	☐ Shooting Range	☐ _____
☐ Boating	☐ Hunting	☐ Stargazing	☐ _____
☐ Camping	☐ Off-Roading	☐ Swimming	☐ _____
☐ Caving	☐ Paddle Boarding	☐ Tennis	☐ _____
☐ Geocaching	☐ Photography	☐ Walking	☐ _____

Traveling by:

Reservation Information:

_____

Places we discovered along the way
_____
_____
_____

Places to stop and see along the way
_____
_____
_____

Add your favorite ticket stub, postcard, photo, stamp or drawing here

LET NEW ADVENTURES
>>> BEGIN →

Succor Creek State Natural Area

Region: Eastern Oregon - **Close to:** Nyssa

Natural Area

Star Rating ☆☆☆☆☆

My favorite thing about this place is... _____

Why I went ... _____

Who I went with ... _____

When I went ... _____

What I did... _____

What I saw... _____

What I learned... _____

An unforgettable moment... _____

A laughable moment... _____

A surprising moment... _____

An unforeseeable moment... _____

Wildlife spotted... _____

Snapped a selfie | Location... _____

Took a park sign photo? - ☐ y ☐ n

The weather was ...

My List

And so the Adventure begins

www.mynaturebookadventures.com

149

Plan Your Trip:

☐ Day Trip ☐ Overnight Stay

Reservations required: ☐ y ☐ n

Date reservations made: _____

Refund Policy: ☐ y ☐ n Site #: _____

Confirmation #: _____

Miles to travel: _____

Time traveling: _____

Dog friendly?: ☐ y ☐ n

Activities Accomplished:

- ☐ Archery
- ☐ Biking
- ☐ Birding
- ☐ Boating
- ☐ Camping
- ☐ Caving
- ☐ Geocaching

- ☐ Fishing
- ☐ Hiking
- ☐ Horseback Riding
- ☐ Hunting
- ☐ Off-Roading
- ☐ Paddle Boarding
- ☐ Photography

- ☐ Picnicking
- ☐ Rock Climbing
- ☐ Shooting Range
- ☐ Stargazing
- ☐ Swimming
- ☐ Tennis
- ☐ Walking

- ☐ Wildlife Watching
- ☐ _____
- ☐ _____
- ☐ _____
- ☐ _____
- ☐ _____
- ☐ _____

Traveling by: ☐ ☐ ☐ ☐ ☐ ☐ ☐ ☐ ☐ ☐ ☐ ☐

Reservation Information:

Places we discovered along the way

Places to stop and see along the way

Add your favorite ticket stub, postcard, photo, stamp or drawing here

LET NEW ADVENTURES ≫ BEGIN →

www.mynaturebookadventures.com

Sumpter Valley Dredge State Heritage Area

Region: Eastern Oregon - **Close to:** Baker City

Heritage Area

Star Rating ☆☆☆☆☆

My favorite thing about this place is... _____

Why I went ... _____

Who I went with ... _____

When I went ... _____

What I did... _____

What I saw... _____

What I learned... _____

An unforgettable moment... _____

A laughable moment... _____

A surprising moment... _____

An unforeseeable moment... _____

Wildlife spotted... _____

Snapped a selfie | Location... _____

Took a park sign photo? - ☐ y ☐ n

The weather was ...

My List
☐ _____
☐ _____
☐ _____
☐ _____
☐ _____
☐ _____
☐ _____
☐ _____
☐ _____
☐ _____
☐ _____
☐ _____
☐ _____
☐ _____
☐ _____

And so the Adventure begins

www.mynaturebookadventures.com

151

Plan Your Trip:

☐ Day Trip ☐ Overnight Stay

Reservations required: ☐ y ☐ n

Date reservations made: _____

Refund Policy: ☐ y ☐ n Site #: _____

Confirmation #: _____

Miles to travel: _____

Time traveling: _____

Dog friendly?: ☐ y ☐ n

Activities Accomplished:

- ☐ Archery
- ☐ Biking
- ☐ Birding
- ☐ Boating
- ☐ Camping
- ☐ Caving
- ☐ Geocaching

- ☐ Fishing
- ☐ Hiking
- ☐ Horseback Riding
- ☐ Hunting
- ☐ Off-Roading
- ☐ Paddle Boarding
- ☐ Photography

- ☐ Picnicking
- ☐ Rock Climbing
- ☐ Shooting Range
- ☐ Stargazing
- ☐ Swimming
- ☐ Tennis
- ☐ Walking

- ☐ Wildlife Watching
- ☐ _____
- ☐ _____
- ☐ _____
- ☐ _____
- ☐ _____
- ☐ _____

Traveling by:

Reservation Information:

Places we discovered along the way

Places to stop and see along the way

Add your favorite ticket stub, postcard, photo, stamp or drawing here

Let New Adventures Begin →

www.mynaturebookadventures.com

Ukiah-Dale Forest State Scenic Corridor

Region: Eastern Oregon - **Close to:** Ukiah
Scenic Corridor

Star Rating

My favorite thing about this place is... _____

Why I went ... _____

Who I went with ... _____

When I went ... _____

What I did... _____

What I saw... _____

What I learned... _____

An unforgettable moment... _____

A laughable moment... _____

A surprising moment... _____

An unforeseeable moment... _____

Wildlife spotted... _____

Snapped a selfie | Location... _____

Took a park sign photo? - ☐ y ☐ n

The weather was ...

My List

And so the Adventure begins

Plan Your Trip:

_____

☐ Day Trip ☐ Overnight Stay

Reservations required: ☐ y ☐ n

Date reservations made: _____

Refund Policy: ☐ y ☐ n Site #: _____

Confirmation #: _____

Miles to travel: _____

Time traveling: _____

Dog friendly?: ☐ y ☐ n

Activities Accomplished:

☐ Archery
☐ Biking
☐ Birding
☐ Boating
☐ Camping
☐ Caving
☐ Geocaching

☐ Fishing
☐ Hiking
☐ Horseback Riding
☐ Hunting
☐ Off-Roading
☐ Paddle Boarding
☐ Photography

☐ Picnicking
☐ Rock Climbing
☐ Shooting Range
☐ Stargazing
☐ Swimming
☐ Tennis
☐ Walking

☐ Wildlife Watching
☐ _____
☐ _____
☐ _____
☐ _____
☐ _____
☐ _____

Traveling by:

☐ ☐ ☐ ☐ ☐ ☐ ☐ ☐ ☐ ☐ ☐ ☐

Reservation Information:

_____

Places we discovered along the way

_____

Places to stop and see along the way

_____

Add your favorite ticket stub, postcard, photo, stamp or drawing here

LET NEW ADVENTURES
»> BEGIN →

Unity Forest State Scenic Corridor

Region: Eastern Oregon - **Close to:** John Day

Scenic Corridor

Star Rating

My favorite thing about this place is...

Why I went ...

Who I went with ...

When I went ...

What I did...

What I saw...

What I learned...

An unforgettable moment...

A laughable moment...

A surprising moment...

An unforeseeable moment...

Wildlife spotted...

Snapped a selfie | Location...

Took a park sign photo? - ☐ y ☐ n

The weather was ...

My List

And so the Adventure begins

Plan Your Trip:

☐ Day Trip ☐ Overnight Stay

Reservations required: ☐ y ☐ n

Date reservations made: _____

Refund Policy: ☐ y ☐ n Site #: _____

Confirmation #: _____

Miles to travel: _____

Time traveling: _____

Dog friendly?: ☐ y ☐ n

Activities Accomplished:

☐ Archery	☐ Fishing	☐ Picnicking	☐ Wildlife Watching
☐ Biking	☐ Hiking	☐ Rock Climbing	☐ _____
☐ Birding	☐ Horseback Riding	☐ Shooting Range	☐ _____
☐ Boating	☐ Hunting	☐ Stargazing	☐ _____
☐ Camping	☐ Off-Roading	☐ Swimming	☐ _____
☐ Caving	☐ Paddle Boarding	☐ Tennis	☐ _____
☐ Geocaching	☐ Photography	☐ Walking	☐ _____

Traveling by: ☐ ☐ ☐ ☐ ☐ ☐ ☐ ☐ ☐ ☐ ☐ ☐

Reservation information:

Places we discovered along the way

Places to stop and see along the way

Add your favorite ticket stub, postcard, photo, stamp or drawing here

LET NEW ADVENTURES ›› BEGIN →

Unity Lake State Recreation Site

Region: Eastern Oregon - *Close to:* John Day

Recreation Site

Star Rating ☆☆☆☆☆

My favorite thing about this place is... _____

Why I went ... _____

Who I went with ... _____

When I went ... _____

What I did... _____

What I saw... _____

What I learned... _____

An unforgettable moment... _____

A laughable moment... _____

A surprising moment... _____

An unforeseeable moment... _____

Wildlife spotted... _____

Snapped a selfie | Location... _____

Took a park sign photo? - ☐ y ☐ n

The weather was ...

My List
☐ _____
☐ _____
☐ _____
☐ _____
☐ _____
☐ _____
☐ _____
☐ _____
☐ _____
☐ _____
☐ _____
☐ _____
☐ _____
☐ _____
☐ _____
☐ _____

And so the Adventure begins

Plan Your Trip:

_____

- ☐ Day Trip ☐ Overnight Stay

Reservations required: ☐ y ☐ n

Date reservations made: _____

Refund Policy: ☐ y ☐ n Site #: _____

Confirmation #: _____

Miles to travel: _____

Time traveling: _____

Dog friendly?: ☐ y ☐ n

Activities Accomplished:

☐ Archery	☐ Fishing	☐ Picnicking	☐ Wildlife Watching
☐ Biking	☐ Hiking	☐ Rock Climbing	☐ _____
☐ Birding	☐ Horseback Riding	☐ Shooting Range	☐ _____
☐ Boating	☐ Hunting	☐ Stargazing	☐ _____
☐ Camping	☐ Off-Roading	☐ Swimming	☐ _____
☐ Caving	☐ Paddle Boarding	☐ Tennis	☐ _____
☐ Geocaching	☐ Photography	☐ Walking	☐ _____

Traveling by:
☐ ☐ ☐ ☐ ☐ ☐ ☐ ☐ ☐ ☐ ☐ ☐

Reservation Information:

_____
_____

Places we discovered along the way

_____
_____

Places to stop and see along the way

_____
_____

Add your favorite ticket stub, postcard, photo, stamp or drawing here

LET NEW ADVENTURES ≫ BEGIN →

www.mynaturebookadventures.com

Wallowa Lake Highway Forest State Scenic Corridor

Region: Eastern Oregon - **Close to:** Enterprise

Scenic Corridor

Star Rating ☆☆☆☆☆

My favorite thing about this place is...

Why I went ...

Who I went with ...

When I went ...

What I did...

What I saw...

What I learned...

An unforgettable moment...

A laughable moment...

A surprising moment...

An unforeseeable moment...

Wildlife spotted...

Snapped a selfie | Location...

Took a park sign photo? - ☐ y ☐ n

The weather was ...

My List
☐
☐
☐
☐
☐
☐
☐
☐
☐
☐
☐
☐
☐
☐
☐

And so the Adventure begins

Plan Your Trip:

☐ Day Trip   ☐ Overnight Stay

Reservations required: ☐ y ☐ n
Date reservations made: _____
Refund Policy: ☐ y ☐ n Site #: _____
Confirmation #: _____
Miles to travel: _____
Time traveling: _____
Dog friendly?: ☐ y ☐ n

Activities Accomplished:

☐ Archery	☐ Fishing	☐ Picnicking	☐ Wildlife Watching
☐ Biking	☐ Hiking	☐ Rock Climbing	☐ _____
☐ Birding	☐ Horseback Riding	☐ Shooting Range	☐ _____
☐ Boating	☐ Hunting	☐ Stargazing	☐ _____
☐ Camping	☐ Off-Roading	☐ Swimming	☐ _____
☐ Caving	☐ Paddle Boarding	☐ Tennis	☐ _____
☐ Geocaching	☐ Photography	☐ Walking	☐ _____

Traveling by:

Reservation Information:

Places we discovered along the way

Places to stop and see along the way

Add your favorite ticket stub, postcard, photo, stamp or drawing here

LET NEW ADVENTURES
»» BEGIN →

www.mynaturebookadventures.com

Wallowa Lake State Recreation Area

Region: Eastern Oregon - ***Close to:*** Joseph

Recreation Area

Star Rating

My favorite thing about this place is...

Why I went ...

Who I went with ...

When I went ...

What I did...

What I saw...

What I learned...

An unforgettable moment...

A laughable moment...

A surprising moment...

An unforeseeable moment...

Wildlife spotted...

Snapped a selfie | Location...

Took a park sign photo? - ☐ y ☐ n

The weather was ...

My List

And so the Adventure begins

www.mynaturebookadventures.com

161

Plan Your Trip:

☐ Day Trip ☐ Overnight Stay

Reservations required: ☐ y ☐ n

Date reservations made: _____

Refund Policy: ☐ y ☐ n Site #: _____

Confirmation #: _____

Miles to travel: _____

Time traveling: _____

Dog friendly?: ☐ y ☐ n

Activities Accomplished:

- ☐ Archery
- ☐ Biking
- ☐ Birding
- ☐ Boating
- ☐ Camping
- ☐ Caving
- ☐ Geocaching

- ☐ Fishing
- ☐ Hiking
- ☐ Horseback Riding
- ☐ Hunting
- ☐ Off-Roading
- ☐ Paddle Boarding
- ☐ Photography

- ☐ Picnicking
- ☐ Rock Climbing
- ☐ Shooting Range
- ☐ Stargazing
- ☐ Swimming
- ☐ Tennis
- ☐ Walking

- ☐ Wildlife Watching
- ☐ _____
- ☐ _____
- ☐ _____
- ☐ _____
- ☐ _____
- ☐ _____

Traveling by:

Reservation Information:

Places we discovered along the way

Places to stop and see along the way

Add your favorite ticket stub, postcard, photo, stamp or drawing here

LET NEW ADVENTURES ›› BEGIN →

www.mynaturebookadventures.com

Wallowa River Rest Area

Region: Eastern Oregon - **Close to:** La Grande

Rest Area

Star Rating ☆☆☆☆☆

My favorite thing about this place is... _____

Why I went ... _____

Who I went with ... _____

When I went ... _____

What I did... _____

What I saw... _____

What I learned... _____

An unforgettable moment... _____

A laughable moment... _____

A surprising moment... _____

An unforeseeable moment... _____

Wildlife spotted... _____

Snapped a selfie | Location... _____

Took a park sign photo? - ☐ y ☐ n

The weather was ...

My List
☐ _____
☐ _____
☐ _____
☐ _____
☐ _____
☐ _____
☐ _____
☐ _____
☐ _____
☐ _____
☐ _____
☐ _____
☐ _____
☐ _____
☐ _____
☐ _____

And so the Adventure begins

Plan Your Trip:

☐ Day Trip ☐ Overnight Stay

Reservations required: ☐ y ☐ n

Date reservations made: _____

Refund Policy: ☐ y ☐ n Site #: _____

Confirmation #: _____

Miles to travel: _____

Time traveling: _____

Dog friendly?: ☐ y ☐ n

Activities Accomplished:

☐ Archery	☐ Fishing	☐ Picnicking	☐ Wildlife Watching
☐ Biking	☐ Hiking	☐ Rock Climbing	☐ _____
☐ Birding	☐ Horseback Riding	☐ Shooting Range	☐ _____
☐ Boating	☐ Hunting	☐ Stargazing	☐ _____
☐ Camping	☐ Off-Roading	☐ Swimming	☐ _____
☐ Caving	☐ Paddle Boarding	☐ Tennis	☐ _____
☐ Geocaching	☐ Photography	☐ Walking	☐ _____

Traveling by:

☐ ☐ ☐ ☐ ☐ ☐ ☐ ☐ ☐ ☐ ☐ ☐

Reservation Information:

Places we discovered along the way

_____
_____
_____

Places to stop and see along the way

_____
_____
_____

Add your favorite ticket stub, postcard, photo, stamp or drawing here

LET NEW ADVENTURES ›› BEGIN →

Arcadia Beach State Recreation Site

Region: North Coast - *Close to:* Cannon Beach
Recreation Site

Star Rating
☆☆☆☆☆

My favorite thing about this place is...

Why I went ...

Who I went with ...

When I went ...

What I did...

What I saw...

What I learned...

An unforgettable moment...

A laughable moment...

A surprising moment...

An unforeseeable moment...

Wildlife spotted...

Snapped a selfie | Location...

Took a park sign photo? - ☐ y ☐ n

My List
☐ ___
☐ ___
☐ ___
☐ ___
☐ ___
☐ ___
☐ ___
☐ ___
☐ ___
☐ ___
☐ ___
☐ ___
☐ ___
☐ ___
☐ ___
☐ ___
☐ ___
☐ ___

And so the Adventure begins

The weather was ...

www.mynaturebookadventures.com

Plan Your Trip:

☐ Day Trip ☐ Overnight Stay

Reservations required: ☐ y ☐ n

Date reservations made: _____

Refund Policy: ☐ y ☐ n Site #: _____

Confirmation #: _____

Miles to travel: _____

Time traveling: _____

Dog friendly?: ☐ y ☐ n

Activities Accomplished:

- ☐ Archery
- ☐ Biking
- ☐ Birding
- ☐ Boating
- ☐ Camping
- ☐ Caving
- ☐ Geocaching

- ☐ Fishing
- ☐ Hiking
- ☐ Horseback Riding
- ☐ Hunting
- ☐ Off-Roading
- ☐ Paddle Boarding
- ☐ Photography

- ☐ Picnicking
- ☐ Rock Climbing
- ☐ Shooting Range
- ☐ Stargazing
- ☐ Swimming
- ☐ Tennis
- ☐ Walking

- ☐ Wildlife Watching
- ☐ _____
- ☐ _____
- ☐ _____
- ☐ _____
- ☐ _____
- ☐ _____

Traveling by: ☐ ☐ ☐ ☐ ☐ ☐ ☐ ☐ ☐ ☐ ☐ ☐

Reservation Information:

Places we discovered along the way

Places to stop and see along the way

Add your favorite ticket stub, postcard, photo, stamp or drawing here

LET NEW ADVENTURES ≫ BEGIN →

www.mynaturebookadventures.com

Bob Straub State Park

Region: North Coast - **Close to:** Pacific City

State Park

Star Rating
☆☆☆☆☆

My favorite thing about this place is...

Why I went ...

Who I went with ...

When I went ...

What I did...

What I saw...

What I learned...

An unforgettable moment...

A laughable moment...

A surprising moment...

An unforeseeable moment...

Wildlife spotted...

Snapped a selfie | Location...

Took a park sign photo? - ☐ y ☐ n

My List

And so the Adventure begins

The weather was ...

www.mynaturebookadventures.com

167

Plan Your Trip:

☐ Day Trip   ☐ Overnight Stay

Reservations required: ☐ y ☐ n

Date reservations made: _____

Refund Policy: ☐ y ☐ n Site #: _____

Confirmation #: _____

Miles to travel: _____

Time traveling: _____

Dog friendly?: ☐ y ☐ n

Activities Accomplished:

- ☐ Archery
- ☐ Biking
- ☐ Birding
- ☐ Boating
- ☐ Camping
- ☐ Caving
- ☐ Geocaching
- ☐ Fishing
- ☐ Hiking
- ☐ Horseback Riding
- ☐ Hunting
- ☐ Off-Roading
- ☐ Paddle Boarding
- ☐ Photography
- ☐ Picnicking
- ☐ Rock Climbing
- ☐ Shooting Range
- ☐ Stargazing
- ☐ Swimming
- ☐ Tennis
- ☐ Walking
- ☐ Wildlife Watching
- ☐ _____
- ☐ _____
- ☐ _____
- ☐ _____
- ☐ _____
- ☐ _____

Traveling by: ☐ car ☐ truck ☐ SUV ☐ van ☐ airplane ☐ trolley ☐ bicycle ☐ bus ☐ train ☐ helicopter ☐ motorcycle ☐ boat

Reservation Information:

Places we discovered along the way

Places to stop and see along the way

Add your favorite ticket stub, postcard, photo, stamp or drawing here

LET NEW ADVENTURES ≫ BEGIN →

168

www.mynaturebookadventures.com

Bradley State Scenic Viewpoint

Region: North Coast - **Close to:** Astoria
Scenic Viewpoint

Star Rating
☆☆☆☆☆

My favorite thing about this place is... _____

Why I went ... _____

Who I went with ... _____

When I went ... _____

What I did... _____

What I saw... _____

What I learned... _____

An unforgettable moment... _____

A laughable moment... _____

A surprising moment... _____

An unforeseeable moment... _____

Wildlife spotted... _____

Snapped a selfie | Location... _____

Took a park sign photo? - ☐ y ☐ n

The weather was ...

My List
☐ _____
☐ _____
☐ _____
☐ _____
☐ _____
☐ _____
☐ _____
☐ _____
☐ _____
☐ _____
☐ _____
☐ _____
☐ _____
☐ _____
☐ _____
☐ _____

And so the Adventure begins

www.mynaturebookadventures.com

Plan Your Trip:

☐ Day Trip ☐ Overnight Stay

Reservations required: ☐ y ☐ n

Date reservations made: _____

Refund Policy: ☐ y ☐ n Site #: _____

Confirmation #: _____

Miles to travel: _____

Time traveling: _____

Dog friendly?: ☐ y ☐ n

Activities Accomplished:

☐ Archery	☐ Fishing	☐ Picnicking	☐ Wildlife Watching
☐ Biking	☐ Hiking	☐ Rock Climbing	☐ _____
☐ Birding	☐ Horseback Riding	☐ Shooting Range	☐ _____
☐ Boating	☐ Hunting	☐ Stargazing	☐ _____
☐ Camping	☐ Off-Roading	☐ Swimming	☐ _____
☐ Caving	☐ Paddle Boarding	☐ Tenn s	☐ _____
☐ Geocaching	☐ Photography	☐ Walking	☐ _____

Traveling by:

Reservation Information:

Places we discovered along the way

Places to stop and see along the way

Add your favorite ticket stub, postcard, photo, stamp or drawing here

LET NEW ADVENTURES
»» BEGIN →

Cape Kiwanda State Natural Area

Region: North Coast - **Close to:** Pacific City

Natural Area

Star Rating
☆☆☆☆☆

My favorite thing about this place is...

Why I went ...

Who I went with ...

When I went ...

What I did...

What I saw...

What I learned...

An unforgettable moment...

A laughable moment...

A surprising moment...

An unforeseeable moment...

Wildlife spotted...

Snapped a selfie | Location...

Took a park sign photo? - ☐ y ☐ n

The weather was ...

My List
☐
☐
☐
☐
☐
☐
☐
☐
☐
☐
☐
☐
☐
☐
☐
☐
☐
☐

And so the Adventure begins

www.mynaturebookadventures.com

Plan Your Trip:

☐ Day Trip ☐ Overnight Stay

Reservations required: ☐y ☐n

Date reservations made: _____

Refund Policy: ☐y ☐n Site #: _____

Confirmation #: _____

Miles to travel: _____

Time traveling: _____

Dog friendly?: ☐y ☐n

Activities Accomplished:

- ☐ Archery
- ☐ Biking
- ☐ Birding
- ☐ Boating
- ☐ Camping
- ☐ Caving
- ☐ Geocaching

- ☐ Fishing
- ☐ Hiking
- ☐ Horseback Riding
- ☐ Hunting
- ☐ Off-Roading
- ☐ Paddle Boarding
- ☐ Photography

- ☐ Picnicking
- ☐ Rock Climbing
- ☐ Shooting Range
- ☐ Stargazing
- ☐ Swimming
- ☐ Tennis
- ☐ Walking

- ☐ Wildlife Watching
- ☐ _____
- ☐ _____
- ☐ _____
- ☐ _____
- ☐ _____
- ☐ _____

Traveling by: ☐ ☐ ☐ ☐ ☐ ☐ ☐ ☐ ☐ ☐ ☐ ☐

Reservation Information:

Places we discovered along the way

Places to stop and see along the way

Add your favorite ticket stub, postcard, photo, stamp or drawing here

LET NEW ADVENTURES
» BEGIN →

www.mynaturebookadventures.com

Cape Lookout State Park

Region: North Coast - **Close to:** Tillamook

State Park

Star Rating
☆☆☆☆☆

My favorite thing about this place is... _____

Why I went ... _____

Who I went with ... _____

When I went ... _____

What I did... _____

What I saw... _____

What I learned... _____

An unforgettable moment... _____

A laughable moment... _____

A surprising moment... _____

An unforeseeable moment... _____

Wildlife spotted... _____

Snapped a selfie | Location... _____

Took a park sign photo? - ☐ y ☐ n

The weather was ...

My List
☐ _____
☐ _____
☐ _____
☐ _____
☐ _____
☐ _____
☐ _____
☐ _____
☐ _____
☐ _____
☐ _____
☐ _____
☐ _____
☐ _____
☐ _____
☐ _____
☐ _____

And so the Adventure begins

www.mynaturebookadventures.com

Plan Your Trip:

☐ Day Trip ☐ Overnight Stay

Reservations required: ☐ y ☐ n

Date reservations made: _____

Refund Policy: ☐ y ☐ n Site #: _____

Confirmation #: _____

Miles to travel: _____

Time traveling: _____

Dog friendly?: ☐ y ☐ n

Activities Accomplished:

☐ Archery
☐ Biking
☐ Birding
☐ Boating
☐ Camping
☐ Caving
☐ Geocaching

☐ Fishing
☐ Hiking
☐ Horseback Riding
☐ Hunting
☐ Off-Roading
☐ Paddle Boarding
☐ Photography

☐ Picnicking
☐ Rock Climbing
☐ Shooting Range
☐ Stargazing
☐ Swimming
☐ Tennis
☐ Walking

☐ Wildlife Watching
☐ _____
☐ _____
☐ _____
☐ _____
☐ _____
☐ _____

Traveling by:

Reservation information:

Places we discovered along the way

Places to stop and see along the way

Add your favorite ticket stub, postcard, photo, stamp or drawing here

LET NEW ADVENTURES
»» BEGIN →

www.mynaturebookadventures.com

Cape Meares State Scenic Viewpoint

Region: North Coast - **Close to:** Tillamook
Scenic Viewpoint

Star Rating
☆☆☆☆☆

My favorite thing about this place is...

Why I went ...

Who I went with ...

When I went ...

What I did...

What I saw...

What I learned...

An unforgettable moment...

A laughable moment...

A surprising moment...

An unforeseeable moment...

Wildlife spotted...

Snapped a selfie | Location...

Took a park sign photo? - ☐ y ☐ n

The weather was ...

My List

And so the Adventure begins

www.mynaturebookadventures.com

175

Plan Your Trip:

☐ Day Trip ☐ Overnight Stay

Reservations required: ☐ y ☐ n

Date reservations made: _____

Refund Policy: ☐ y ☐ n Site #: _____

Confirmation #: _____

Miles to travel: _____

Time traveling: _____

Dog friendly?: ☐ y ☐ n

Activities Accomplished:

- ☐ Archery
- ☐ Biking
- ☐ Birding
- ☐ Boating
- ☐ Camping
- ☐ Caving
- ☐ Geocaching
- ☐ Fishing
- ☐ Hiking
- ☐ Horseback Riding
- ☐ Hunting
- ☐ Off-Roading
- ☐ Paddle Boarding
- ☐ Photography
- ☐ Picnicking
- ☐ Rock Climbing
- ☐ Shooting Range
- ☐ Stargazing
- ☐ Swimming
- ☐ Tennis
- ☐ Walking
- ☐ Wildlife Watching
- ☐ _____
- ☐ _____
- ☐ _____
- ☐ _____
- ☐ _____
- ☐ _____

Traveling by:

Reservation Information:

Places we discovered along the way

Places to stop and see along the way

Add your favorite ticket stub, postcard, photo, stamp or drawing here

LET NEW ADVENTURES
»> BEGIN →

Clay Myers State Natural Area at Whalen Island

Region: North Coast - **Close to:** Pacific City

Natural Area

Star Rating
☆☆☆☆☆

My favorite thing about this place is... _____

Why I went ... _____

Who I went with ... _____

When I went ... _____

What I did... _____

What I saw... _____

What I learned... _____

An unforgettable moment... _____

A laughable moment... _____

A surprising moment... _____

An unforeseeable moment... _____

Wildlife spotted... _____

Snapped a selfie | Location... _____

Took a park sign photo? - ☐ y ☐ n

The weather was ...

My List
☐ _____
☐ _____
☐ _____
☐ _____
☐ _____
☐ _____
☐ _____
☐ _____
☐ _____
☐ _____
☐ _____
☐ _____
☐ _____
☐ _____
☐ _____
☐ _____
☐ _____
☐ _____

And so the Adventure begins

Plan Your Trip:

☐ Day Trip ☐ Overnight Stay

Reservations required: ☐ y ☐ n

Date reservations made: _____

Refund Policy: ☐ y ☐ n Site #: _____

Confirmation #: _____

Miles to travel: _____

Time traveling: _____

Dog friendly?: ☐ y ☐ n

Activities Accomplished:

☐ Archery	☐ Fishing	☐ Picnicking	☐ Wildlife Watching
☐ Biking	☐ Hiking	☐ Rock Climbing	☐ _____
☐ Birding	☐ Horseback Riding	☐ Shooting Range	☐ _____
☐ Boating	☐ Hunting	☐ Stargazing	☐ _____
☐ Camping	☐ Off-Roading	☐ Swimming	☐ _____
☐ Caving	☐ Paddle Boarding	☐ Tennis	☐ _____
☐ Geocaching	☐ Photography	☐ Walking	☐ _____

Traveling by:
☐ ☐ ☐ ☐ ☐ ☐ ☐ ☐ ☐ ☐ ☐ ☐ ☐

Reservation Information:

Places we discovered along the way

Places to stop and see along the way

Add your favorite ticket stub, postcard, photo, drawing or stamp here

LET NEW ADVENTURES ≫ BEGIN →

178

www.mynaturebookadventures.com

D River State Recreation Site

Region: North Coast - **Close to:** Lincoln City
Recreation Site

Star Rating
☆☆☆☆☆

My favorite thing about this place is... _____

Why I went ... _____

Who I went with ... _____

When I went ... _____

What I did... _____

What I saw... _____

What I learned... _____

An unforgettable moment... _____

A laughable moment... _____

A surprising moment... _____

An unforeseeable moment... _____

Wildlife spotted... _____

Snapped a selfie | Location... _____

Took a park sign photo? - ☐ y ☐ n

The weather was ...

My List
☐ _____
☐ _____
☐ _____
☐ _____
☐ _____
☐ _____
☐ _____
☐ _____
☐ _____
☐ _____
☐ _____
☐ _____
☐ _____
☐ _____
☐ _____
☐ _____
☐ _____

And so the Adventure begins

www.mynaturebookadventures.com

Plan Your Trip:

☐ Day Trip　　☐ Overnight Stay

Reservations required: ☐ y ☐ n

Date reservations made: _____

Refund Policy: ☐ y ☐ n　Site #: _____

Confirmation #: _____

Miles to travel: _____

Time traveling: _____

Dog friendly?: ☐ y ☐ n

Activities Accomplished:

☐ Archery
☐ Biking
☐ Birding
☐ Boating
☐ Camping
☐ Caving
☐ Geocaching

☐ Fishing
☐ Hiking
☐ Horseback Riding
☐ Hunting
☐ Off-Roading
☐ Paddle Boarding
☐ Photography

☐ Picnicking
☐ Rock Climbing
☐ Shooting Range
☐ Stargazing
☐ Swimming
☐ Tennis
☐ Walking

☐ Wildlife Watching
☐ _____
☐ _____
☐ _____
☐ _____
☐ _____
☐ _____

Traveling by:

Reservation information:

Places we discovered along the way

Places to stop and see along the way

Add your favorite ticket stub, postcard, photo, stamp or drawing here

LET NEW ADVENTURES ≫ BEGIN →

180　　www.mynaturebookadventures.com

Del Rey Beach State Recreation Site

Region: North Coast - **Close to:** Gearhart
Recreation Site

Star Rating
☆☆☆☆☆

My favorite thing about this place is... _____

Why I went ... _____

Who I went with ... _____

When I went ... _____

What I did... _____

What I saw... _____

What I learned... _____

An unforgettable moment... _____

A laughable moment... _____

A surprising moment... _____

An unforeseeable moment... _____

Wildlife spotted... _____

Snapped a selfie | Location... _____

Took a park sign photo? - ☐ y ☐ n

The weather was ...

My List
☐ _____
☐ _____
☐ _____
☐ _____
☐ _____
☐ _____
☐ _____
☐ _____
☐ _____
☐ _____
☐ _____
☐ _____
☐ _____
☐ _____
☐ _____
☐ _____
☐ _____
☐ _____
☐ _____

And so the Adventure begins

www.mynaturebookadventures.com

Plan Your Trip:

☐ Day Trip ☐ Overnight Stay

Reservations required: ☐ y ☐ n

Date reservations made: _____

Refund Policy: ☐ y ☐ n Site #: _____

Confirmation #: _____

Miles to travel: _____

Time traveling: _____

Dog friendly?: ☐ y ☐ n

Activities Accomplished:

☐ Archery	☐ Fishing	☐ Picnicking	☐ Wildlife Watching
☐ Biking	☐ Hiking	☐ Rock Climbing	☐ _____
☐ Birding	☐ Horseback Riding	☐ Shooting Range	☐ _____
☐ Boating	☐ Hunting	☐ Stargazing	☐ _____
☐ Camping	☐ Off-Roading	☐ Swimming	☐ _____
☐ Caving	☐ Paddle Boarding	☐ Tennis	☐ _____
☐ Geocaching	☐ Photography	☐ Walking	☐ _____

Traveling by: ☐ ☐ ☐ ☐ ☐ ☐ ☐ ☐ ☐ ☐ ☐ ☐

Reservation Information:

Places we discovered along the way

Places to stop and see along the way

Add your favorite ticket stub, postcard, photo, stamp or drawing here

LET NEW ADVENTURES ≫ BEGIN →

Devils Lake State Recreation Area

Region: North Coast - **Close to:** Lincoln City

Recreation Area

Star Rating

My favorite thing about this place is...

Why I went ...

Who I went with ...

When I went ...

What I did...

What I saw...

What I learned...

An unforgettable moment...

A laughable moment...

A surprising moment...

An unforeseeable moment...

Wildlife spotted...

Snapped a selfie | Location...

Took a park sign photo? - ☐ y ☐ n

The weather was ...

My List

And so the Adventure begins

Plan Your Trip:

☐ Day Trip   ☐ Overnight Stay

Reservations required: ☐ y ☐ n

Date reservations made: _____

Refund Policy: ☐ y ☐ n Site #: _____

Confirmation #: _____

Miles to travel: _____

Time traveling: _____

Dog friendly?: ☐ y ☐ n

Activities Accomplished:

☐ Archery	☐ Fishing	☐ Picnicking	☐ Wildlife Watching
☐ Biking	☐ Hiking	☐ Rock Climbing	☐ _____
☐ Birding	☐ Horseback Riding	☐ Shooting Range	☐ _____
☐ Boating	☐ Hunting	☐ Stargazing	☐ _____
☐ Camping	☐ Off-Roading	☐ Swimming	☐ _____
☐ Caving	☐ Paddle Boarding	☐ Tennis	☐ _____
☐ Geocaching	☐ Photography	☐ Walking	☐ _____

Traveling by:

☐ ☐ ☐ ☐ ☐ ☐ ☐ ☐ ☐ ☐ ☐ ☐

Reservation Information:

Places we discovered along the way

Places to stop and see along the way

Add your favorite ticket stub, postcard, photo, stamp or drawing here

LET NEW ADVENTURES ≫ BEGIN →

Ecola State Park

Region: North Coast - **Close to:** Cannon Beach

State Park

Star Rating
☆☆☆☆☆

My favorite thing about this place is... _____

Why I went ... _____

Who I went with ... _____

When I went ... _____

What I did... _____

What I saw... _____

What I learned... _____

An unforgettable moment... _____

A laughable moment... _____

A surprising moment... _____

An unforeseeable moment... _____

Wildlife spotted... _____

Snapped a selfie | Location... _____

Took a park sign photo? - ☐ y ☐ n

The weather was ...

My List
☐ _____
☐ _____
☐ _____
☐ _____
☐ _____
☐ _____
☐ _____
☐ _____
☐ _____
☐ _____
☐ _____
☐ _____
☐ _____
☐ _____
☐ _____
☐ _____
☐ _____
☐ _____

And so the Adventure begins

www.mynaturebookadventures.com

Plan Your Trip:

☐ Day Trip ☐ Overnight Stay

Reservations required: ☐ y ☐ n

Date reservations made: _____

Refund Policy: ☐ y ☐ n   Site #: _____

Confirmation #: _____

Miles to travel: _____

Time traveling: _____

Dog friendly?: ☐ y ☐ n

Activities Accomplished:

- ☐ Archery
- ☐ Biking
- ☐ Birding
- ☐ Boating
- ☐ Camping
- ☐ Caving
- ☐ Geocaching
- ☐ Fishing
- ☐ Hiking
- ☐ Horseback Riding
- ☐ Hunting
- ☐ Off-Roading
- ☐ Paddle Boarding
- ☐ Photography
- ☐ Picnicking
- ☐ Rock Climbing
- ☐ Shooting Range
- ☐ Stargazing
- ☐ Swimming
- ☐ Tennis
- ☐ Walking
- ☐ Wildlife Watching
- ☐ _____
- ☐ _____
- ☐ _____
- ☐ _____
- ☐ _____
- ☐ _____

Traveling by:

Reservation Information:

Places we discovered along the way

Places to stop and see along the way

Add your favorite ticket stub, postcard, photo, stamp or drawing here

LET NEW ADVENTURES ≫ BEGIN →

186   www.mynaturebookadventures.com

Fort Stevens State Park

Region: North Coast - **Close to:** Astoria
State Park

Star Rating ☆☆☆☆☆

My favorite thing about this place is... _____
Why I went ... _____
Who I went with ... _____
When I went ... _____
What I did... _____
What I saw... _____

What I learned... _____

An unforgettable moment... _____

A laughable moment... _____

A surprising moment... _____

An unforeseeable moment... _____

Wildlife spotted... _____

Snapped a selfie | Location... _____
Took a park sign photo? - ☐ y ☐ n

The weather was ...

My List
☐ _____
☐ _____
☐ _____
☐ _____
☐ _____
☐ _____
☐ _____
☐ _____
☐ _____
☐ _____
☐ _____
☐ _____
☐ _____
☐ _____
☐ _____
☐ _____
☐ _____
☐ _____

And so the Adventure begins

www.mynaturebookadventures.com
187

Plan Your Trip:

☐ Day Trip ☐ Overnight Stay

Reservations required: ☐ y ☐ n

Date reservations made: _____

Refund Policy: ☐ y ☐ n Site #: _____

Confirmation #: _____

Miles to travel: _____

Time traveling: _____

Dog friendly?: ☐ y ☐ n

Activities Accomplished:

- ☐ Archery
- ☐ Biking
- ☐ Birding
- ☐ Boating
- ☐ Camping
- ☐ Caving
- ☐ Geocaching
- ☐ Fishing
- ☐ Hiking
- ☐ Horseback Riding
- ☐ Hunting
- ☐ Off-Roading
- ☐ Paddle Boarding
- ☐ Photography
- ☐ Picnicking
- ☐ Rock Climbing
- ☐ Shooting Range
- ☐ Stargazing
- ☐ Swimming
- ☐ Tennis
- ☐ Walking
- ☐ Wildlife Watching
- ☐ _____
- ☐ _____
- ☐ _____
- ☐ _____
- ☐ _____
- ☐ _____

Traveling by: ☐ ☐ ☐ ☐ ☐ ☐ ☐ ☐ ☐ ☐ ☐ ☐

Reservation Information:

Places we discovered along the way

Places to stop and see along the way

Add your favorite ticket stub, postcard, photo, stamp or drawing here

LET NEW ADVENTURES BEGIN →

H. B. Van Duzer Forest State Scenic Corridor

Region: North Coast - **Close to:** Lincoln City
Scenic Corridor

Star Rating ☆☆☆☆☆

My favorite thing about this place is... _____

Why I went ... _____

Who I went with ... _____

When I went ... _____

What I did... _____

What I saw... _____

What I learned... _____

An unforgettable moment... _____

A laughable moment... _____

A surprising moment... _____

An unforeseeable moment... _____

Wildlife spotted... _____

Snapped a selfie | Location... _____

Took a park sign photo? - ☐ y ☐ n

The weather was ...

My List
☐ _____
☐ _____
☐ _____
☐ _____
☐ _____
☐ _____
☐ _____
☐ _____
☐ _____
☐ _____
☐ _____
☐ _____
☐ _____
☐ _____
☐ _____

And so the Adventure begins

Plan Your Trip:

☐ Day Trip   ☐ Overnight Stay

Reservations required: ☐ y ☐ n

Date reservations made: _____

Refund Policy: ☐ y ☐ n   Site #: _____

Confirmation #: _____

Miles to travel: _____

Time traveling: _____

Dog friendly?: ☐ y ☐ n

Activities Accomplished:

- ☐ Archery
- ☐ Biking
- ☐ Birding
- ☐ Boating
- ☐ Camping
- ☐ Caving
- ☐ Geocaching

- ☐ Fishing
- ☐ Hiking
- ☐ Horseback Riding
- ☐ Hunting
- ☐ Off-Roading
- ☐ Paddle Boarding
- ☐ Photography

- ☐ Picnicking
- ☐ Rock Climbing
- ☐ Shooting Range
- ☐ Stargazing
- ☐ Swimming
- ☐ Tennis
- ☐ Walking

- ☐ Wildlife Watching
- ☐ _____
- ☐ _____
- ☐ _____
- ☐ _____
- ☐ _____
- ☐ _____

Traveling by:

Reservation Information:

Places we discovered along the way

Places to stop and see along the way

Add your favorite ticket stub, postcard, photo, stamp or drawing here

LET NEW ADVENTURES ≫ BEGIN →

Hug Point State Recreation Site

Region: North Coast - **Close to:** Cannon Beach

Recreation Site

Star Rating
☆☆☆☆☆

My favorite thing about this place is... _____

Why I went ... _____

Who I went with ... _____

When I went ... _____

What I did... _____

What I saw... _____

What I learned... _____

An unforgettable moment... _____

A laughable moment... _____

A surprising moment... _____

An unforeseeable moment... _____

Wildlife spotted... _____

Snapped a selfie | Location... _____

Took a park sign photo? - ☐ y ☐ n

The weather was ... ☐ ☐ ☐ ☐ ☐ ☐ ☐

My List
- ☐ _____
- ☐ _____
- ☐ _____
- ☐ _____
- ☐ _____
- ☐ _____
- ☐ _____
- ☐ _____
- ☐ _____
- ☐ _____
- ☐ _____
- ☐ _____
- ☐ _____
- ☐ _____
- ☐ _____
- ☐ _____
- ☐ _____

And so the Adventure begins

www.mynaturebookadventures.com

Plan Your Trip:

☐ Day Trip   ☐ Overnight Stay

Reservations required: ☐ y ☐ n

Date reservations made: _____

Refund Policy: ☐ y ☐ n Site #: _____

Confirmation #: _____

Miles to travel: _____

Time traveling: _____

Dog friendly?: ☐ y ☐ n

Activities Accomplished:

☐ Archery	☐ Fishing	☐ Picnicking	☐ Wildlife Watching
☐ Biking	☐ Hiking	☐ Rock Climbing	☐ _____
☐ Birding	☐ Horseback Riding	☐ Shooting Range	☐ _____
☐ Boating	☐ Hunting	☐ Stargazing	☐ _____
☐ Camping	☐ Off-Roading	☐ Swimming	☐ _____
☐ Caving	☐ Paddle Boarding	☐ Tennis	☐ _____
☐ Geocaching	☐ Photography	☐ Walking	☐ _____

Traveling by:

Reservation Information:

Places we discovered along the way

_____
_____
_____

Places to stop and see along the way

_____
_____
_____

Add your favorite ticket stub, postcard, photo, stamp or drawing here

LET NEW ADVENTURES ›› BEGIN →

www.mynaturebookadventures.com

Manhattan Beach State Recreation Site

Region: North Coast - **Close to:** Rockaway Beach
Recreation Site

Star Rating ☆☆☆☆☆

My favorite thing about this place is... _____

Why I went ... _____

Who I went with ... _____

When I went ... _____

What I did... _____

What I saw... _____

What I learned... _____

An unforgettable moment... _____

A laughable moment... _____

A surprising moment... _____

An unforeseeable moment... _____

Wildlife spotted... _____

Snapped a selfie | Location... _____

Took a park sign photo? - ☐ y ☐ n

The weather was ...

My List
☐ _____
☐ _____
☐ _____
☐ _____
☐ _____
☐ _____
☐ _____
☐ _____
☐ _____
☐ _____
☐ _____
☐ _____
☐ _____
☐ _____
☐ _____
☐ _____
☐ _____
☐ _____

And so the Adventure begins

Plan Your Trip:

☐ Day Trip   ☐ Overnight Stay

Reservations required: ☐ y ☐ n
Date reservations made: _____
Refund Policy: ☐ y ☐ n Site #: _____
Confirmation #: _____
Miles to travel: _____
Time traveling: _____
Dog friendly?: ☐ y ☐ n

Activities Accomplished:

☐ Archery   ☐ Fishing   ☐ Picnicking   ☐ Wildlife Watching
☐ Biking   ☐ Hiking   ☐ Rock Climbing   ☐ _____
☐ Birding   ☐ Horseback Riding   ☐ Shooting Range   ☐ _____
☐ Boating   ☐ Hunting   ☐ Stargazing   ☐ _____
☐ Camping   ☐ Off-Roading   ☐ Swimming   ☐ _____
☐ Caving   ☐ Paddle Boarding   ☐ Tenn s   ☐ _____
☐ Geocaching   ☐ Photography   ☐ Walking   ☐ _____

Traveling by:
☐ ☐ ☐ ☐ ☐ ☐ ☐ ☐ ☐ ☐ ☐ ☐

Reservation Information:

_____

Places we discovered along the way

_____
_____
_____

Places to stop and see along the way

_____
_____
_____

Add your favorite ticket stub, postcard, photo, stamp or drawing here

LET NEW ADVENTURES
» BEGIN →

194   www.mynaturebookadventures.com

Munson Creek Falls State Natural Site

Region: North Coast - ***Close to:*** Tillamook
Natural Site

Star Rating
☆☆☆☆☆

My favorite thing about this place is... _____

Why I went ... _____

Who I went with ... _____

When I went ... _____

What I did... _____

What I saw... _____

What I learned... _____

An unforgettable moment... _____

A laughable moment... _____

A surprising moment... _____

An unforeseeable moment... _____

Wildlife spotted... _____

Snapped a selfie | Location... _____

Took a park sign photo? - ☐ y ☐ n

My List
☐ _____
☐ _____
☐ _____
☐ _____
☐ _____
☐ _____
☐ _____
☐ _____
☐ _____
☐ _____
☐ _____
☐ _____
☐ _____
☐ _____
☐ _____
☐ _____

And so the Adventure begins

The weather was ...

www.mynaturebookadventures.com

Plan Your Trip:

☐ Day Trip ☐ Overnight Stay

Reservations required: ☐ y ☐ n

Date reservations made: _____

Refund Policy: ☐ y ☐ n Site #: _____

Confirmation #: _____

Miles to travel: _____

Time traveling: _____

Dog friendly?: ☐ y ☐ n

Activities Accomplished:

☐ Archery	☐ Fishing	☐ Picnicking	☐ Wildlife Watching
☐ Biking	☐ Hiking	☐ Rock Climbing	☐ _____
☐ Birding	☐ Horseback Riding	☐ Shooting Range	☐ _____
☐ Boating	☐ Hunting	☐ Stargazing	☐ _____
☐ Camping	☐ Off-Roading	☐ Swimming	☐ _____
☐ Caving	☐ Paddle Boarding	☐ Tennis	☐ _____
☐ Geocaching	☐ Photography	☐ Walking	☐ _____

Traveling by:

Reservation Information:

Places we discovered along the way

Places to stop and see along the way

Add your favorite ticket stub, postcard, photo, stamp or drawing here

LET NEW ADVENTURES
»› BEGIN →

Nehalem Bay State Park

Region: North Coast - **Close to:** Manzanita
State Park

Star Rating
☆☆☆☆☆

My favorite thing about this place is… _____

Why I went … _____

Who I went with … _____

When I went … _____

What I did… _____

What I saw… _____

What I learned… _____

An unforgettable moment… _____

A laughable moment… _____

A surprising moment… _____

An unforeseeable moment… _____

Wildlife spotted… _____

Snapped a selfie | Location… _____

Took a park sign photo? - ☐ y ☐ n

The weather was …

My List
☐ _____
☐ _____
☐ _____
☐ _____
☐ _____
☐ _____
☐ _____
☐ _____
☐ _____
☐ _____
☐ _____
☐ _____
☐ _____
☐ _____
☐ _____
☐ _____

And so the Adventure begins

www.mynaturebookadventures.com

Plan Your Trip:

☐ Day Trip ☐ Overnight Stay

Reservations required: ☐ y ☐ n

Date reservations made: _____

Refund Policy: ☐ y ☐ n Site #: _____

Confirmation #: _____

Miles to travel: _____

Time traveling: _____

Dog friendly?: ☐ y ☐ n

Activities Accomplished:

☐ Archery	☐ Fishing	☐ Picnicking	☐ Wildlife Watching
☐ Biking	☐ Hiking	☐ Rock Climbing	☐ _____
☐ Birding	☐ Horseback Riding	☐ Shooting Range	☐ _____
☐ Boating	☐ Hunting	☐ Stargazing	☐ _____
☐ Camping	☐ Off-Roading	☐ Swimming	☐ _____
☐ Caving	☐ Paddle Boarding	☐ Tennis	☐ _____
☐ Geocaching	☐ Photography	☐ Walking	☐ _____

Traveling by:

Reservation Information:

_____

Places we discovered along the way

_____
_____
_____

Places to stop and see along the way

_____
_____
_____

Add your favorite ticket stub, postcard, photo, stamp or drawing here

LET NEW ADVENTURES BEGIN →

www.mynaturebookadventures.com

Neskowin Beach State Recreation Site

Region: North Coast - *Close to:* Neskowin
Recreation Site

Star Rating
☆☆☆☆☆

My favorite thing about this place is... _____

Why I went ... _____

Who I went with ... _____

When I went ... _____

What I did... _____

What I saw... _____

What I learned... _____

An unforgettable moment... _____

A laughable moment... _____

A surprising moment... _____

An unforeseeable moment... _____

Wildlife spotted... _____

Snapped a selfie | Location... _____

Took a park sign photo? - ☐ y ☐ n

The weather was ...

My List
☐ _____
☐ _____
☐ _____
☐ _____
☐ _____
☐ _____
☐ _____
☐ _____
☐ _____
☐ _____
☐ _____
☐ _____
☐ _____
☐ _____
☐ _____
☐ _____
☐ _____

And so the Adventure begins

www.mynaturebookadventures.com

Plan Your Trip:

☐ Day Trip   ☐ Overnight Stay

Reservations required: ☐ y ☐ n

Date reservations made: _____

Refund Policy: ☐ y ☐ n   Site #: _____

Confirmation #: _____

Miles to travel: _____

Time traveling: _____

Dog friendly?: ☐ y ☐ n

Activities Accomplished:

- ☐ Archery
- ☐ Biking
- ☐ Birding
- ☐ Boating
- ☐ Camping
- ☐ Caving
- ☐ Geocaching

- ☐ Fishing
- ☐ Hiking
- ☐ Horseback Riding
- ☐ Hunting
- ☐ Off-Roading
- ☐ Paddle Boarding
- ☐ Photography

- ☐ Picnicking
- ☐ Rock Climbing
- ☐ Shooting Range
- ☐ Stargazing
- ☐ Swimming
- ☐ Tennis
- ☐ Walking

- ☐ Wildlife Watching
- ☐ _____
- ☐ _____
- ☐ _____
- ☐ _____
- ☐ _____
- ☐ _____

Traveling by:

Reservation Information:

Places we discovered along the way

Places to stop and see along the way

Add your favorite ticket stub, postcard, photo, stamp or drawing here

LET NEW ADVENTURES BEGIN →

200   www.mynaturebookadventures.com

Oceanside Beach State Recreation Site

Region: North Coast - *Close to:* Tillamook
Recreation Site

Star Rating
☆☆☆☆☆

My favorite thing about this place is... _____

Why I went ... _____

Who I went with ... _____

When I went ... _____

What I did... _____

What I saw... _____

What I learned... _____

An unforgettable moment... _____

A laughable moment... _____

A surprising moment... _____

An unforeseeable moment... _____

Wildlife spotted... _____

Snapped a selfie | Location... _____

Took a park sign photo? - ☐ y ☐ n

The weather was ...

My List
☐ _____
☐ _____
☐ _____
☐ _____
☐ _____
☐ _____
☐ _____
☐ _____
☐ _____
☐ _____
☐ _____
☐ _____
☐ _____
☐ _____
☐ _____

And so the Adventure begins

www.mynaturebookadventures.com

Plan Your Trip:

☐ Day Trip   ☐ Overnight Stay

Reservations required: ☐ y ☐ n

Date reservations made: _____

Refund Policy: ☐ y ☐ n   Site #: _____

Confirmation #: _____

Miles to travel: _____

Time traveling: _____

Dog friendly?: ☐ y ☐ n

Activities Accomplished:

☐ Archery	☐ Fishing	☐ Picnicking	☐ Wildlife Watching
☐ Biking	☐ Hiking	☐ Rock Climbing	☐ _____
☐ Birding	☐ Horseback Riding	☐ Shooting Range	☐ _____
☐ Boating	☐ Hunting	☐ Stargazing	☐ _____
☐ Camping	☐ Off-Roading	☐ Swimming	☐ _____
☐ Caving	☐ Paddle Boarding	☐ Tennis	☐ _____
☐ Geocaching	☐ Photography	☐ Walking	☐ _____

Traveling by:

☐ car ☐ truck ☐ SUV ☐ van ☐ plane ☐ trolley ☐ bike ☐ bus ☐ train ☐ helicopter ☐ motorcycle ☐ boat

Reservation Information:

_____

Places we discovered along the way
_____
_____
_____

Places to stop and see along the way
_____
_____
_____

Add your favorite ticket stub, postcard, photo, stamp or drawing here

LET NEW ADVENTURES
»» BEGIN →

Oswald West State Park

Region: North Coast - **Close to:** Cannon Beach

State Park

Star Rating
☆☆☆☆☆

My favorite thing about this place is... _____

Why I went ... _____

Who I went with ... _____

When I went ... _____

What I did... _____

What I saw... _____

What I learned... _____

An unforgettable moment... _____

A laughable moment... _____

A surprising moment... _____

An unforeseeable moment... _____

Wildlife spotted... _____

Snapped a selfie | Location... _____

Took a park sign photo? - ☐ y ☐ n

The weather was ...

My List
☐ _____
☐ _____
☐ _____
☐ _____
☐ _____
☐ _____
☐ _____
☐ _____
☐ _____
☐ _____
☐ _____
☐ _____
☐ _____
☐ _____
☐ _____
☐ _____
☐ _____

And so the Adventure begins

Plan Your Trip:

☐ Day Trip   ☐ Overnight Stay

Reservations required: ☐ y ☐ n

Date reservations made: _____

Refund Policy: ☐ y ☐ n   Site #: _____

Confirmation #: _____

Miles to travel: _____

Time traveling: _____

Dog friendly?: ☐ y ☐ n

Activities Accomplished:

- ☐ Archery
- ☐ Biking
- ☐ Birding
- ☐ Boating
- ☐ Camping
- ☐ Caving
- ☐ Geocaching

- ☐ Fishing
- ☐ Hiking
- ☐ Horseback Riding
- ☐ Hunting
- ☐ Off-Roading
- ☐ Paddle Boarding
- ☐ Photography

- ☐ Picnicking
- ☐ Rock Climbing
- ☐ Shooting Range
- ☐ Stargazing
- ☐ Swimming
- ☐ Tennis
- ☐ Walking

- ☐ Wildlife Watching
- ☐ _____
- ☐ _____
- ☐ _____
- ☐ _____
- ☐ _____
- ☐ _____

Traveling by:

Reservation Information:

Places we discovered along the way

Places to stop and see along the way

Add your favorite ticket stub, postcard, photo, stamp or drawing here

Let New Adventures Begin →

204   www.mynaturebookadventures.com

Roads End State Recreation Site

Region: North Coast - **Close to:** Lincoln City
Recreation Site

Star Rating
☆☆☆☆☆

My favorite thing about this place is... _____

Why I went ... _____

Who I went with ... _____

When I went ... _____

What I did... _____

What I saw... _____

What I learned... _____

An unforgettable moment... _____

A laughable moment... _____

A surprising moment... _____

An unforeseeable moment... _____

Wildlife spotted... _____

Snapped a selfie | Location... _____

Took a park sign photo? - ☐ y ☐ n

The weather was ...

My List
☐ _____
☐ _____
☐ _____
☐ _____
☐ _____
☐ _____
☐ _____
☐ _____
☐ _____
☐ _____
☐ _____
☐ _____
☐ _____
☐ _____
☐ _____
☐ _____

And so the Adventure begins

www.mynaturebookadventures.com

Plan Your Trip:

☐ Day Trip ☐ Overnight Stay

Reservations required: ☐ y ☐ n

Date reservations made: _____

Refund Policy: ☐ y ☐ n Site #: _____

Confirmation #: _____

Miles to travel: _____

Time traveling: _____

Dog friendly?: ☐ y ☐ n

Activities Accomplished:

- ☐ Archery
- ☐ Biking
- ☐ Birding
- ☐ Boating
- ☐ Camping
- ☐ Caving
- ☐ Geocaching

- ☐ Fishing
- ☐ Hiking
- ☐ Horseback Riding
- ☐ Hunting
- ☐ Off-Roading
- ☐ Paddle Boarding
- ☐ Photography

- ☐ Picnicking
- ☐ Rock Climbing
- ☐ Shooting Range
- ☐ Stargazing
- ☐ Swimming
- ☐ Tennis
- ☐ Walking

- ☐ Wildlife Watching
- ☐ _____
- ☐ _____
- ☐ _____
- ☐ _____
- ☐ _____
- ☐ _____

Traveling by:

☐ car ☐ truck ☐ SUV ☐ van ☐ airplane ☐ trolley ☐ bicycle ☐ bus ☐ train ☐ helicopter ☐ motorcycle ☐ boat

Reservation Information:

Places we discovered along the way

Places to stop and see along the way

Add your favorite ticket stub, postcard, photo, stamp or drawing here

LET NEW ADVENTURES ≫ BEGIN →

www.mynaturebookadventures.com

Saddle Mountain State Natural Area

Region: North Coast - ***Close to:*** Seaside
Natural Area

Star Rating

My favorite thing about this place is...

Why I went ...

Who I went with ...

When I went ...

What I did...

What I saw...

What I learned...

An unforgettable moment...

A laughable moment...

A surprising moment...

An unforeseeable moment...

Wildlife spotted...

Snapped a selfie | Location...

Took a park sign photo? - ☐ y ☐ n

The weather was ...

My List

And so the Adventure begins

www.mynaturebookadventures.com

207

Plan Your Trip:

☐ Day Trip ☐ Overnight Stay

Reservations required: ☐ y ☐ n

Date reservations made: _____

Refund Policy: ☐ y ☐ n Site #: _____

Confirmation #: _____

Miles to travel: _____

Time traveling: _____

Dog friendly?: ☐ y ☐ n

Activities Accomplished:

☐ Archery	☐ Fishing	☐ Picnicking	☐ Wildlife Watching
☐ Biking	☐ Hiking	☐ Rock Climbing	☐ _____
☐ Birding	☐ Horseback Riding	☐ Shooting Range	☐ _____
☐ Boating	☐ Hunting	☐ Stargazing	☐ _____
☐ Camping	☐ Off-Roading	☐ Swimming	☐ _____
☐ Caving	☐ Paddle Boarding	☐ Tennis	☐ _____
☐ Geocaching	☐ Photography	☐ Walking	☐ _____

Traveling by:

Reservation Information:

Places we discovered along the way

Places to stop and see along the way

Add your favorite ticket stub, postcard, photo, stamp or drawing here

LET NEW ADVENTURES ≫ BEGIN →

Sitka Sedge State Natural Area

Region: North Coast - **Close to:** Tillamook

Natural Site

Star Rating
☆☆☆☆☆

My favorite thing about this place is... _____

Why I went ... _____

Who I went with ... _____

When I went ... _____

What I did... _____

What I saw... _____

What I learned... _____

An unforgettable moment... _____

A laughable moment... _____

A surprising moment... _____

An unforeseeable moment... _____

Wildlife spotted... _____

Snapped a selfie | Location... _____

Took a park sign photo? - ☐ y ☐ n

The weather was ...

My List
☐ _____
☐ _____
☐ _____
☐ _____
☐ _____
☐ _____
☐ _____
☐ _____
☐ _____
☐ _____
☐ _____
☐ _____
☐ _____
☐ _____
☐ _____
☐ _____
☐ _____

And so the Adventure begins

Plan Your Trip:

☐ Day Trip ☐ Overnight Stay

Reservations required: ☐ y ☐ n

Date reservations made: _____

Refund Policy: ☐ y ☐ n Site #: _____

Confirmation #: _____

Miles to travel: _____

Time traveling: _____

Dog friendly?: ☐ y ☐ n

Activities Accomplished:

- ☐ Archery
- ☐ Biking
- ☐ Birding
- ☐ Boating
- ☐ Camping
- ☐ Caving
- ☐ Geocaching
- ☐ Fishing
- ☐ Hiking
- ☐ Horseback Riding
- ☐ Hunting
- ☐ Off-Roading
- ☐ Paddle Boarding
- ☐ Photography
- ☐ Picnicking
- ☐ Rock Climbing
- ☐ Shooting Range
- ☐ Stargazing
- ☐ Swimming
- ☐ Tennis
- ☐ Walking
- ☐ Wildlife Watching
- ☐ _____
- ☐ _____
- ☐ _____
- ☐ _____
- ☐ _____
- ☐ _____

Traveling by: ☐ ☐ ☐ ☐ ☐ ☐ ☐ ☐ ☐ ☐ ☐ ☐

Reservation Information:

Places we discovered along the way

Places to stop and see along the way

Add your favorite ticket stub, postcard, photo, stamp or drawing here

LET NEW ADVENTURES BEGIN →

www.mynaturebookadventures.com

Sunset Beach State Recreation Site

Region: North Coast - **Close to:** Astoria
Recreation Site

Star Rating
☆☆☆☆☆

My favorite thing about this place is... _____

Why I went ... _____

Who I went with ... _____

When I went ... _____

What I did... _____

What I saw... _____

What I learned... _____

An unforgettable moment... _____

A laughable moment... _____

A surprising moment... _____

An unforeseeable moment... _____

Wildlife spotted... _____

Snapped a selfie | Location... _____

Took a park sign photo? - ☐ y ☐ n

The weather was ...

My List
☐ _____
☐ _____
☐ _____
☐ _____
☐ _____
☐ _____
☐ _____
☐ _____
☐ _____
☐ _____
☐ _____
☐ _____
☐ _____
☐ _____
☐ _____
☐ _____
☐ _____
☐ _____

And so the Adventure begins

www.mynaturebookadventures.com

Plan Your Trip:

_____

☐ Day Trip ☐ Overnight Stay
Reservations required: ☐ y ☐ n
Date reservations made: _____
Refund Policy: ☐ y ☐ n Site #: _____
Confirmation #: _____
Miles to travel: _____
Time traveling: _____
Dog friendly?: ☐ y ☐ n

Activities Accomplished:

☐ Archery ☐ Fishing ☐ Picnicking ☐ Wildlife Watching
☐ Biking ☐ Hiking ☐ Rock Climbing ☐ _____
☐ Birding ☐ Horseback Riding ☐ Shooting Range ☐ _____
☐ Boating ☐ Hunting ☐ Stargazing ☐ _____
☐ Camping ☐ Off-Roading ☐ Swimming ☐ _____
☐ Caving ☐ Paddle Boarding ☐ Tennis ☐ _____
☐ Geocaching ☐ Photography ☐ Walking ☐ _____

Traveling by:
☐ ☐ ☐ ☐ ☐ ☐ ☐ ☐ ☐ ☐ ☐ ☐

Reservation Information:

_____
_____

Places we discovered along the way

_____
_____
_____

Places to stop and see along the way

_____
_____
_____

Add your favorite ticket stub, postcard, photo, stamp or drawing here

LET NEW ADVENTURES
»› BEGIN →

Tolovana Beach State Recreation Site

Region: North Coast - **Close to:** Cannon Beach
Recreation Site

Star Rating
☆☆☆☆☆

My favorite thing about this place is...

Why I went ...

Who I went with ...

When I went ...

What I did...

What I saw...

What I learned...

An unforgettable moment...

A laughable moment...

A surprising moment...

An unforeseeable moment...

Wildlife spotted...

Snapped a selfie | Location...

Took a park sign photo? - ☐ y ☐ n

My List
☐
☐
☐
☐
☐
☐
☐
☐
☐
☐
☐
☐
☐
☐
☐

And so the Adventure begins

The weather was ...

www.mynaturebookadventures.com

213

Plan Your Trip:

☐ Day Trip ☐ Overnight Stay

Reservations required: ☐ y ☐ n

Date reservations made: _____

Refund Policy: ☐ y ☐ n Site #: _____

Confirmation #: _____

Miles to travel: _____

Time traveling: _____

Dog friendly?: ☐ y ☐ n

Activities Accomplished:

- ☐ Archery
- ☐ Biking
- ☐ Birding
- ☐ Boating
- ☐ Camping
- ☐ Caving
- ☐ Geocaching

- ☐ Fishing
- ☐ Hiking
- ☐ Horseback Riding
- ☐ Hunting
- ☐ Off-Roading
- ☐ Paddle Boarding
- ☐ Photography

- ☐ Picnicking
- ☐ Rock Climbing
- ☐ Shooting Range
- ☐ Stargazing
- ☐ Swimming
- ☐ Tennis
- ☐ Walking

- ☐ Wildlife Watching
- ☐ _____
- ☐ _____
- ☐ _____
- ☐ _____
- ☐ _____
- ☐ _____

Traveling by:

Reservation Information:

Places we discovered along the way

Places to stop and see along the way

Add your favorite ticket stub, postcard, photo, stamp or drawing here

LET NEW ADVENTURES ≫ BEGIN →

Ainsworth State Park

Region: Portland/Columbia Gorge - **Close to:** Multnomah Falls
State Park

Star Rating
☆☆☆☆☆

My favorite thing about this place is... _____
Why I went ... _____
Who I went with ... _____
When I went ... _____
What I did... _____
What I saw... _____

What I learned... _____

An unforgettable moment... _____

A laughable moment... _____

A surprising moment... _____

An unforeseeable moment... _____

Wildlife spotted... _____

Snapped a selfie | Location... _____
Took a park sign photo? - ☐ y ☐ n

The weather was ... ☐ ☐ ☐ ☐ ☐ ☐

My List
☐ _____
☐ _____
☐ _____
☐ _____
☐ _____
☐ _____
☐ _____
☐ _____
☐ _____
☐ _____
☐ _____
☐ _____
☐ _____
☐ _____
☐ _____
☐ _____
☐ _____
☐ _____

And so the Adventure begins

www.mynaturebookadventures.com

Plan Your Trip:

☐ Day Trip   ☐ Overnight Stay

Reservations required: ☐ y ☐ n

Date reservations made: _____

Refund Policy: ☐ y ☐ n Site #: _____

Confirmation #: _____

Miles to travel: _____

Time traveling: _____

Dog friendly?: ☐ y ☐ n

Activities Accomplished:

- ☐ Archery
- ☐ Biking
- ☐ Birding
- ☐ Boating
- ☐ Camping
- ☐ Caving
- ☐ Geocaching

- ☐ Fishing
- ☐ Hiking
- ☐ Horseback Riding
- ☐ Hunting
- ☐ Off-Roading
- ☐ Paddle Boarding
- ☐ Photography

- ☐ Picnicking
- ☐ Rock Climbing
- ☐ Shooting Range
- ☐ Stargazing
- ☐ Swimming
- ☐ Tennis
- ☐ Walking

- ☐ Wildlife Watching
- ☐ _____
- ☐ _____
- ☐ _____
- ☐ _____
- ☐ _____
- ☐ _____

Traveling by: ☐ ☐ ☐ ☐ ☐ ☐ ☐ ☐ ☐ ☐ ☐ ☐

Reservation Information:

Places we discovered along the way

Places to stop and see along the way

Add your favorite ticket stub, postcard, photo, stamp or drawing here

LET NEW ADVENTURES ›› BEGIN →

BALD PEAK STATE SCENIC VIEWPOINT

Region: Portland/Columbia Gorge - **Close to:** Newberg

Scenic Viewpoint

Star Rating
☆☆☆☆☆

My favorite thing about this place is... _____

Why I went ... _____

Who I went with ... _____

When I went ... _____

What I did... _____

What I saw... _____

What I learned... _____

An unforgettable moment... _____

A laughable moment... _____

A surprising moment... _____

An unforeseeable moment... _____

Wildlife spotted... _____

Snapped a selfie | Location... _____

Took a park sign photo? - ☐ y ☐ n

The weather was ... ☀ ⛅ 🌧 ⛈ 🌫 ❄ 🌡

My List
☐ _____
☐ _____
☐ _____
☐ _____
☐ _____
☐ _____
☐ _____
☐ _____
☐ _____
☐ _____
☐ _____
☐ _____
☐ _____
☐ _____
☐ _____
☐ _____
☐ _____
☐ _____

And so the Adventure begins

Plan Your Trip:

☐ Day Trip ☐ Overnight Stay

Reservations required: ☐ y ☐ n

Date reservations made: _____

Refund Policy: ☐ y ☐ n Site #: _____

Confirmation #: _____

Miles to travel: _____

Time traveling: _____

Dog friendly?: ☐ y ☐ n

Activities Accomplished:

- ☐ Archery
- ☐ Biking
- ☐ Birding
- ☐ Boating
- ☐ Camping
- ☐ Caving
- ☐ Geocaching
- ☐ Fishing
- ☐ Hiking
- ☐ Horseback Riding
- ☐ Hunting
- ☐ Off-Roading
- ☐ Paddle Boarding
- ☐ Photography
- ☐ Picnicking
- ☐ Rock Climbing
- ☐ Shooting Range
- ☐ Stargazing
- ☐ Swimming
- ☐ Tennis
- ☐ Walking
- ☐ Wildlife Watching
- ☐ _____
- ☐ _____
- ☐ _____
- ☐ _____
- ☐ _____
- ☐ _____

Traveling by:

Reservation Information:

Places we discovered along the way

Places to stop and see along the way

Add your favorite ticket stub, postcard, photo, stamp or drawing here

LET NEW ADVENTURES
>> BEGIN →

www.mynaturebookadventures.com

Banks-Vernonia State Trail

Region: Portland/Columbia Gorge - **Close to:** Vernonia

State Trail

Star Rating
☆☆☆☆☆

My favorite thing about this place is... _____

Why I went ... _____

Who I went with ... _____

When I went ... _____

What I did... _____

What I saw... _____

What I learned... _____

An unforgettable moment... _____

A laughable moment... _____

A surprising moment... _____

An unforeseeable moment... _____

Wildlife spotted... _____

Snapped a selfie | Location... _____

Took a park sign photo? - ☐ y ☐ n

The weather was ...

My List
☐ _____
☐ _____
☐ _____
☐ _____
☐ _____
☐ _____
☐ _____
☐ _____
☐ _____
☐ _____
☐ _____
☐ _____
☐ _____
☐ _____
☐ _____
☐ _____

And so the Adventure begins

www.mynaturebookadventures.com

219

Plan Your Trip:

☐ Day Trip ☐ Overnight Stay

Reservations required: ☐ y ☐ n

Date reservations made: _____

Refund Policy: ☐ y ☐ n Site #: _____

Confirmation #: _____

Miles to travel: _____

Time traveling: _____

Dog friendly?: ☐ y ☐ n

Activities Accomplished:

☐ Archery	☐ Fishing	☐ Picnicking	☐ Wildlife Watching
☐ Biking	☐ Hiking	☐ Rock Climbing	☐ _____
☐ Birding	☐ Horseback Riding	☐ Shooting Range	☐ _____
☐ Boating	☐ Hunting	☐ Stargazing	☐ _____
☐ Camping	☐ Off-Roading	☐ Swimming	☐ _____
☐ Caving	☐ Paddle Boarding	☐ Tennis	☐ _____
☐ Geocaching	☐ Photography	☐ Walking	☐ _____

Traveling by: ☐ ☐ ☐ ☐ ☐ ☐ ☐ ☐ ☐ ☐ ☐ ☐

Add your favorite ticket stub, postcard, photo, stamp or drawing here

LET NEW ADVENTURES ›› BEGIN →

Reservation Information:

_____

Places we discovered along the way

_____
_____
_____

Places to stop and see along the way

_____
_____
_____

Benson State Recreation Area

Region: Portland/Columbia Gorge - **Close to:** Multnomah Falls

Recreation Area

Star Rating ☆☆☆☆☆

My favorite thing about this place is... _____

Why I went ... _____

Who I went with ... _____

When I went ... _____

What I did... _____

What I saw... _____

What I learned... _____

An unforgettable moment... _____

A laughable moment... _____

A surprising moment... _____

An unforeseeable moment... _____

Wildlife spotted... _____

Snapped a selfie | Location... _____

Took a park sign photo? - ☐ y ☐ n

The weather was ...

My List
- ☐ _____
- ☐ _____
- ☐ _____
- ☐ _____
- ☐ _____
- ☐ _____
- ☐ _____
- ☐ _____
- ☐ _____
- ☐ _____
- ☐ _____
- ☐ _____
- ☐ _____
- ☐ _____
- ☐ _____
- ☐ _____

And so the Adventure begins

www.mynaturebookadventures.com

Plan Your Trip:

☐ Day Trip   ☐ Overnight Stay

Reservations required: ☐ y ☐ n
Date reservations made: _____
Refund Policy: ☐ y ☐ n Site #: _____
Confirmation #: _____
Miles to travel: _____
Time traveling: _____
Dog friendly?: ☐ y ☐ n

Reservation Information:

Places we discovered along the way

_____
_____
_____

Places to stop and see along the way

_____
_____
_____

Activities Accomplished:

☐ Archery   ☐ Fishing   ☐ Picnicking   ☐ Wildlife Watching
☐ Biking   ☐ Hiking   ☐ Rock Climbing   ☐ _____
☐ Birding   ☐ Horseback Riding   ☐ Shooting Range   ☐ _____
☐ Boating   ☐ Hunting   ☐ Stargazing   ☐ _____
☐ Camping   ☐ Off-Roading   ☐ Swimming   ☐ _____
☐ Caving   ☐ Paddle Boarding   ☐ Tennis   ☐ _____
☐ Geocaching   ☐ Photography   ☐ Walking   ☐ _____

Traveling by:

Add your favorite ticket stub, postcard, photo, stamp or drawing here

LET NEW ADVENTURES ≫ BEGIN →

Bonnie Lure State Recreation Area

Region: Portland/Columbia Gorge - **Close to:** Estacada

Recreation Area

Star Rating
☆☆☆☆☆

My favorite thing about this place is...

Why I went ...

Who I went with ...

When I went ...

What I did...

What I saw...

What I learned...

An unforgettable moment...

A laughable moment...

A surprising moment...

An unforeseeable moment...

Wildlife spotted...

Snapped a selfie | Location...

Took a park sign photo? - ☐ y ☐ n

The weather was ...

My List
☐ ___
☐ ___
☐ ___
☐ ___
☐ ___
☐ ___
☐ ___
☐ ___
☐ ___
☐ ___
☐ ___
☐ ___
☐ ___
☐ ___
☐ ___
☐ ___
☐ ___
☐ ___

And so the Adventure begins

Plan Your Trip:

☐ Day Trip   ☐ Overnight Stay

Reservations required: ☐ y ☐ n

Date reservations made: _____

Refund Policy: ☐ y ☐ n Site #: _____

Confirmation #: _____

Miles to travel: _____

Time traveling: _____

Dog friendly?: ☐ y ☐ n

Activities Accomplished:

☐ Archery	☐ Fishing	☐ Picnicking	☐ Wildlife Watching
☐ Biking	☐ Hiking	☐ Rock Climbing	☐ _____
☐ Birding	☐ Horseback Riding	☐ Shooting Range	☐ _____
☐ Boating	☐ Hunting	☐ Stargazing	☐ _____
☐ Camping	☐ Off-Roading	☐ Swimming	☐ _____
☐ Caving	☐ Paddle Boarding	☐ Tennis	☐ _____
☐ Geocaching	☐ Photography	☐ Walking	☐ _____

Traveling by:

☐ ☐ ☐ ☐ ☐ ☐ ☐ ☐ ☐ ☐ ☐ ☐

Reservation Information:

_____

Places we discovered along the way

_____
_____
_____

Places to stop and see along the way

_____
_____
_____

Add your favorite ticket stub, postcard, photo, stamp or drawing here

LET NEW ADVENTURES ›› BEGIN →

Bridal Veil Falls State Scenic Viewpoint

Region: Portland/Columbia Gorge - **Close to:** Multnomah Falls
Scenic Viewpoint

Star Rating
☆☆☆☆☆

My favorite thing about this place is...

Why I went ...

Who I went with ...

When I went ...

What I did...

What I saw...

What I learned...

An unforgettable moment...

A laughable moment...

A surprising moment...

An unforeseeable moment...

Wildlife spotted...

 Snapped a selfie | Location...

 Took a park sign photo? - ☐ y ☐ n

My List
☐ ___
☐ ___
☐ ___
☐ ___
☐ ___
☐ ___
☐ ___
☐ ___
☐ ___
☐ ___
☐ ___
☐ ___
☐ ___
☐ ___
☐ ___
☐ ___
☐ ___
☐ ___

And so the Adventure begins

The weather was ...
☐ ☐ ☐ ☐ ☐ ☐ ☐

www.mynaturebookadventures.com

Plan Your Trip:

☐ Day Trip ☐ Overnight Stay

Reservations required: ☐ y ☐ n

Date reservations made: _____

Refund Policy: ☐ y ☐ n Site #: _____

Confirmation #: _____

Miles to travel: _____

Time traveling: _____

Dog friendly?: ☐ y ☐ n

Activities Accomplished:

☐ Archery	☐ Fishing	☐ Picnicking	☐ Wildlife Watching
☐ Biking	☐ Hiking	☐ Rock Climbing	☐ _____
☐ Birding	☐ Horseback Riding	☐ Shooting Range	☐ _____
☐ Boating	☐ Hunting	☐ Stargazing	☐ _____
☐ Camping	☐ Off-Roading	☐ Swimming	☐ _____
☐ Caving	☐ Paddle Boarding	☐ Tennis	☐ _____
☐ Geocaching	☐ Photography	☐ Walking	☐ _____

Reservation Information:

Places we discovered along the way

_____

Places to stop and see along the way

_____

Traveling by:

Add your favorite ticket stub, postcard, photo, stamp or drawing here

LET NEW ADVENTURES ≫ BEGIN →

Crown Point State Scenic Corridor

Region: Portland/Columbia Gorge - **Close to:** Troutdale

Scenic Corridor

Star Rating ☆☆☆☆☆

My favorite thing about this place is... _____

Why I went ... _____

Who I went with ... _____

When I went ... _____

What I did... _____

What I saw... _____

What I learned... _____

An unforgettable moment... _____

A laughable moment... _____

A surprising moment... _____

An unforeseeable moment... _____

Wildlife spotted... _____

Snapped a selfie | Location... _____

Took a park sign photo? - ☐ y ☐ n

The weather was ...

My List
☐ _____
☐ _____
☐ _____
☐ _____
☐ _____
☐ _____
☐ _____
☐ _____
☐ _____
☐ _____
☐ _____
☐ _____
☐ _____
☐ _____
☐ _____
☐ _____
☐ _____

And so the Adventure begins

Plan Your Trip:

☐ Day Trip ☐ Overnight Stay

Reservations required: ☐ y ☐ n

Date reservations made: _____

Refund Policy: ☐ y ☐ n Site #: _____

Confirmation #: _____

Miles to travel: _____

Time traveling: _____

Dog friendly?: ☐ y ☐ n

Activities Accomplished:

☐ Archery	☐ Fishing	☐ Picnicking	☐ Wildlife Watching
☐ Biking	☐ Hiking	☐ Rock Climbing	☐ _____
☐ Birding	☐ Horseback Riding	☐ Shooting Range	☐ _____
☐ Boating	☐ Hunting	☐ Stargazing	☐ _____
☐ Camping	☐ Off-Roading	☐ Swimming	☐ _____
☐ Caving	☐ Paddle Boarding	☐ Tennis	☐ _____
☐ Geocaching	☐ Photography	☐ Walking	☐ _____

Traveling by:

Reservation Information:

Places we discovered along the way

Places to stop and see along the way

Add your favorite ticket stub, postcard, photo, stamp or drawing here

228   www.mynaturebookadventures.com

Dabney State Recreation Area

Region: Portland/Columbia Gorge - **Close to:** Troutdale

Recreation Area

Star Rating
☆☆☆☆☆

My favorite thing about this place is... _____

Why I went ... _____

Who I went with ... _____

When I went ... _____

What I did... _____

What I saw... _____

What I learned... _____

An unforgettable moment... _____

A laughable moment... _____

A surprising moment... _____

An unforeseeable moment... _____

Wildlife spotted... _____

Snapped a selfie | Location... _____

Took a park sign photo? - ☐ y ☐ n

The weather was ...

My List
☐ _____
☐ _____
☐ _____
☐ _____
☐ _____
☐ _____
☐ _____
☐ _____
☐ _____
☐ _____
☐ _____
☐ _____
☐ _____
☐ _____
☐ _____
☐ _____
☐ _____

And so the Adventure begins

Plan Your Trip:

☐ Day Trip   ☐ Overnight Stay

Reservations required: ☐ y ☐ n

Date reservations made: _____

Refund Policy: ☐ y ☐ n Site #: _____

Confirmation #: _____

Miles to travel: _____

Time traveling: _____

Dog friendly?: ☐ y ☐ n

Activities Accomplished:

☐ Archery ☐ Fishing ☐ Picnicking ☐ Wildlife Watching
☐ Biking ☐ Hiking ☐ Rock Climbing ☐ _____
☐ Birding ☐ Horseback Riding ☐ Shooting Range ☐ _____
☐ Boating ☐ Hunting ☐ Stargazing ☐ _____
☐ Camping ☐ Off-Roading ☐ Swimming ☐ _____
☐ Caving ☐ Paddle Boarding ☐ Tennis ☐ _____
☐ Geocaching ☐ Photography ☐ Walking ☐ _____

Traveling by:

Reservation Information:

Places we discovered along the way

Places to stop and see along the way

Add your favorite ticket stub, postcard, photo, stamp or drawing here

LET NEW ADVENTURES
»› BEGIN →

www.mynaturebookadventures.com

Deschutes River State Recreation Area

Region: Portland/Columbia Gorge - **Close to:** The Dalles

Recreation Area

Star Rating
☆☆☆☆☆

My favorite thing about this place is... _____

Why I went ... _____

Who I went with ... _____

When I went ... _____

What I did... _____

What I saw... _____

What I learned... _____

An unforgettable moment... _____

A laughable moment... _____

A surprising moment... _____

An unforeseeable moment... _____

Wildlife spotted... _____

Snapped a selfie | Location... _____

Took a park sign photo? - ☐ y ☐ n

The weather was ...

My List
- ☐ _____
- ☐ _____
- ☐ _____
- ☐ _____
- ☐ _____
- ☐ _____
- ☐ _____
- ☐ _____
- ☐ _____
- ☐ _____
- ☐ _____
- ☐ _____
- ☐ _____
- ☐ _____
- ☐ _____
- ☐ _____
- ☐ _____

And so the Adventure begins

Plan Your Trip:

☐ Day Trip ☐ Overnight Stay

Reservations required: ☐ y ☐ n

Date reservations made: _____

Refund Policy: ☐ y ☐ n Site #: _____

Confirmation #: _____

Miles to travel: _____

Time traveling: _____

Dog friendly?: ☐ y ☐ n

Activities Accomplished:

☐ Archery	☐ Fishing	☐ Picnicking	☐ Wildlife Watching
☐ Biking	☐ Hiking	☐ Rock Climbing	☐ _____
☐ Birding	☐ Horseback Riding	☐ Shooting Range	☐ _____
☐ Boating	☐ Hunting	☐ Stargazing	☐ _____
☐ Camping	☐ Off-Roading	☐ Swimming	☐ _____
☐ Caving	☐ Paddle Boarding	☐ Tennis	☐ _____
☐ Geocaching	☐ Photography	☐ Walking	☐ _____

Traveling by:

Reservation Information:

Places we discovered along the way

Places to stop and see along the way

Add your favorite ticket stub, postcard, photo, stamp or drawing here

LET NEW ADVENTURES
»» BEGIN →

George W. Joseph State Natural Area (accessible from Guy W. Talbot State Park)

Region: Portland/Columbia Gorge - **Close to:** Troutdale

Natural Area

Star Rating ☆☆☆☆☆

My favorite thing about this place is...

Why I went ...

Who I went with ...

When I went ...

What I did...

What I saw...

What I learned...

An unforgettable moment...

A laughable moment...

A surprising moment...

An unforeseeable moment...

Wildlife spotted...

Snapped a selfie | Location...

Took a park sign photo? - ☐y ☐n

The weather was ...

My List

And so the Adventure begins

www.mynaturebookadventures.com

233

Plan Your Trip:

☐ Day Trip ☐ Overnight Stay

Reservations required: ☐ y ☐ n
Date reservations made: _____
Refund Policy: ☐ y ☐ n Site #: _____
Confirmation #: _____
Miles to travel: _____
Time traveling: _____
Dog friendly?: ☐ y ☐ n

Activities Accomplished:

- ☐ Archery
- ☐ Biking
- ☐ Birding
- ☐ Boating
- ☐ Camping
- ☐ Caving
- ☐ Geocaching

- ☐ Fishing
- ☐ Hiking
- ☐ Horseback Riding
- ☐ Hunting
- ☐ Off-Roading
- ☐ Paddle Boarding
- ☐ Photography

- ☐ Picnicking
- ☐ Rock Climbing
- ☐ Shooting Range
- ☐ Stargazing
- ☐ Swimming
- ☐ Tennis
- ☐ Walking

- ☐ Wildlife Watching
- ☐ _____
- ☐ _____
- ☐ _____
- ☐ _____
- ☐ _____
- ☐ _____

Traveling by:

Add your favorite ticket stub, postcard, photo, stamp or drawing here

LET NEW ADVENTURES ›› BEGIN →

Reservation Information:

Places we discovered along the way

Places to stop and see along the way

Government Island State Recreation Area

Region: Portland/Columbia Gorge - **Close to:** Portland

Recreation Area

Star Rating
☆☆☆☆☆

My favorite thing about this place is... _____

Why I went ... _____

Who I went with ... _____

When I went ... _____

What I did... _____

What I saw... _____

What I learned... _____

An unforgettable moment... _____

A laughable moment... _____

A surprising moment... _____

An unforeseeable moment... _____

Wildlife spotted... _____

Snapped a selfie | Location... _____

Took a park sign photo? - ☐ y ☐ n

The weather was ...

My List
- ☐ _____
- ☐ _____
- ☐ _____
- ☐ _____
- ☐ _____
- ☐ _____
- ☐ _____
- ☐ _____
- ☐ _____
- ☐ _____
- ☐ _____
- ☐ _____
- ☐ _____
- ☐ _____
- ☐ _____
- ☐ _____

And so the Adventure begins

www.mynaturebookadventures.com

Plan Your Trip:

☐ Day Trip ☐ Overnight Stay

Reservations required: ☐y ☐n

Date reservations made: _____

Refund Policy: ☐y ☐n Site #: _____

Confirmation #: _____

Miles to travel: _____

Time traveling: _____

Dog friendly?: ☐y ☐n

Activities Accomplished:

☐ Archery	☐ Fishing	☐ Picnicking	☐ Wildlife Watching
☐ Biking	☐ Hiking	☐ Rock Climbing	☐ _____
☐ Birding	☐ Horseback Riding	☐ Shooting Range	☐ _____
☐ Boating	☐ Hunting	☐ Stargazing	☐ _____
☐ Camping	☐ Off-Roading	☐ Swimming	☐ _____
☐ Caving	☐ Paddle Boarding	☐ Tennis	☐ _____
☐ Geocaching	☐ Photography	☐ Walking	☐ _____

Traveling by:

☐ ☐ ☐ ☐ ☐ ☐ ☐ ☐ ☐ ☐ ☐ ☐

Reservation Information:

Places we discovered along the way

Places to stop and see along the way

Add your favorite ticket stub, postcard, photo, stamp or drawing here

LET NEW ADVENTURES
»› BEGIN →

www.mynaturebookadventures.com

Guy W. Talbot State Park

Region: Portland/Columbia Gorge - **Close to:** Troutdale

State Park

Star Rating
☆☆☆☆☆

My favorite thing about this place is... _____

Why I went ... _____

Who I went with ... _____

When I went ... _____

What I did... _____

What I saw... _____

What I learned... _____

An unforgettable moment... _____

A laughable moment... _____

A surprising moment... _____

An unforeseeable moment... _____

Wildlife spotted... _____

Snapped a selfie | Location... _____

Took a park sign photo? - ☐ y ☐ n

The weather was ...

My List
☐ _____
☐ _____
☐ _____
☐ _____
☐ _____
☐ _____
☐ _____
☐ _____
☐ _____
☐ _____
☐ _____
☐ _____
☐ _____
☐ _____
☐ _____
☐ _____
☐ _____

And so the Adventure begins

www.mynaturebookadventures.com

Plan Your Trip:

☐ Day Trip ☐ Overnight Stay

Reservations required: ☐ y ☐ n

Date reservations made: _____

Refund Policy: ☐ y ☐ n   Site #: _____

Confirmation #: _____

Miles to travel: _____

Time traveling: _____

Dog friendly?: ☐ y ☐ n

Activities Accomplished:

- ☐ Archery
- ☐ Biking
- ☐ Birding
- ☐ Boating
- ☐ Camping
- ☐ Caving
- ☐ Geocaching
- ☐ Fishing
- ☐ Hiking
- ☐ Horseback Riding
- ☐ Hunting
- ☐ Off-Roading
- ☐ Paddle Boarding
- ☐ Photography
- ☐ Picnicking
- ☐ Rock Climbing
- ☐ Shooting Range
- ☐ Stargazing
- ☐ Swimming
- ☐ Tennis
- ☐ Walking
- ☐ Wildlife Watching
- ☐ _____
- ☐ _____
- ☐ _____
- ☐ _____
- ☐ _____
- ☐ _____

Traveling by:

Reservation information:

Places we discovered along the way

Places to stop and see along the way

Add your favorite ticket stub, postcard, photo, stamp or drawing here

LET NEW ADVENTURES ≫ BEGIN →

Heritage Landing (Deschutes)

Region: Portland/Columbia Gorge - **Close to:** The Dalles
Boat launch (across from Deschutes River SRA)

Star Rating
☆☆☆☆☆

My favorite thing about this place is...
Why I went ...
Who I went with ...
When I went ...
What I did...
What I saw...
What I learned...
An unforgettable moment...
A laughable moment...
A surprising moment...
An unforeseeable moment...
Wildlife spotted...
Snapped a selfie | Location...
Took a park sign photo? - ☐ y ☐ n

My List

And so the Adventure begins

The weather was ...

www.mynaturebookadventures.com
239

Plan Your Trip:

☐ Day Trip ☐ Overnight Stay

Reservations required: ☐ y ☐ n

Date reservations made: _____

Refund Policy: ☐ y ☐ n Site #: _____

Confirmation #: _____

Miles to travel: _____

Time traveling: _____

Dog friendly?: ☐ y ☐ n

Activities Accomplished:

☐ Archery	☐ Fishing	☐ Picnicking	☐ Wildlife Watching
☐ Biking	☐ Hiking	☐ Rock Climbing	☐ _____
☐ Birding	☐ Horseback Riding	☐ Shooting Range	☐ _____
☐ Boating	☐ Hunting	☐ Stargazing	☐ _____
☐ Camping	☐ Off-Roading	☐ Swimming	☐ _____
☐ Caving	☐ Paddle Boarding	☐ Tennis	☐ _____
☐ Geocaching	☐ Photography	☐ Walking	☐ _____

Traveling by:
☐ ☐ ☐ ☐ ☐ ☐ ☐ ☐ ☐ ☐ ☐ ☐

Reservation Information:

Places we discovered along the way

Places to stop and see along the way

Add your favorite ticket stub, postcard, photo, stamp or drawing here

LET NEW ADVENTURES ≫ BEGIN →

Historic Columbia River Highway State Trail

Region: Portland/Columbia Gorge - **Close to:** Cascade Locks
State Trail

Star Rating
☆☆☆☆☆

My favorite thing about this place is... _____

Why I went ... _____

Who I went with ... _____

When I went ... _____

What I did... _____

What I saw... _____

What I learned... _____

An unforgettable moment... _____

A laughable moment... _____

A surprising moment... _____

An unforeseeable moment... _____

Wildlife spotted... _____

Snapped a selfie | Location... _____

Took a park sign photo? - ☐ y ☐ n

The weather was ...

My List
☐ _____
☐ _____
☐ _____
☐ _____
☐ _____
☐ _____
☐ _____
☐ _____
☐ _____
☐ _____
☐ _____
☐ _____
☐ _____
☐ _____
☐ _____
☐ _____
☐ _____
☐ _____

And so the Adventure begins

www.mynaturebookadventures.com

Plan Your Trip:

☐ Day Trip ☐ Overnight Stay

Reservations required: ☐ y ☐ n

Date reservations made: _____

Refund Policy: ☐ y ☐ n Site #: _____

Confirmation #: _____

Miles to travel: _____

Time traveling: _____

Dog friendly?: ☐ y ☐ n

Activities Accomplished:

- ☐ Archery
- ☐ Biking
- ☐ Birding
- ☐ Boating
- ☐ Camping
- ☐ Caving
- ☐ Geocaching
- ☐ Fishing
- ☐ Hiking
- ☐ Horseback Riding
- ☐ Hunting
- ☐ Off-Roading
- ☐ Paddle Boarding
- ☐ Photography
- ☐ Picnicking
- ☐ Rock Climbing
- ☐ Shooting Range
- ☐ Stargazing
- ☐ Swimming
- ☐ Tennis
- ☐ Walking
- ☐ Wildlife Watching
- ☐ _____
- ☐ _____
- ☐ _____
- ☐ _____
- ☐ _____
- ☐ _____

Traveling by:

Reservation Information:

Places we discovered along the way

Places to stop and see along the way

Add your favorite ticket stub, postcard, photo, stamp or drawing here

LET NEW ADVENTURES
»> BEGIN →

www.mynaturebookadventures.com

John B. Yeon State Scenic Corridor

Region: Portland/Columbia Gorge - **Close to:** Cascade Locks

Scenic Corridor

Star Rating
☆☆☆☆☆

My favorite thing about this place is... _____

Why I went ... _____

Who I went with ... _____

When I went ... _____

What I did... _____

What I saw... _____

What I learned... _____

An unforgettable moment... _____

A laughable moment... _____

A surprising moment... _____

An unforeseeable moment... _____

Wildlife spotted... _____

Snapped a selfie | Location... _____

Took a park sign photo? - ☐ y ☐ n

The weather was ...

My List
☐ _____
☐ _____
☐ _____
☐ _____
☐ _____
☐ _____
☐ _____
☐ _____
☐ _____
☐ _____
☐ _____
☐ _____
☐ _____
☐ _____
☐ _____

And so the Adventure begins

www.mynaturebookadventures.com

Plan Your Trip:

☐ Day Trip   ☐ Overnight Stay

Reservations required: ☐ y ☐ n
Date reservations made: _____
Refund Policy: ☐ y ☐ n Site #: _____
Confirmation #: _____
Miles to travel: _____
Time traveling: _____
Dog friendly?: ☐ y ☐ n

Activities Accomplished:

- ☐ Archery
- ☐ Biking
- ☐ Birding
- ☐ Boating
- ☐ Camping
- ☐ Caving
- ☐ Geocaching
- ☐ Fishing
- ☐ Hiking
- ☐ Horseback Riding
- ☐ Hunting
- ☐ Off-Roading
- ☐ Paddle Boarding
- ☐ Photography
- ☐ Picnicking
- ☐ Rock Climbing
- ☐ Shooting Range
- ☐ Stargazing
- ☐ Swimming
- ☐ Tennis
- ☐ Walking
- ☐ Wildlife Watching
- ☐ _____
- ☐ _____
- ☐ _____
- ☐ _____
- ☐ _____
- ☐ _____

Traveling by: ☐ ☐ ☐ ☐ ☐ ☐ ☐ ☐ ☐ ☐ ☐ ☐

Reservation Information:

Places we discovered along the way

Places to stop and see along the way

Add your favorite ticket stub, postcard, photo, stamp or drawing here

LET NEW ADVENTURES BEGIN →

244

www.mynaturebookadventures.com

Koberg Beach State Recreation Site

Region: Portland/Columbia Gorge - **Close to:** Hood River

Recreation Site

Star Rating
☆☆☆☆☆

My favorite thing about this place is... _____

Why I went ... _____

Who I went with ... _____

When I went ... _____

What I did... _____

What I saw... _____

What I learned... _____

An unforgettable moment... _____

A laughable moment... _____

A surprising moment... _____

An unforeseeable moment... _____

Wildlife spotted... _____

Snapped a selfie | Location... _____

Took a park sign photo? - ☐ y ☐ n

The weather was ...

My List
☐ _____
☐ _____
☐ _____
☐ _____
☐ _____
☐ _____
☐ _____
☐ _____
☐ _____
☐ _____
☐ _____
☐ _____
☐ _____
☐ _____
☐ _____
☐ _____
☐ _____
☐ _____

And so the Adventure begins

www.mynaturebookadventures.com

Plan Your Trip:

☐ Day Trip　　　☐ Overnight Stay

Reservations required: ☐ y ☐ n

Date reservations made: _____

Refund Policy: ☐ y ☐ n　Site #: _____

Confirmation #: _____

Miles to travel: _____

Time traveling: _____

Dog friendly?: ☐ y ☐ n

Activities Accomplished:

☐ Archery	☐ Fishing	☐ Picnicking	☐ Wildlife Watching
☐ Biking	☐ Hiking	☐ Rock Climbing	☐ _____
☐ Birding	☐ Horseback Riding	☐ Shooting Range	☐ _____
☐ Boating	☐ Hunting	☐ Stargazing	☐ _____
☐ Camping	☐ Off-Roading	☐ Swimming	☐ _____
☐ Caving	☐ Paddle Boarding	☐ Tennis	☐ _____
☐ Geocaching	☐ Photography	☐ Walking	☐ _____

Traveling by:

☐ ☐ ☐ ☐ ☐ ☐ ☐ ☐ ☐ ☐ ☐ ☐

Reservation Information:

_____

Places we discovered along the way

_____
_____
_____

Places to stop and see along the way

_____
_____
_____

Add your favorite ticket stub, postcard, photo, stamp or drawing here

LET NEW ADVENTURES ≫ BEGIN →

246　　www.mynaturebookadventures.com

L. L. "Stub" Stewart State Park

Region: Portland/Columbia Gorge - **Close to:** Vernonia

State Park

Star Rating
☆☆☆☆☆

My favorite thing about this place is...

Why I went ...

Who I went with ...

When I went ...

What I did...

What I saw...

What I learned...

An unforgettable moment...

A laughable moment...

A surprising moment...

An unforeseeable moment...

Wildlife spotted...

Snapped a selfie | Location...

Took a park sign photo? - ☐ y ☐ n

The weather was ...

My List
☐
☐
☐
☐
☐
☐
☐
☐
☐
☐
☐
☐
☐
☐
☐
☐
☐
☐

And so the Adventure begins

www.mynaturebookadventures.com

247

Plan Your Trip:

☐ Day Trip ☐ Overnight Stay

Reservations required: ☐ y ☐ n

Date reservations made: _____

Refund Policy: ☐ y ☐ n Site #: _____

Confirmation #: _____

Miles to travel: _____

Time traveling: _____

Dog friendly?: ☐ y ☐ n

Activities Accomplished:

☐ Archery	☐ Fishing	☐ Picnicking	☐ Wildlife Watching
☐ Biking	☐ Hiking	☐ Rock Climbing	☐ _____
☐ Birding	☐ Horseback Riding	☐ Shooting Range	☐ _____
☐ Boating	☐ Hunting	☐ Stargazing	☐ _____
☐ Camping	☐ Off-Roading	☐ Swimming	☐ _____
☐ Caving	☐ Paddle Boarding	☐ Tennis	☐ _____
☐ Geocaching	☐ Photography	☐ Walking	☐ _____

Traveling by:

Reservation Information:

_____

Places we discovered along the way

_____
_____
_____

Places to stop and see along the way

_____
_____
_____

Add your favorite ticket stub, postcard, photo, stamp or drawing here

LET NEW ADVENTURES ≫ BEGIN →

248

Lewis and Clark State Recreation Site

Region: Portland/Columbia Gorge - ***Close to:*** Troutdale

Recreation Site

Star Rating ☆☆☆☆☆

My favorite thing about this place is...

Why I went ...

Who I went with ...

When I went ...

What I did...

What I saw...

What I learned...

An unforgettable moment...

A laughable moment...

A surprising moment...

An unforeseeable moment...

Wildlife spotted...

Snapped a selfie | Location...

Took a park sign photo? - ☐ y ☐ n

The weather was ...

My List
☐ ....
☐ ....
☐ ....
☐ ....
☐ ....
☐ ....
☐ ....
☐ ....
☐ ....
☐ ....
☐ ....
☐ ....
☐ ....
☐ ....
☐ ....
☐ ....

And so the Adventure begins

www.mynaturebookadventures.com

249

Plan Your Trip:

☐ Day Trip ☐ Overnight Stay

Reservations required: ☐ y ☐ n

Date reservations made: _____

Refund Policy: ☐ y ☐ n Site #: _____

Confirmation #: _____

Miles to travel: _____

Time traveling: _____

Dog friendly?: ☐ y ☐ n

Activities Accomplished:

☐ Archery	☐ Fishing	☐ Picnicking	☐ Wildlife Watching
☐ Biking	☐ Hiking	☐ Rock Climbing	☐ _____
☐ Birding	☐ Horseback Riding	☐ Shooting Range	☐ _____
☐ Boating	☐ Hunting	☐ Stargazing	☐ _____
☐ Camping	☐ Off-Roading	☐ Swimming	☐ _____
☐ Caving	☐ Paddle Boarding	☐ Tennis	☐ _____
☐ Geocaching	☐ Photography	☐ Walking	☐ _____

Traveling by:

Reservation Information:

Places we discovered along the way

Places to stop and see along the way

Add your favorite ticket stub, postcard, photo, stamp or drawing here

LET NEW ADVENTURES ≫ BEGIN →

Mary S. Young State Recreation Area

Region: Portland/Columbia Gorge - **Close to:** West Linn
Recreation Area

Star Rating
☆☆☆☆☆

My favorite thing about this place is... _____

Why I went ... _____

Who I went with ... _____

When I went ... _____

What I did... _____

What I saw... _____

What I learned... _____

An unforgettable moment... _____

A laughable moment... _____

A surprising moment... _____

An unforeseeable moment... _____

Wildlife spotted... _____

Snapped a selfie | Location... _____

Took a park sign photo? - ☐ y ☐ n

The weather was ...

My List
☐ _____
☐ _____
☐ _____
☐ _____
☐ _____
☐ _____
☐ _____
☐ _____
☐ _____
☐ _____
☐ _____
☐ _____
☐ _____
☐ _____
☐ _____
☐ _____
☐ _____

And so the Adventure begins

www.mynaturebookadventures.com

Plan Your Trip:

_____

☐ Day Trip   ☐ Overnight Stay

Reservations required: ☐ y ☐ n

Date reservations made: _____

Refund Policy: ☐ y ☐ n Site #: _____

Confirmation #: _____

Miles to travel: _____

Time traveling: _____

Dog friendly?: ☐ y ☐ n

Activities Accomplished:

☐ Archery	☐ Fishing	☐ Picnicking	☐ Wildlife Watching
☐ Biking	☐ Hiking	☐ Rock Climbing	☐ _____
☐ Birding	☐ Horseback Riding	☐ Shooting Range	☐ _____
☐ Boating	☐ Hunting	☐ Stargazing	☐ _____
☐ Camping	☐ Off-Roading	☐ Swimming	☐ _____
☐ Caving	☐ Paddle Boarding	☐ Tennis	☐ _____
☐ Geocaching	☐ Photography	☐ Walking	☐ _____

Traveling by: ☐ ☐ ☐ ☐ ☐ ☐ ☐ ☐ ☐ ☐ ☐ ☐

Reservation Information:

_____

Places we discovered along the way

_____
_____
_____

Places to stop and see along the way

_____
_____
_____

Add your favorite ticket stub, postcard, photo, stamp or drawing here

LET NEW ADVENTURES ≫ BEGIN →

Mayer State Park

Region: Portland/Columbia Gorge - **Close to:** The Dalles
State Park

Star Rating
☆☆☆☆☆

My favorite thing about this place is... _____

Why I went ... _____

Who I went with ... _____

When I went ... _____

What I did... _____

What I saw... _____

What I learned... _____

An unforgettable moment... _____

A laughable moment... _____

A surprising moment... _____

An unforeseeable moment... _____

Wildlife spotted... _____

Snapped a selfie | Location... _____

Took a park sign photo? - ☐ y ☐ n

The weather was ...

My List
☐ _____
☐ _____
☐ _____
☐ _____
☐ _____
☐ _____
☐ _____
☐ _____
☐ _____
☐ _____
☐ _____
☐ _____
☐ _____
☐ _____
☐ _____
☐ _____
☐ _____

And so the Adventure begins

www.mynaturebookadventures.com

Plan Your Trip:

☐ Day Trip ☐ Overnight Stay

Reservations required: ☐ y ☐ n

Date reservations made: _____

Refund Policy: ☐ y ☐ n Site #: _____

Confirmation #: _____

Miles to travel: _____

Time traveling: _____

Dog friendly?: ☐ y ☐ n

Activities Accomplished:

- ☐ Archery
- ☐ Biking
- ☐ Birding
- ☐ Boating
- ☐ Camping
- ☐ Caving
- ☐ Geocaching

- ☐ Fishing
- ☐ Hiking
- ☐ Horseback Riding
- ☐ Hunting
- ☐ Off-Roading
- ☐ Paddle Boarding
- ☐ Photography

- ☐ Picnicking
- ☐ Rock Climbing
- ☐ Shooting Range
- ☐ Stargazing
- ☐ Swimming
- ☐ Tennis
- ☐ Walking

- ☐ Wildlife Watching
- ☐ _____
- ☐ _____
- ☐ _____
- ☐ _____
- ☐ _____
- ☐ _____

Traveling by: ☐ ☐ ☐ ☐ ☐ ☐ ☐ ☐ ☐ ☐ ☐ ☐

Reservation Information:

Places we discovered along the way

Places to stop and see along the way

Add your favorite ticket stub, postcard, photo, stamp or drawing here

LET NEW ADVENTURES ›› BEGIN →

www.mynaturebookadventures.com

Memaloose State Park

Region: Portland/Columbia Gorge - *Close to:* The Dalles
State Park

Star Rating
☆☆☆☆☆

My favorite thing about this place is... _____

Why I went ... _____

Who I went with ... _____

When I went ... _____

What I did... _____

What I saw... _____

What I learned... _____

An unforgettable moment... _____

A laughable moment... _____

A surprising moment... _____

An unforeseeable moment... _____

Wildlife spotted... _____

Snapped a selfie | Location... _____

Took a park sign photo? - ☐ y ☐ n

The weather was ...

My List
☐ _____
☐ _____
☐ _____
☐ _____
☐ _____
☐ _____
☐ _____
☐ _____
☐ _____
☐ _____
☐ _____
☐ _____
☐ _____
☐ _____
☐ _____
☐ _____
☐ _____
☐ _____

And so the Adventure begins

www.mynaturebookadventures.com

Plan Your Trip:

_____

☐ Day Trip   ☐ Overnight Stay

Reservations required: ☐ y ☐ n

Date reservations made: _____

Refund Policy: ☐ y ☐ n Site #: _____

Confirmation #: _____

Miles to travel: _____

Time traveling: _____

Dog friendly?: ☐ y ☐ n

Activities Accomplished:

- ☐ Archery
- ☐ Biking
- ☐ Birding
- ☐ Boating
- ☐ Camping
- ☐ Caving
- ☐ Geocaching
- ☐ Fishing
- ☐ Hiking
- ☐ Horseback Riding
- ☐ Hunting
- ☐ Off-Roading
- ☐ Paddle Boarding
- ☐ Photography
- ☐ Picnicking
- ☐ Rock Climbing
- ☐ Shooting Range
- ☐ Stargazing
- ☐ Swimming
- ☐ Tennis
- ☐ Walking
- ☐ Wildlife Watching
- ☐ _____
- ☐ _____
- ☐ _____
- ☐ _____
- ☐ _____
- ☐ _____

Traveling by: ☐ ☐ ☐ ☐ ☐ ☐ ☐ ☐ ☐ ☐ ☐ ☐

Reservation Information:

_____
_____

Places we discovered along the way

_____
_____
_____

Places to stop and see along the way

_____
_____
_____

Add your favorite ticket stub, postcard, photo, stamp or drawing here

LET NEW ADVENTURES ›› BEGIN →

256   www.mynaturebookadventures.com

Milo McIver State Park

Region: Portland/Columbia Gorge - **Close to:** Estacada
State Park

Star Rating
☆☆☆☆☆

My favorite thing about this place is...

Why I went ...

Who I went with ...

When I went ...

What I did...

What I saw...

What I learned...

An unforgettable moment...

A laughable moment...

A surprising moment...

An unforeseeable moment...

Wildlife spotted...

Snapped a selfie | Location...

Took a park sign photo? - ☐ y ☐ n

The weather was ...

My List

And so the Adventure begins

www.mynaturebookadventures.com

257

Plan Your Trip:

☐ Day Trip   ☐ Overnight Stay

Reservations required: ☐ y ☐ n

Date reservations made: _____

Refund Policy: ☐ y ☐ n   Site #: _____

Confirmation #: _____

Miles to travel: _____

Time traveling: _____

Dog friendly?: ☐ y ☐ n

Activities Accomplished:

- ☐ Archery
- ☐ Biking
- ☐ Birding
- ☐ Boating
- ☐ Camping
- ☐ Caving
- ☐ Geocaching

- ☐ Fishing
- ☐ Hiking
- ☐ Horseback Riding
- ☐ Hunting
- ☐ Off-Roading
- ☐ Paddle Boarding
- ☐ Photography

- ☐ Picnicking
- ☐ Rock Climbing
- ☐ Shooting Range
- ☐ Stargazing
- ☐ Swimming
- ☐ Tennis
- ☐ Walking

- ☐ Wildlife Watching
- ☐ _____
- ☐ _____
- ☐ _____
- ☐ _____
- ☐ _____
- ☐ _____

Traveling by:

Reservation Information:

Places we discovered along the way

Places to stop and see along the way

Add your favorite ticket stub, postcard, photo, stamp or drawing here

LET NEW ADVENTURES ≫ BEGIN →

258

www.mynaturebookadventures.com

Molalla River State Park

Region: Portland/Columbia Gorge - **Close to:** Canby

State Park

Star Rating
☆☆☆☆☆

My favorite thing about this place is... _____

Why I went ... _____

Who I went with ... _____

When I went ... _____

What I did... _____

What I saw... _____

What I learned... _____

An unforgettable moment... _____

A laughable moment... _____

A surprising moment... _____

An unforeseeable moment... _____

Wildlife spotted... _____

Snapped a selfie | Location... _____

Took a park sign photo? - ☐ y ☐ n

The weather was ...

My List
☐ _____
☐ _____
☐ _____
☐ _____
☐ _____
☐ _____
☐ _____
☐ _____
☐ _____
☐ _____
☐ _____
☐ _____
☐ _____
☐ _____
☐ _____
☐ _____
☐ _____
☐ _____

And so the Adventure begins

www.mynaturebookadventures.com

Plan Your Trip:

☐ Day Trip ☐ Overnight Stay
Reservations required: ☐ y ☐ n
Date reservations made: _____
Refund Policy: ☐ y ☐ n Site #: _____
Confirmation #: _____
Miles to travel: _____
Time traveling: _____
Dog friendly?: ☐ y ☐ n

Activities Accomplished:

☐ Archery	☐ Fishing	☐ Picnicking	☐ Wildlife Watching
☐ Biking	☐ Hiking	☐ Rock Climbing	☐ _____
☐ Birding	☐ Horseback Riding	☐ Shooting Range	☐ _____
☐ Boating	☐ Hunting	☐ Stargazing	☐ _____
☐ Camping	☐ Off-Roading	☐ Swimming	☐ _____
☐ Caving	☐ Paddle Boarding	☐ Tennis	☐ _____
☐ Geocaching	☐ Photography	☐ Walking	☐ _____

Traveling by:
☐ ☐ ☐ ☐ ☐ ☐ ☐ ☐ ☐ ☐ ☐ ☐

Reservation Information:

Places we discovered along the way

Places to stop and see along the way

Add your favorite ticket stub, postcard, photo, stamp or drawing here

LET NEW ADVENTURES ≫ BEGIN →

Portland Women's Forum State Scenic Viewpoint

Region: Portland/Columbia Gorge - **Close to:** Troutdale

Scenic Viewpoint

Star Rating
☆☆☆☆☆

My favorite thing about this place is... _____

Why I went ... _____

Who I went with ... _____

When I went ... _____

What I did... _____

What I saw... _____

What I learned... _____

An unforgettable moment... _____

A laughable moment... _____

A surprising moment... _____

An unforeseeable moment... _____

Wildlife spotted... _____

Snapped a selfie | Location... _____

Took a park sign photo? - ☐ y ☐ n

The weather was ...

My List
☐ _____
☐ _____
☐ _____
☐ _____
☐ _____
☐ _____
☐ _____
☐ _____
☐ _____
☐ _____
☐ _____
☐ _____
☐ _____
☐ _____
☐ _____
☐ _____
☐ _____

And so the Adventure begins

www.mynaturebookadventures.com

261

Plan Your Trip:

_____

☐ Day Trip ☐ Overnight Stay

Reservations required: ☐ y ☐ n

Date reservations made: _____

Refund Policy: ☐ y ☐ n Site #: _____

Confirmation #: _____

Miles to travel: _____

Time traveling: _____

Dog friendly?: ☐ y ☐ n

Activities Accomplished:

☐ Archery	☐ Fishing	☐ Picnicking	☐ Wildlife Watching
☐ Biking	☐ Hiking	☐ Rock Climbing	☐ _____
☐ Birding	☐ Horseback Riding	☐ Shooting Range	☐ _____
☐ Boating	☐ Hunting	☐ Stargazing	☐ _____
☐ Camping	☐ Off-Roading	☐ Swimming	☐ _____
☐ Caving	☐ Paddle Boarding	☐ Tennis	☐ _____
☐ Geocaching	☐ Photography	☐ Walking	☐ _____

Traveling by:

Reservation Information:

_____
_____

Places we discovered along the way

_____
_____
_____

Places to stop and see along the way

_____
_____
_____

Add your favorite ticket stub, postcard, photo, stamp or drawing here

LET NEW ADVENTURES
»» BEGIN →

Rooster Rock State Park

Region: Portland/Columbia Gorge - **Close to:** Multnomah Falls
State Park

Star Rating
☆☆☆☆☆

My favorite thing about this place is... _____
Why I went ... _____
Who I went with ... _____
When I went ... _____
What I did... _____
What I saw... _____

What I learned... _____

An unforgettable moment... _____

A laughable moment... _____

A surprising moment... _____

An unforeseeable moment... _____

Wildlife spotted... _____

Snapped a selfie | Location... _____
Took a park sign photo? - ☐ y ☐ n

The weather was ...

My List
☐ _____
☐ _____
☐ _____
☐ _____
☐ _____
☐ _____
☐ _____
☐ _____
☐ _____
☐ _____
☐ _____
☐ _____
☐ _____
☐ _____
☐ _____
☐ _____
☐ _____
☐ _____

And so the Adventure begins

www.mynaturebookadventures.com

Plan Your Trip:

☐ Day Trip   ☐ Overnight Stay

Reservations required: ☐ y ☐ n

Date reservations made: _____

Refund Policy: ☐ y ☐ n Site #: _____

Confirmation #: _____

Miles to travel: _____

Time traveling: _____

Dog friendly?: ☐ y ☐ n

Activities Accomplished:

☐ Archery	☐ Fishing	☐ Picnicking	☐ Wildlife Watching
☐ Biking	☐ Hiking	☐ Rock Climbing	☐ _____
☐ Birding	☐ Horseback Riding	☐ Shooting Range	☐ _____
☐ Boating	☐ Hunting	☐ Stargazing	☐ _____
☐ Camping	☐ Off-Roading	☐ Swimming	☐ _____
☐ Caving	☐ Paddle Boarding	☐ Tennis	☐ _____
☐ Geocaching	☐ Photography	☐ Walking	☐ _____

Traveling by:

Reservation Information:

Places we discovered along the way

Places to stop and see along the way

Add your favorite ticket stub, postcard, photo, stamp or drawing here

LET NEW ADVENTURES
»» BEGIN →

Seneca Fouts Memorial State Natural Area

Region: Portland/Columbia Gorge - **Close to:** Hood River

Natural Area

Star Rating ☆☆☆☆☆

My favorite thing about this place is... _____

Why I went ... _____

Who I went with ... _____

When I went ... _____

What I did... _____

What I saw... _____

What I learned... _____

An unforgettable moment... _____

A laughable moment... _____

A surprising moment... _____

An unforeseeable moment... _____

Wildlife spotted... _____

Snapped a selfie | Location... _____

Took a park sign photo? - ☐ y ☐ n

The weather was ...

My List
☐ _____
☐ _____
☐ _____
☐ _____
☐ _____
☐ _____
☐ _____
☐ _____
☐ _____
☐ _____
☐ _____
☐ _____
☐ _____
☐ _____
☐ _____
☐ _____
☐ _____
☐ _____

And so the Adventure begins

www.mynaturebookadventures.com

265

Plan Your Trip:

☐ Day Trip ☐ Overnight Stay
Reservations required: ☐ y ☐ n
Date reservations made: _____
Refund Policy: ☐ y ☐ n Site #: _____
Confirmation #: _____
Miles to travel: _____
Time traveling: _____
Dog friendly?: ☐ y ☐ n

Activities Accomplished:

☐ Archery	☐ Fishing	☐ Picnicking	☐ Wildlife Watching
☐ Biking	☐ Hiking	☐ Rock Climbing	☐ _____
☐ Birding	☐ Horseback Riding	☐ Shooting Range	☐ _____
☐ Boating	☐ Hunting	☐ Stargazing	☐ _____
☐ Camping	☐ Off-Roading	☐ Swimming	☐ _____
☐ Caving	☐ Paddle Boarding	☐ Tennis	☐ _____
☐ Geocaching	☐ Photography	☐ Walking	☐ _____

Traveling by:

Reservation Information:

Places we discovered along the way

Places to stop and see along the way

Add your favorite ticket stub, postcard, photo, stamp or drawing here

LET NEW ADVENTURES ≫ BEGIN →

Shepperd's Dell State Natural Area

Region: Portland/Columbia Gorge - **Close to:** Multnomah Falls

Natural Area

Star Rating ☆☆☆☆☆

My favorite thing about this place is... _____

Why I went ... _____

Who I went with ... _____

When I went ... _____

What I did... _____

What I saw... _____

What I learned... _____

An unforgettable moment... _____

A laughable moment... _____

A surprising moment... _____

An unforeseeable moment... _____

Wildlife spotted... _____

Snapped a selfie | Location... _____

Took a park sign photo? - ☐ y ☐ n

The weather was ...

My List
☐ _____
☐ _____
☐ _____
☐ _____
☐ _____
☐ _____
☐ _____
☐ _____
☐ _____
☐ _____
☐ _____
☐ _____
☐ _____
☐ _____
☐ _____
☐ _____
☐ _____

And so the Adventure begins

Plan Your Trip:

☐ Day Trip ☐ Overnight Stay

Reservations required: ☐ y ☐ n

Date reservations made: _____

Refund Policy: ☐ y ☐ n Site #: _____

Confirmation #: _____

Miles to travel: _____

Time traveling: _____

Dog friendly?: ☐ y ☐ n

Activities Accomplished:

☐ Archery	☐ Fishing	☐ Picnicking	☐ Wildlife Watching
☐ Biking	☐ Hiking	☐ Rock Climbing	☐ _____
☐ Birding	☐ Horseback Riding	☐ Shooting Range	☐ _____
☐ Boating	☐ Hunting	☐ Stargazing	☐ _____
☐ Camping	☐ Off-Roading	☐ Swimming	☐ _____
☐ Caving	☐ Paddle Boarding	☐ Tennis	☐ _____
☐ Geocaching	☐ Photography	☐ Walking	☐ _____

Traveling by:

Reservation Information:

Places we discovered along the way

Places to stop and see along the way

Add your favorite ticket stub, postcard, photo, stamp or drawing here

LET NEW ADVENTURES
»> BEGIN →

www.mynaturebookadventures.com

Sheridan State Scenic Corridor

Region: Portland/Columbia Gorge - **Close to:** Cascade Locks

Scenic Corridor

Star Rating
☆☆☆☆☆

My favorite thing about this place is... _____

Why I went ... _____

Who I went with ... _____

When I went ... _____

What I did... _____

What I saw... _____

What I learned... _____

An unforgettable moment... _____

A laughable moment... _____

A surprising moment... _____

An unforeseeable moment... _____

Wildlife spotted... _____

Snapped a selfie | Location... _____

Took a park sign photo? - ☐ y ☐ n

The weather was ...

My List
☐ _____
☐ _____
☐ _____
☐ _____
☐ _____
☐ _____
☐ _____
☐ _____
☐ _____
☐ _____
☐ _____
☐ _____
☐ _____
☐ _____
☐ _____
☐ _____
☐ _____

And so the Adventure begins

Plan Your Trip:

☐ Day Trip ☐ Overnight Stay

Reservations required: ☐ y ☐ n

Date reservations made: _____

Refund Policy: ☐ y ☐ n   Site #: _____

Confirmation #: _____

Miles to travel: _____

Time traveling: _____

Dog friendly?: ☐ y ☐ n

Activities Accomplished:

- ☐ Archery
- ☐ Biking
- ☐ Birding
- ☐ Boating
- ☐ Camping
- ☐ Caving
- ☐ Geocaching

- ☐ Fishing
- ☐ Hiking
- ☐ Horseback Riding
- ☐ Hunting
- ☐ Off-Roading
- ☐ Paddle Boarding
- ☐ Photography

- ☐ Picnicking
- ☐ Rock Climbing
- ☐ Shooting Range
- ☐ Stargazing
- ☐ Swimming
- ☐ Tennis
- ☐ Walking

- ☐ Wildlife Watching
- ☐ _____
- ☐ _____
- ☐ _____
- ☐ _____
- ☐ _____
- ☐ _____

Traveling by: ☐ car ☐ truck ☐ SUV ☐ van ☐ airplane ☐ trolley ☐ bicycle ☐ bus ☐ train ☐ helicopter ☐ motorcycle ☐ boat

Reservation Information:

Places we discovered along the way

_____
_____

Places to stop and see along the way

_____
_____

Add your favorite ticket stub, postcard, photo, stamp or drawing here

LET NEW ADVENTURES ›› BEGIN →

270   www.mynaturebookadventures.com

Starvation Creek State Park

Region: Portland/Columbia Gorge - **Close to:** Hood River

State Park

Star Rating ☆☆☆☆☆

My favorite thing about this place is... _____

Why I went ... _____

Who I went with ... _____

When I went ... _____

What I did... _____

What I saw... _____

What I learned... _____

An unforgettable moment... _____

A laughable moment... _____

A surprising moment... _____

An unforeseeable moment... _____

Wildlife spotted... _____

Snapped a selfie | Location... _____

Took a park sign photo? - ☐ y ☐ n

The weather was ...

My List
- ☐ _____
- ☐ _____
- ☐ _____
- ☐ _____
- ☐ _____
- ☐ _____
- ☐ _____
- ☐ _____
- ☐ _____
- ☐ _____
- ☐ _____
- ☐ _____
- ☐ _____
- ☐ _____
- ☐ _____
- ☐ _____
- ☐ _____

And so the Adventure begins

Plan Your Trip:

☐ Day Trip ☐ Overnight Stay

Reservations required: ☐y ☐n
Date reservations made: _____
Refund Policy: ☐y ☐n Site #: _____
Confirmation #: _____
Miles to travel: _____
Time traveling: _____
Dog friendly?: ☐y ☐n

Activities Accomplished:

☐ Archery	☐ Fishing	☐ Picnicking	☐ Wildlife Watching
☐ Biking	☐ Hiking	☐ Rock Climbing	☐ _____
☐ Birding	☐ Horseback Riding	☐ Shooting Range	☐ _____
☐ Boating	☐ Hunting	☐ Stargazing	☐ _____
☐ Camping	☐ Off-Roading	☐ Swimming	☐ _____
☐ Caving	☐ Paddle Boarding	☐ Tennis	☐ _____
☐ Geocaching	☐ Photography	☐ Walking	☐ _____

Traveling by:
☐ ☐ ☐ ☐ ☐ ☐ ☐ ☐ ☐ ☐ ☐ ☐

Reservation Information:

Places we discovered along the way

Places to stop and see along the way

Add your favorite ticket stub, postcard, photo, stamp or drawing here

LET NEW ADVENTURES ≫ BEGIN →

www.mynaturebookadventures.com

Tryon Creek State Natural Area

Region: Portland/Columbia Gorge - **Close to:** Lake Oswego

Natural Area

Star Rating
☆☆☆☆☆

My favorite thing about this place is... _____

Why I went ... _____

Who I went with ... _____

When I went ... _____

What I did... _____

What I saw... _____

What I learned... _____

An unforgettable moment... _____

A laughable moment... _____

A surprising moment... _____

An unforeseeable moment... _____

Wildlife spotted... _____

Snapped a selfie | Location... _____

Took a park sign photo? - ☐ y ☐ n

The weather was ...

My List
☐ _____
☐ _____
☐ _____
☐ _____
☐ _____
☐ _____
☐ _____
☐ _____
☐ _____
☐ _____
☐ _____
☐ _____
☐ _____
☐ _____
☐ _____
☐ _____
☐ _____
☐ _____

And so the Adventure begins

Plan Your Trip:

_____

☐ Day Trip ☐ Overnight Stay

Reservations required: ☐ y ☐ n

Date reservations made: _____

Refund Policy: ☐ y ☐ n Site #: _____

Confirmation #: _____

Miles to travel: _____

Time traveling: _____

Dog friendly?: ☐ y ☐ n

Activities Accomplished:

_____

☐ Archery	☐ Fishing	☐ Picnicking	☐ Wildlife Watching
☐ Biking	☐ Hiking	☐ Rock Climbing	☐ _____
☐ Birding	☐ Horseback Riding	☐ Shooting Range	☐ _____
☐ Boating	☐ Hunting	☐ Stargazing	☐ _____
☐ Camping	☐ Off-Roading	☐ Swimming	☐ _____
☐ Caving	☐ Paddle Boarding	☐ Tennis	☐ _____
☐ Geocaching	☐ Photography	☐ Walking	☐ _____

Traveling by:

☐ ☐ ☐ ☐ ☐ ☐ ☐ ☐ ☐ ☐ ☐ ☐

Reservation Information:

_____

Places we discovered along the way

_____
_____
_____

Places to stop and see along the way

_____
_____
_____

Add your favorite ticket stub, postcard, photo, stamp or drawing here

LET NEW ADVENTURES ≫ BEGIN →

274   www.mynaturebookadventures.com

Viento State Park

Region: Portland/Columbia Gorge - **Close to:** Hood River
State Park

Star Rating
☆☆☆☆☆

My favorite thing about this place is... _____

Why I went ... _____

Who I went with ... _____

When I went ... _____

What I did... _____

What I saw... _____

What I learned... _____

An unforgettable moment... _____

A laughable moment... _____

A surprising moment... _____

An unforeseeable moment... _____

Wildlife spotted... _____

Snapped a selfie | Location... _____

Took a park sign photo? - ☐ y ☐ n

The weather was ...

My List
☐ _____
☐ _____
☐ _____
☐ _____
☐ _____
☐ _____
☐ _____
☐ _____
☐ _____
☐ _____
☐ _____
☐ _____
☐ _____
☐ _____
☐ _____
☐ _____
☐ _____
☐ _____
☐ _____
☐ _____

And so the Adventure begins

www.mynaturebookadventures.com

Plan Your Trip:

☐ Day Trip   ☐ Overnight Stay

Reservations required: ☐y ☐n

Date reservations made: _____

Refund Policy: ☐y ☐n Site #: _____

Confirmation #: _____

Miles to travel: _____

Time traveling: _____

Dog friendly?: ☐y ☐n

Activities Accomplished:

☐ Archery	☐ Fishing	☐ Picnicking	☐ Wildlife Watching
☐ Biking	☐ Hiking	☐ Rock Climbing	☐ _____
☐ Birding	☐ Horseback Riding	☐ Shooting Range	☐ _____
☐ Boating	☐ Hunting	☐ Stargazing	☐ _____
☐ Camping	☐ Off-Roading	☐ Swimming	☐ _____
☐ Caving	☐ Paddle Boarding	☐ Tennis	☐ _____
☐ Geocaching	☐ Photography	☐ Walking	☐ _____

Traveling by:

☐ ☐ ☐ ☐ ☐ ☐ ☐ ☐ ☐ ☐ ☐ ☐

Reservation Information:

Places we discovered along the way

_____

_____

Places to stop and see along the way

_____

_____

Add your favorite ticket stub, postcard, photo, stamp or drawing here

LET NEW ADVENTURES
»» BEGIN →

Vinzenz Lausmann Memorial State Natural Area

Region: Portland/Columbia Gorge - **Close to:** Hood River

Natural Area

Star Rating
☆☆☆☆☆

My favorite thing about this place is...

Why I went ...

Who I went with ...

When I went ...

What I did...

What I saw...

What I learned...

An unforgettable moment...

A laughable moment...

A surprising moment...

An unforeseeable moment...

Wildlife spotted...

Snapped a selfie | Location...

Took a park sign photo? - ☐ y ☐ n

The weather was ...

My List
☐ ___
☐ ___
☐ ___
☐ ___
☐ ___
☐ ___
☐ ___
☐ ___
☐ ___
☐ ___
☐ ___
☐ ___
☐ ___
☐ ___
☐ ___
☐ ___
☐ ___

And so the Adventure begins

www.mynaturebookadventures.com

Plan Your Trip:

☐ Day Trip ☐ Overnight Stay

Reservations required: ☐ y ☐ n

Date reservations made: _____

Refund Policy: ☐ y ☐ n Site #: _____

Confirmation #: _____

Miles to travel: _____

Time traveling: _____

Dog friendly?: ☐ y ☐ n

Activities Accomplished:

☐ Archery	☐ Fishing	☐ Picnicking	☐ Wildlife Watching
☐ Biking	☐ Hiking	☐ Rock Climbing	☐ _____
☐ Birding	☐ Horseback Riding	☐ Shooting Range	☐ _____
☐ Boating	☐ Hunting	☐ Stargazing	☐ _____
☐ Camping	☐ Off-Roading	☐ Swimming	☐ _____
☐ Caving	☐ Paddle Boarding	☐ Tennis	☐ _____
☐ Geocaching	☐ Photography	☐ Walking	☐ _____

Traveling by:

☐ ☐ ☐ ☐ ☐ ☐ ☐ ☐ ☐ ☐ ☐ ☐

Add your favorite ticket stub, postcard, photo, stamp or drawing here

LET NEW ADVENTURES BEGIN →

Reservation Information:

_____

Places we discovered along the way

_____
_____

Places to stop and see along the way

_____
_____

White River Falls State Park

Region: Portland/Columbia Gorge - **Close to:** The Dalles

State Park

Star Rating
☆☆☆☆☆

My favorite thing about this place is... _____

Why I went ... _____

Who I went with ... _____

When I went ... _____

What I did... _____

What I saw... _____

What I learned... _____

An unforgettable moment... _____

A laughable moment... _____

A surprising moment... _____

An unforeseeable moment... _____

Wildlife spotted... _____

Snapped a selfie | Location... _____

Took a park sign photo? - ☐ y ☐ n

The weather was ...

My List
☐ _____
☐ _____
☐ _____
☐ _____
☐ _____
☐ _____
☐ _____
☐ _____
☐ _____
☐ _____
☐ _____
☐ _____
☐ _____
☐ _____
☐ _____
☐ _____
☐ _____
☐ _____

And so the Adventure begins

www.mynaturebookadventures.com

Plan Your Trip:

☐ Day Trip   ☐ Overnight Stay

Reservations required: ☐ y ☐ n

Date reservations made: _____

Refund Policy: ☐ y ☐ n   Site #: _____

Confirmation #: _____

Miles to travel: _____

Time traveling: _____

Dog friendly?: ☐ y ☐ n

Activities Accomplished:

☐ Archery	☐ Fishing	☐ Picnicking	☐ Wildlife Watching
☐ Biking	☐ Hiking	☐ Rock Climbing	☐ _____
☐ Birding	☐ Horseback Riding	☐ Shooting Range	☐ _____
☐ Boating	☐ Hunting	☐ Stargazing	☐ _____
☐ Camping	☐ Off-Roading	☐ Swimming	☐ _____
☐ Caving	☐ Paddle Boarding	☐ Tennis	☐ _____
☐ Geocaching	☐ Photography	☐ Walking	☐ _____

Traveling by:

☐ ☐ ☐ ☐ ☐ ☐ ☐ ☐ ☐ ☐ ☐ ☐

Reservation Information:

Places we discovered along the way

Places to stop and see along the way

Add your favorite ticket stub, postcard, photo, stamp or drawing here

LET NEW ADVENTURES ≫ BEGIN →

www.mynaturebookadventures.com

Willamette Stone State Heritage Site

Region: Portland/Columbia Gorge - **Close to:** Portland

Heritage Site

Star Rating ☆☆☆☆☆

My favorite thing about this place is… _____

Why I went … _____

Who I went with … _____

When I went … _____

What I did… _____

What I saw… _____

What I learned… _____

An unforgettable moment… _____

A laughable moment… _____

A surprising moment… _____

An unforeseeable moment… _____

Wildlife spotted… _____

Snapped a selfie | Location… _____

Took a park sign photo? - ☐ y ☐ n

The weather was … ☐ ☐ ☐ ☐ ☐ ☐ ☐

My List
☐ _____
☐ _____
☐ _____
☐ _____
☐ _____
☐ _____
☐ _____
☐ _____
☐ _____
☐ _____
☐ _____
☐ _____
☐ _____
☐ _____
☐ _____
☐ _____
☐ _____
☐ _____
☐ _____

And so the Adventure begins

www.mynaturebookadventures.com

Plan Your Trip:

☐ Day Trip   ☐ Overnight Stay

Reservations required: ☐ y ☐ n

Date reservations made: _____

Refund Policy: ☐ y ☐ n Site #: _____

Confirmation #: _____

Miles to travel: _____

Time traveling: _____

Dog friendly?: ☐ y ☐ n

Activities Accomplished:

☐ Archery	☐ Fishing	☐ Picnicking	☐ Wildlife Watching
☐ Biking	☐ Hiking	☐ Rock Climbing	☐ _____
☐ Birding	☐ Horseback Riding	☐ Shooting Range	☐ _____
☐ Boating	☐ Hunting	☐ Stargazing	☐ _____
☐ Camping	☐ Off-Roading	☐ Swimming	☐ _____
☐ Caving	☐ Paddle Boarding	☐ Tennis	☐ _____
☐ Geocaching	☐ Photography	☐ Walking	☐ _____

Traveling by:

☐ car ☐ truck ☐ SUV ☐ van ☐ plane ☐ trolley ☐ bike ☐ bus ☐ train ☐ helicopter ☐ motorcycle ☐ boat

Reservation Information:

_____

Places we discovered along the way

_____
_____
_____

Places to stop and see along the way

_____
_____
_____

Add your favorite ticket stub, postcard, photo, stamp or drawing here

LET NEW ADVENTURES
»» BEGIN →

www.mynaturebookadventures.com

Wygant State Natural Area

Region: Portland/Columbia Gorge - **Close to:** Hood River

Natural Area

Star Rating ☆☆☆☆☆

My favorite thing about this place is... _____

Why I went ... _____

Who I went with ... _____

When I went ... _____

What I did... _____

What I saw... _____

What I learned... _____

An unforgettable moment... _____

A laughable moment... _____

A surprising moment... _____

An unforeseeable moment... _____

Wildlife spotted... _____

Snapped a selfie | Location... _____

Took a park sign photo? - ☐ y ☐ n

The weather was ...

My List
- ☐ _____
- ☐ _____
- ☐ _____
- ☐ _____
- ☐ _____
- ☐ _____
- ☐ _____
- ☐ _____
- ☐ _____
- ☐ _____
- ☐ _____
- ☐ _____
- ☐ _____
- ☐ _____
- ☐ _____
- ☐ _____
- ☐ _____
- ☐ _____

And so the Adventure begins

Plan Your Trip:

☐ Day Trip ☐ Overnight Stay
Reservations required: ☐ y ☐ n
Date reservations made: _____
Refund Policy: ☐ y ☐ n Site #: _____
Confirmation #: _____
Miles to travel: _____
Time traveling: _____
Dog friendly?: ☐ y ☐ n

Activities Accomplished:

☐ Archery
☐ Biking
☐ Birding
☐ Boating
☐ Camping
☐ Caving
☐ Geocaching

☐ Fishing
☐ Hiking
☐ Horseback Riding
☐ Hunting
☐ Off-Roading
☐ Paddle Boarding
☐ Photography

☐ Picnicking
☐ Rock Climbing
☐ Shooting Range
☐ Stargazing
☐ Swimming
☐ Tennis
☐ Walking

☐ Wildlife Watching
☐ _____
☐ _____
☐ _____
☐ _____
☐ _____
☐ _____

Traveling by:

Reservation Information:

Places we discovered along the way

Places to stop and see along the way

Add your favorite ticket stub, postcard, photo, stamp or drawing here

LET NEW ADVENTURES ≫ BEGIN →

www.mynaturebookadventures.com

Alfred A. Loeb State Park

Region: South Coast - **Close to:** Brookings

State Park

Star Rating
☆☆☆☆☆

My favorite thing about this place is... _____

Why I went ... _____

Who I went with ... _____

When I went ... _____

What I did... _____

What I saw... _____

What I learned... _____

An unforgettable moment... _____

A laughable moment... _____

A surprising moment... _____

An unforeseeable moment... _____

Wildlife spotted... _____

Snapped a selfie | Location... _____

Took a park sign photo? - ☐ y ☐ n

The weather was ...

My List
☐ _____
☐ _____
☐ _____
☐ _____
☐ _____
☐ _____
☐ _____
☐ _____
☐ _____
☐ _____
☐ _____
☐ _____
☐ _____
☐ _____
☐ _____
☐ _____
☐ _____
☐ _____

And so the Adventure begins

Plan Your Trip:

_____

☐ Day Trip ☐ Overnight Stay
Reservations required: ☐ y ☐ n
Date reservations made: _____
Refund Policy: ☐ y ☐ n Site #: _____
Confirmation #: _____
Miles to travel: _____
Time traveling: _____
Dog friendly?: ☐ y ☐ n

Activities Accomplished:

- ☐ Archery
- ☐ Biking
- ☐ Birding
- ☐ Boating
- ☐ Camping
- ☐ Caving
- ☐ Geocaching

- ☐ Fishing
- ☐ Hiking
- ☐ Horseback Riding
- ☐ Hunting
- ☐ Off-Roading
- ☐ Paddle Boarding
- ☐ Photography

- ☐ Picnicking
- ☐ Rock Climbing
- ☐ Shooting Range
- ☐ Stargazing
- ☐ Swimming
- ☐ Tennis
- ☐ Walking

- ☐ Wildlife Watching
- ☐ _____
- ☐ _____
- ☐ _____
- ☐ _____
- ☐ _____
- ☐ _____

Traveling by:

Reservation Information:

_____
_____
_____

Places we discovered along the way

_____
_____
_____

Places to stop and see along the way

_____
_____
_____

Add your favorite ticket stub, postcard, photo, stamp or drawing here

LET NEW ADVENTURES ≫ BEGIN →

286 www.mynaturebookadventures.com

Arizona Beach State Recreation Site

Region: South Coast - **Close to:** Port Orford
Recreation Site

Star Rating

My favorite thing about this place is...

Why I went ...

Who I went with ...

When I went ...

What I did...

What I saw...

What I learned...

An unforgettable moment...

A laughable moment...

A surprising moment...

An unforeseeable moment...

Wildlife spotted...

Snapped a selfie | Location...

Took a park sign photo? - ☐ y ☐ n

My List

And so the Adventure begins

The weather was ...

www.mynaturebookadventures.com

Plan Your Trip:

☐ Day Trip ☐ Overnight Stay

Reservations required: ☐ y ☐ n
Date reservations made: _____
Refund Policy: ☐ y ☐ n Site #: _____
Confirmation #: _____
Miles to travel: _____
Time traveling: _____
Dog friendly?: ☐ y ☐ n

Activities Accomplished:

- ☐ Archery
- ☐ Biking
- ☐ Birding
- ☐ Boating
- ☐ Camping
- ☐ Caving
- ☐ Geocaching

- ☐ Fishing
- ☐ Hiking
- ☐ Horseback Riding
- ☐ Hunting
- ☐ Off-Roading
- ☐ Paddle Boarding
- ☐ Photography

- ☐ Picnicking
- ☐ Rock Climbing
- ☐ Shooting Range
- ☐ Stargazing
- ☐ Swimming
- ☐ Tennis
- ☐ Walking

- ☐ Wildlife Watching
- ☐ _____
- ☐ _____
- ☐ _____
- ☐ _____
- ☐ _____
- ☐ _____

Traveling by: ☐ car ☐ truck ☐ SUV ☐ van ☐ airplane ☐ bus ☐ bike ☐ school bus ☐ train ☐ helicopter ☐ motorcycle ☐ boat

Reservation Information:

Places we discovered along the way

Places to stop and see along the way

Add your favorite ticket stub, postcard, photo, stamp or drawing here

LET NEW ADVENTURES BEGIN →

Bandon State Natural Area

Region: South Coast - **Close to:** Bandon

Natural Area

Star Rating ☆☆☆☆☆

My favorite thing about this place is… _____

Why I went … _____

Who I went with … _____

When I went … _____

What I did… _____

What I saw… _____

What I learned… _____

An unforgettable moment… _____

A laughable moment… _____

A surprising moment… _____

An unforeseeable moment… _____

Wildlife spotted… _____

Snapped a selfie | Location… _____

Took a park sign photo? - ☐ y ☐ n

The weather was …

My List
☐ _____
☐ _____
☐ _____
☐ _____
☐ _____
☐ _____
☐ _____
☐ _____
☐ _____
☐ _____
☐ _____
☐ _____
☐ _____
☐ _____
☐ _____
☐ _____

And so the Adventure begins

www.mynaturebookadventures.com

Plan Your Trip:

☐ Day Trip ☐ Overnight Stay

Reservations required: ☐ y ☐ n

Date reservations made: _____

Refund Policy: ☐ y ☐ n Site #: _____

Confirmation #: _____

Miles to travel: _____

Time traveling: _____

Dog friendly?: ☐ y ☐ n

Activities Accomplished:

☐ Archery	☐ Fishing	☐ Picnicking	☐ Wildlife Watching
☐ Biking	☐ Hiking	☐ Rock Climbing	☐ _____
☐ Birding	☐ Horseback Riding	☐ Shooting Range	☐ _____
☐ Boating	☐ Hunting	☐ Stargazing	☐ _____
☐ Camping	☐ Off-Roading	☐ Swimming	☐ _____
☐ Caving	☐ Paddle Boarding	☐ Tennis	☐ _____
☐ Geocaching	☐ Photography	☐ Walking	☐ _____

Traveling by:

Reservation Information:

Places we discovered along the way

Places to stop and see along the way

Add your favorite ticket stub, postcard, photo, stamp or drawing here

LET NEW ADVENTURES
»» BEGIN →

Bullards Beach State Park

Region: South Coast - **Close to:** Bandon
State Park

Star Rating
☆☆☆☆☆

My favorite thing about this place is...

Why I went ...

Who I went with ...

When I went ...

What I did...

What I saw...

What I learned...

An unforgettable moment...

A laughable moment...

A surprising moment...

An unforeseeable moment...

Wildlife spotted...

Snapped a selfie | Location...

Took a park sign photo? - ☐ y ☐ n

The weather was ...

My List
☐
☐
☐
☐
☐
☐
☐
☐
☐
☐
☐
☐
☐
☐
☐
☐
☐
☐

And so the Adventure begins

www.mynaturebookadventures.com
291

Plan Your Trip:

☐ Day Trip ☐ Overnight Stay

Reservations required: ☐ y ☐ n
Date reservations made: _____
Refund Policy: ☐ y ☐ n Site #: _____
Confirmation #: _____
Miles to travel: _____
Time traveling: _____
Dog friendly?: ☐ y ☐ n

Activities Accomplished:

- ☐ Archery
- ☐ Biking
- ☐ Birding
- ☐ Boating
- ☐ Camping
- ☐ Caving
- ☐ Geocaching
- ☐ Fishing
- ☐ Hiking
- ☐ Horseback Riding
- ☐ Hunting
- ☐ Off-Roading
- ☐ Paddle Boarding
- ☐ Photography
- ☐ Picnicking
- ☐ Rock Climbing
- ☐ Shooting Range
- ☐ Stargazing
- ☐ Swimming
- ☐ Tennis
- ☐ Walking
- ☐ Wildlife Watching
- ☐ _____
- ☐ _____
- ☐ _____
- ☐ _____
- ☐ _____
- ☐ _____

Traveling by:

Reservation Information:

Places we discovered along the way

Places to stop and see along the way

Add your favorite ticket stub, postcard, photo, stamp or drawing here

LET NEW ADVENTURES ›› BEGIN →

www.mynaturebookadventures.com

Cape Arago State Park

Region: South Coast - **Close to:** Coos Bay

State Park

Star Rating

My favorite thing about this place is...

Why I went ...

Who I went with ...

When I went ...

What I did...

What I saw...

What I learned...

An unforgettable moment...

A laughable moment...

A surprising moment...

An unforeseeable moment...

Wildlife spotted...

Snapped a selfie | Location...

Took a park sign photo? - ☐ y ☐ n

The weather was ...

My List

And so the Adventure begins

www.mynaturebookadventures.com

293

Plan Your Trip:

☐ Day Trip ☐ Overnight Stay

Reservations required: ☐ y ☐ n

Date reservations made: _____

Refund Policy: ☐ y ☐ n   Site #: _____

Confirmation #: _____

Miles to travel: _____

Time traveling: _____

Dog friendly?: ☐ y ☐ n

Activities Accomplished:

- ☐ Archery
- ☐ Biking
- ☐ Birding
- ☐ Boating
- ☐ Camping
- ☐ Caving
- ☐ Geocaching

- ☐ Fishing
- ☐ Hiking
- ☐ Horseback Riding
- ☐ Hunting
- ☐ Off-Roading
- ☐ Paddle Boarding
- ☐ Photography

- ☐ Picnicking
- ☐ Rock Climbing
- ☐ Shooting Range
- ☐ Stargazing
- ☐ Swimming
- ☐ Tennis
- ☐ Walking

- ☐ Wildlife Watching
- ☐ _____
- ☐ _____
- ☐ _____
- ☐ _____
- ☐ _____
- ☐ _____

Traveling by: ☐ ☐ ☐ ☐ ☐ ☐ ☐ ☐ ☐ ☐ ☐ ☐

Reservation Information:

Places we discovered along the way

Places to stop and see along the way

Add your favorite ticket stub, postcard, photo, stamp or drawing here

LET NEW ADVENTURES ›› BEGIN →

www.mynaturebookadventures.com

Cape Blanco State Park

Region: South Coast - **Close to:** Port Orford
State Park

Star Rating
☆☆☆☆☆

My favorite thing about this place is... _____
Why I went ... _____
Who I went with ... _____
When I went ... _____
What I did... _____
What I saw... _____

What I learned... _____

An unforgettable moment... _____

A laughable moment... _____

A surprising moment... _____

An unforeseeable moment... _____

Wildlife spotted... _____

Snapped a selfie | Location... _____
Took a park sign photo? - ☐ y ☐ n

The weather was ...

My List
☐ _____
☐ _____
☐ _____
☐ _____
☐ _____
☐ _____
☐ _____
☐ _____
☐ _____
☐ _____
☐ _____
☐ _____
☐ _____
☐ _____
☐ _____
☐ _____
☐ _____

And so the Adventure begins

Plan Your Trip:

☐ Day Trip ☐ Overnight Stay

Reservations required: ☐ y ☐ n
Date reservations made: _____
Refund Policy: ☐ y ☐ n Site #: _____
Confirmation #: _____
Miles to travel: _____
Time traveling: _____
Dog friendly?: ☐ y ☐ n

Activities Accomplished:

☐ Archery	☐ Fishing	☐ Picnicking	☐ Wildlife Watching
☐ Biking	☐ Hiking	☐ Rock Climbing	☐ _____
☐ Birding	☐ Horseback Riding	☐ Shooting Range	☐ _____
☐ Boating	☐ Hunting	☐ Stargazing	☐ _____
☐ Camping	☐ Off-Roading	☐ Swimming	☐ _____
☐ Caving	☐ Paddle Boarding	☐ Tennis	☐ _____
☐ Geocaching	☐ Photography	☐ Walking	☐ _____

Traveling by:

Reservation Information:

Places we discovered along the way

Places to stop and see along the way

Add your favorite ticket stub, postcard, photo, stamp or drawing here

LET NEW ADVENTURES
»› BEGIN →

296

Cape Sebastian State Scenic Corridor

Region: South Coast - **Close to:** Gold Beach

Scenic Corridor

Star Rating
☆☆☆☆☆

My favorite thing about this place is...

Why I went ...

Who I went with ...

When I went ...

What I did...

What I saw...

What I learned...

An unforgettable moment...

A laughable moment...

A surprising moment...

An unforeseeable moment...

Wildlife spotted...

Snapped a selfie | Location...

Took a park sign photo? - ☐ y ☐ n

The weather was ...

My List

And so the Adventure begins

www.mynaturebookadventures.com

297

Plan Your Trip:

☐ Day Trip ☐ Overnight Stay

Reservations required: ☐y ☐n

Date reservations made: _____

Refund Policy: ☐y ☐n Site #: _____

Confirmation #: _____

Miles to travel: _____

Time traveling: _____

Dog friendly?: ☐y ☐n

Activities Accomplished:

- ☐ Archery
- ☐ Biking
- ☐ Birding
- ☐ Boating
- ☐ Camping
- ☐ Caving
- ☐ Geocaching
- ☐ Fishing
- ☐ Hiking
- ☐ Horseback Riding
- ☐ Hunting
- ☐ Off-Roading
- ☐ Paddle Boarding
- ☐ Photography
- ☐ Picnicking
- ☐ Rock Climbing
- ☐ Shooting Range
- ☐ Stargazing
- ☐ Swimming
- ☐ Tennis
- ☐ Walking
- ☐ Wildlife Watching
- ☐ _____
- ☐ _____
- ☐ _____
- ☐ _____
- ☐ _____
- ☐ _____

Traveling by:

Reservation Information:

Places we discovered along the way

Places to stop and see along the way

Add your favorite ticket stub, postcard, photo, stamp or drawing here

LET NEW ADVENTURES
»› BEGIN →

Coquille Myrtle Grove State Natural Site

Region: South Coast - **Close to:** Myrtle Point
Natural Site

Star Rating
☆☆☆☆☆

My favorite thing about this place is... _____

Why I went ... _____

Who I went with ... _____

When I went ... _____

What I did... _____

What I saw... _____

What I learned... _____

An unforgettable moment... _____

A laughable moment... _____

A surprising moment... _____

An unforeseeable moment... _____

Wildlife spotted... _____

Snapped a selfie | Location... _____

Took a park sign photo? - ☐ y ☐ n

The weather was ...

My List
☐ _____
☐ _____
☐ _____
☐ _____
☐ _____
☐ _____
☐ _____
☐ _____
☐ _____
☐ _____
☐ _____
☐ _____
☐ _____
☐ _____
☐ _____
☐ _____

And so the Adventure begins

Plan Your Trip:

☐ Day Trip ☐ Overnight Stay

Reservations required: ☐ y ☐ n

Date reservations made: _____

Refund Policy: ☐ y ☐ n Site #: _____

Confirmation #: _____

Miles to travel: _____

Time traveling: _____

Dog friendly?: ☐ y ☐ n

Activities Accomplished:

☐ Archery
☐ Biking
☐ Birding
☐ Boating
☐ Camping
☐ Caving
☐ Geocaching

☐ Fishing
☐ Hiking
☐ Horseback Riding
☐ Hunting
☐ Off-Roading
☐ Paddle Boarding
☐ Photography

☐ Picnicking
☐ Rock Climbing
☐ Shooting Range
☐ Stargazing
☐ Swimming
☐ Tennis
☐ Walking

☐ Wildlife Watching
☐ _____
☐ _____
☐ _____
☐ _____
☐ _____
☐ _____

Traveling by:

☐ ☐ ☐ ☐ ☐ ☐ ☐ ☐ ☐ ☐ ☐ ☐ ☐

Reservation Information:

Places we discovered along the way

Places to stop and see along the way

Add your favorite ticket stub, postcard, photo, stamp or drawing here

LET NEW ADVENTURES ≫ BEGIN →

CRISSEY FIELD STATE RECREATION SITE

Region: South Coast - *Close to:* Brookings

Recreation Site

Star Rating
☆☆☆☆☆

My favorite thing about this place is... _____

Why I went ... _____

Who I went with ... _____

When I went ... _____

What I did... _____

What I saw... _____

What I learned... _____

An unforgettable moment... _____

A laughable moment... _____

A surprising moment... _____

An unforeseeable moment... _____

Wildlife spotted... _____

Snapped a selfie | Location... _____

Took a park sign photo? - ☐ y ☐ n

The weather was ...

My List
☐ _____
☐ _____
☐ _____
☐ _____
☐ _____
☐ _____
☐ _____
☐ _____
☐ _____
☐ _____
☐ _____
☐ _____
☐ _____
☐ _____
☐ _____

AND SO the Adventure begins

www.mynaturebookadventures.com

Plan Your Trip:

☐ Day Trip ☐ Overnight Stay

Reservations required: ☐ y ☐ n

Date reservations made: _____

Refund Policy: ☐ y ☐ n Site #: _____

Confirmation #: _____

Miles to travel: _____

Time traveling: _____

Dog friendly?: ☐ y ☐ n

Activities Accomplished:

- ☐ Archery
- ☐ Biking
- ☐ Birding
- ☐ Boating
- ☐ Camping
- ☐ Caving
- ☐ Geocaching

- ☐ Fishing
- ☐ Hiking
- ☐ Horseback Riding
- ☐ Hunting
- ☐ Off-Roading
- ☐ Paddle Boarding
- ☐ Photography

- ☐ Picnicking
- ☐ Rock Climbing
- ☐ Shooting Range
- ☐ Stargazing
- ☐ Swimming
- ☐ Tennis
- ☐ Walking

- ☐ Wildlife Watching
- ☐ _____
- ☐ _____
- ☐ _____
- ☐ _____
- ☐ _____
- ☐ _____

Traveling by:

Reservation Information:

Places we discovered along the way

Places to stop and see along the way

Add your favorite ticket stub, postcard, photo, stamp or drawing here

LET NEW ADVENTURES ›› BEGIN →

Face Rock State Scenic Viewpoint

Region: South Coast - *Close to:* Bandon

Scenic Viewpoint

Star Rating
☆☆☆☆☆

My favorite thing about this place is...

Why I went ...

Who I went with ...

When I went ...

What I did...

What I saw...

What I learned...

An unforgettable moment...

A laughable moment...

A surprising moment...

An unforeseeable moment...

Wildlife spotted...

Snapped a selfie | Location...

Took a park sign photo? - ☐ y ☐ n

The weather was ...

My List
☐
☐
☐
☐
☐
☐
☐
☐
☐
☐
☐
☐
☐
☐
☐
☐
☐
☐
☐
☐

And so the Adventure begins

Plan Your Trip:

☐ Day Trip   ☐ Overnight Stay

Reservations required: ☐ y ☐ n

Date reservations made: _____

Refund Policy: ☐ y ☐ n   Site #: _____

Confirmation #: _____

Miles to travel: _____

Time traveling: _____

Dog friendly?: ☐ y ☐ n

Activities Accomplished:

☐ Archery	☐ Fishing	☐ Picnicking	☐ Wildlife Watching
☐ Biking	☐ Hiking	☐ Rock Climbing	☐ _____
☐ Birding	☐ Horseback Riding	☐ Shooting Range	☐ _____
☐ Boating	☐ Hunting	☐ Stargazing	☐ _____
☐ Camping	☐ Off-Roading	☐ Swimming	☐ _____
☐ Caving	☐ Paddle Boarding	☐ Tennis	☐ _____
☐ Geocaching	☐ Photography	☐ Walking	☐ _____

Traveling by:

Reservation Information:

Places we discovered along the way

Places to stop and see along the way

Add your favorite ticket stub, postcard, photo, stamp or drawing here

LET NEW ADVENTURES ≫ BEGIN →

304   www.mynaturebookadventures.com

Geisel Monument State Heritage Site

Region: South Coast - *Close to:* Gold Beach
Heritage Site

_____
Star Rating
☆☆☆☆☆

My favorite thing about this place is... _____

Why I went ... _____

Who I went with ... _____

When I went ... _____

What I did... _____

What I saw... _____

What I learned... _____

An unforgettable moment... _____

A laughable moment... _____

A surprising moment... _____

An unforeseeable moment... _____

Wildlife spotted... _____

Snapped a selfie | Location... _____

Took a park sign photo? - ☐ y ☐ n

The weather was ...

My List
☐ _____
☐ _____
☐ _____
☐ _____
☐ _____
☐ _____
☐ _____
☐ _____
☐ _____
☐ _____
☐ _____
☐ _____
☐ _____
☐ _____
☐ _____

And so the Adventure begins

www.mynaturebookadventures.com

Plan Your Trip:

☐ Day Trip ☐ Overnight Stay

Reservations required: ☐ y ☐ n

Date reservations made: _____

Refund Policy: ☐ y ☐ n Site #: _____

Confirmation #: _____

Miles to travel: _____

Time traveling: _____

Dog friendly?: ☐ y ☐ n

Activities Accomplished:

- ☐ Archery
- ☐ Biking
- ☐ Birding
- ☐ Boating
- ☐ Camping
- ☐ Caving
- ☐ Geocaching
- ☐ Fishing
- ☐ Hiking
- ☐ Horseback Riding
- ☐ Hunting
- ☐ Off-Roading
- ☐ Paddle Boarding
- ☐ Photography
- ☐ Picnicking
- ☐ Rock Climbing
- ☐ Shooting Range
- ☐ Stargazing
- ☐ Swimming
- ☐ Tennis
- ☐ Walking
- ☐ Wildlife Watching
- ☐ _____
- ☐ _____
- ☐ _____
- ☐ _____
- ☐ _____
- ☐ _____

Traveling by:

Reservation Information:

Places we discovered along the way

Places to stop and see along the way

Add your favorite ticket stub, postcard, photo, stamp or drawing here

LET NEW ADVENTURES
» BEGIN →

www.mynaturebookadventures.com

Golden and Silver Falls State Natural Area

Region: South Coast - **Close to:** Coos Bay

Natural Area

Star Rating ☆☆☆☆☆

My favorite thing about this place is...

Why I went ...

Who I went with ...

When I went ...

What I did...

What I saw...

What I learned...

An unforgettable moment...

A laughable moment...

A surprising moment...

An unforeseeable moment...

Wildlife spotted...

Snapped a selfie | Location...

Took a park sign photo? - ☐ y ☐ n

The weather was ...

My List

And so the Adventure begins

www.mynaturebookadventures.com

Plan Your Trip:

☐ Day Trip ☐ Overnight Stay

Reservations required: ☐ y ☐ n

Date reservations made: _____

Refund Policy: ☐ y ☐ n Site #: _____

Confirmation #: _____

Miles to travel: _____

Time traveling: _____

Dog friendly?: ☐ y ☐ n

Activities Accomplished:

- ☐ Archery
- ☐ Biking
- ☐ Birding
- ☐ Boating
- ☐ Camping
- ☐ Caving
- ☐ Geocaching
- ☐ Fishing
- ☐ Hiking
- ☐ Horseback Riding
- ☐ Hunting
- ☐ Off-Roading
- ☐ Paddle Boarding
- ☐ Photography
- ☐ Picnicking
- ☐ Rock Climbing
- ☐ Shooting Range
- ☐ Stargazing
- ☐ Swimming
- ☐ Tennis
- ☐ Walking
- ☐ Wildlife Watching
- ☐ _____
- ☐ _____
- ☐ _____
- ☐ _____
- ☐ _____
- ☐ _____

Traveling by:

Reservation Information:

Places we discovered along the way

Places to stop and see along the way

Add your favorite ticket stub, postcard, photo, stamp or drawing here

LET NEW ADVENTURES BEGIN →

www.mynaturebookadventures.com

Harris Beach State Recreation Area

Region: South Coast - ***Close to:*** Brookings
Recreation Area

Star Rating
☆☆☆☆☆

My favorite thing about this place is... _____

Why I went ... _____

Who I went with ... _____

When I went ... _____

What I did... _____

What I saw... _____

What I learned... _____

An unforgettable moment... _____

A laughable moment... _____

A surprising moment... _____

An unforeseeable moment... _____

Wildlife spotted... _____

Snapped a selfie | Location... _____

Took a park sign photo? - ☐ y ☐ n

The weather was ...

My List
☐ _____
☐ _____
☐ _____
☐ _____
☐ _____
☐ _____
☐ _____
☐ _____
☐ _____
☐ _____
☐ _____
☐ _____
☐ _____
☐ _____
☐ _____
☐ _____
☐ _____

And so the Adventure begins

www.mynaturebookadventures.com

Plan Your Trip:

☐ Day Trip ☐ Overnight Stay

Reservations required: ☐ y ☐ n

Date reservations made: _____

Refund Policy: ☐ y ☐ n Site #: _____

Confirmation #: _____

Miles to travel: _____

Time traveling: _____

Dog friendly?: ☐ y ☐ n

Activities Accomplished:

☐ Archery	☐ Fishing	☐ Picnicking	☐ Wildlife Watching
☐ Biking	☐ Hiking	☐ Rock Climbing	☐ _____
☐ Birding	☐ Horseback Riding	☐ Shooting Range	☐ _____
☐ Boating	☐ Hunting	☐ Stargazing	☐ _____
☐ Camping	☐ Off-Roading	☐ Swimming	☐ _____
☐ Caving	☐ Paddle Boarding	☐ Tennis	☐ _____
☐ Geocaching	☐ Photography	☐ Walking	☐ _____

Traveling by: ☐ ☐ ☐ ☐ ☐ ☐ ☐ ☐ ☐ ☐ ☐ ☐

Add your favorite ticket stub, postcard, photo, stamp or drawing here

LET NEW ADVENTURES ≫ BEGIN →

Reservation information:

_____

Places we discovered along the way

_____
_____

Places to stop and see along the way

_____
_____

Hoffman Memorial State Wayside

Region: South Coast - **Close to:** Myrtle Point

Wayside

Star Rating ☆☆☆☆☆

My favorite thing about this place is... _____

Why I went ... _____

Who I went with ... _____

When I went ... _____

What I did... _____

What I saw... _____

What I learned... _____

An unforgettable moment... _____

A laughable moment... _____

A surprising moment... _____

An unforeseeable moment... _____

Wildlife spotted... _____

Snapped a selfie | Location... _____

Took a park sign photo? - ☐ y ☐ n

The weather was ...

My List
- _____
- _____
- _____
- _____
- _____
- _____
- _____
- _____
- _____
- _____
- _____
- _____
- _____
- _____
- _____
- _____

And so the Adventure begins

Plan Your Trip:

_____

☐ Day Trip ☐ Overnight Stay

Reservations required: ☐ y ☐ n

Date reservations made: _____

Refund Policy: ☐ y ☐ n Site #: _____

Confirmation #: _____

Miles to travel: _____

Time traveling: _____

Dog friendly?: ☐ y ☐ n

Activities Accomplished:

☐ Archery	☐ Fishing	☐ Picnicking	☐ Wildlife Watching
☐ Biking	☐ Hiking	☐ Rock Climbing	☐ _____
☐ Birding	☐ Horseback Riding	☐ Shooting Range	☐ _____
☐ Boating	☐ Hunting	☐ Stargazing	☐ _____
☐ Camping	☐ Off-Roading	☐ Swimming	☐ _____
☐ Caving	☐ Paddle Boarding	☐ Tennis	☐ _____
☐ Geocaching	☐ Photography	☐ Walking	☐ _____

Traveling by:

Reservation Information:

_____

Places we discovered along the way

_____
_____
_____

Places to stop and see along the way

_____
_____
_____

Add your favorite ticket stub, postcard, photo, stamp or drawing here

LET NEW ADVENTURES ≫ BEGIN →

Humbug Mountain State Park

Region: South Coast - **Close to:** Port Orford
State Park

Star Rating
☆☆☆☆☆

My favorite thing about this place is... _____

Why I went ... _____

Who I went with ... _____

When I went ... _____

What I did... _____

What I saw... _____

What I learned... _____

An unforgettable moment... _____

A laughable moment... _____

A surprising moment... _____

An unforeseeable moment... _____

Wildlife spotted... _____

Snapped a selfie | Location... _____

Took a park sign photo? - ☐ y ☐ n

The weather was ...

My List
☐ _____
☐ _____
☐ _____
☐ _____
☐ _____
☐ _____
☐ _____
☐ _____
☐ _____
☐ _____
☐ _____
☐ _____
☐ _____
☐ _____
☐ _____
☐ _____
☐ _____

And so the Adventure begins

www.mynaturebookadventures.com

Plan Your Trip:

☐ Day Trip ☐ Overnight Stay

Reservations required: ☐y ☐n
Date reservations made: _____
Refund Policy: ☐y ☐n Site #: _____
Confirmation #: _____
Miles to travel: _____
Time traveling: _____
Dog friendly?: ☐y ☐n

Activities Accomplished:

☐ Archery	☐ Fishing	☐ Picnicking	☐ Wildlife Watching
☐ Biking	☐ Hiking	☐ Rock Climbing	☐ _____
☐ Birding	☐ Horseback Riding	☐ Shooting Range	☐ _____
☐ Boating	☐ Hunting	☐ Stargazing	☐ _____
☐ Camping	☐ Off-Roading	☐ Swimming	☐ _____
☐ Caving	☐ Paddle Boarding	☐ Tennis	☐ _____
☐ Geocaching	☐ Photography	☐ Walking	☐ _____

Traveling by: ☐ ☐ ☐ ☐ ☐ ☐ ☐ ☐ ☐ ☐ ☐ ☐

Reservation Information:

Places we discovered along the way

Places to stop and see along the way

Add your favorite ticket stub, postcard, photo, stamp or drawing here

LET NEW ADVENTURES ›› BEGIN →

McVay Rock State Recreation Site

Region: South Coast - **Close to:** Brookings
Recreation Site

Star Rating
☆☆☆☆☆

My favorite thing about this place is... _____
Why I went ... _____
Who I went with ... _____
When I went ... _____
What I did... _____
What I saw... _____

What I learned... _____

An unforgettable moment... _____

A laughable moment... _____

A surprising moment... _____

An unforeseeable moment... _____

Wildlife spotted... _____

Snapped a selfie | Location... _____
Took a park sign photo? - ☐ y ☐ n
The weather was ...

My List
☐ _____
☐ _____
☐ _____
☐ _____
☐ _____
☐ _____
☐ _____
☐ _____
☐ _____
☐ _____
☐ _____
☐ _____
☐ _____
☐ _____
☐ _____
☐ _____

And so the Adventure begins

www.mynaturebookadventures.com
315

Plan Your Trip:

☐ Day Trip   ☐ Overnight Stay

Reservations required: ☐ y ☐ n

Date reservations made: _____

Refund Policy: ☐ y ☐ n Site #: _____

Confirmation #: _____

Miles to travel: _____

Time traveling: _____

Dog friendly?: ☐ y ☐ n

Activities Accomplished:

☐ Archery	☐ Fishing	☐ Picnicking	☐ Wildlife Watching
☐ Biking	☐ Hiking	☐ Rock Climbing	☐ _____
☐ Birding	☐ Horseback Riding	☐ Shooting Range	☐ _____
☐ Boating	☐ Hunting	☐ Stargazing	☐ _____
☐ Camping	☐ Off-Roading	☐ Swimming	☐ _____
☐ Caving	☐ Paddle Boarding	☐ Tennis	☐ _____
☐ Geocaching	☐ Photography	☐ Walking	☐ _____

Traveling by: 🚗 🛻 🚙 🚐 ✈️ 🚊 🚲 🚌 🚂 🚁 🏍️ 🛥️

Reservation Information:

_____

Places we discovered along the way
_____
_____
_____

Places to stop and see along the way
_____
_____
_____

Add your favorite ticket stub, postcard, photo, stamp or drawing here

LET NEW ADVENTURES ›› BEGIN →

316   www.mynaturebookadventures.com

Otter Point State Recreation Site

Region: South Coast - **Close to:** Gold Beach

Recreation Site

Star Rating
☆☆☆☆☆

My favorite thing about this place is... _____

Why I went ... _____

Who I went with ... _____

When I went ... _____

What I did... _____

What I saw... _____

What I learned... _____

An unforgettable moment... _____

A laughable moment... _____

A surprising moment... _____

An unforeseeable moment... _____

Wildlife spotted... _____

Snapped a selfie | Location... _____

Took a park sign photo? - ☐ y ☐ n

The weather was ... ☐ ☐ ☐ ☐ ☐ ☐ ☐

My List
- ☐ _____
- ☐ _____
- ☐ _____
- ☐ _____
- ☐ _____
- ☐ _____
- ☐ _____
- ☐ _____
- ☐ _____
- ☐ _____
- ☐ _____
- ☐ _____
- ☐ _____
- ☐ _____
- ☐ _____
- ☐ _____
- ☐ _____
- ☐ _____

And so the Adventure begins

Plan Your Trip:

☐ Day Trip ☐ Overnight Stay

Reservations required: ☐ y ☐ n

Date reservations made: _____

Refund Policy: ☐ y ☐ n Site #: _____

Confirmation #: _____

Miles to travel: _____

Time traveling: _____

Dog friendly?: ☐ y ☐ n

Activities Accomplished:

☐ Archery
☐ Biking
☐ Birding
☐ Boating
☐ Camping
☐ Caving
☐ Geocaching

☐ Fishing
☐ Hiking
☐ Horseback Riding
☐ Hunting
☐ Off-Roading
☐ Paddle Boarding
☐ Photography

☐ Picnicking
☐ Rock Climbing
☐ Shooting Range
☐ Stargazing
☐ Swimming
☐ Tennis
☐ Walking

☐ Wildlife Watching
☐ _____
☐ _____
☐ _____
☐ _____
☐ _____
☐ _____

Traveling by:

☐ ☐ ☐ ☐ ☐ ☐ ☐ ☐ ☐ ☐ ☐ ☐

Reservation Information:

_____

Places we discovered along the way

_____
_____
_____
_____

Places to stop and see along the way

_____
_____
_____

Add your favorite ticket stub, postcard, photo, stamp or drawing here

LET NEW ADVENTURES
»› BEGIN →

Paradise Point State Recreation Site

Region: South Coast - **Close to:** Port Orford
Recreation Site

Star Rating
☆☆☆☆☆

My favorite thing about this place is... _____

Why I went ... _____

Who I went with ... _____

When I went ... _____

What I did... _____

What I saw... _____

What I learned... _____

An unforgettable moment... _____

A laughable moment... _____

A surprising moment... _____

An unforeseeable moment... _____

Wildlife spotted... _____

Snapped a selfie | Location... _____

Took a park sign photo? - ☐ y ☐ n

The weather was ...

My List
☐ _____
☐ _____
☐ _____
☐ _____
☐ _____
☐ _____
☐ _____
☐ _____
☐ _____
☐ _____
☐ _____
☐ _____
☐ _____
☐ _____
☐ _____
☐ _____

And so the Adventure begins

Plan Your Trip:

☐ Day Trip ☐ Overnight Stay

Reservations required: ☐ y ☐ n

Date reservations made: _____

Refund Policy: ☐ y ☐ n Site #: _____

Confirmation #: _____

Miles to travel: _____

Time traveling: _____

Dog friendly?: ☐ y ☐ n

Activities Accomplished:

☐ Archery	☐ Fishing	☐ Picnicking	☐ Wildlife Watching
☐ Biking	☐ Hiking	☐ Rock Climbing	☐ _____
☐ Birding	☐ Horseback Riding	☐ Shooting Range	☐ _____
☐ Boating	☐ Hunting	☐ Stargazing	☐ _____
☐ Camping	☐ Off-Roading	☐ Swimming	☐ _____
☐ Caving	☐ Paddle Boarding	☐ Tennis	☐ _____
☐ Geocaching	☐ Photography	☐ Walking	☐ _____

Traveling by:

Reservation Information:

Places we discovered along the way

Places to stop and see along the way

Add your favorite ticket stub, postcard, photo, stamp or drawing here

LET NEW ADVENTURES BEGIN →

Pistol River State Scenic Viewpoint

Region: South Coast - **Close to:** Gold Beach
Scenic Viewpoint

Star Rating
☆☆☆☆☆

My favorite thing about this place is... _____

Why I went ... _____

Who I went with ... _____

When I went ... _____

What I did... _____

What I saw... _____

What I learned... _____

An unforgettable moment... _____

A laughable moment... _____

A surprising moment... _____

An unforeseeable moment... _____

Wildlife spotted... _____

Snapped a selfie | Location... _____

Took a park sign photo? - ☐ y ☐ n

The weather was ... ☐ ☐ ☐ ☐ ☐ ☐ ☐

My List
☐ _____
☐ _____
☐ _____
☐ _____
☐ _____
☐ _____
☐ _____
☐ _____
☐ _____
☐ _____
☐ _____
☐ _____
☐ _____
☐ _____
☐ _____
☐ _____

And so the Adventure begins

www.mynaturebookadventures.com

321

Plan Your Trip:

☐ Day Trip   ☐ Overnight Stay

Reservations required: ☐ y ☐ n

Date reservations made: _____

Refund Policy: ☐ y ☐ n Site #: _____

Confirmation #: _____

Miles to travel: _____

Time traveling: _____

Dog friendly?: ☐ y ☐ n

Activities Accomplished:

☐ Archery	☐ Fishing	☐ Picnicking	☐ Wildlife Watching
☐ Biking	☐ Hiking	☐ Rock Climbing	☐ _____
☐ Birding	☐ Horseback Riding	☐ Shooting Range	☐ _____
☐ Boating	☐ Hunting	☐ Stargazing	☐ _____
☐ Camping	☐ Off-Roading	☐ Swimming	☐ _____
☐ Caving	☐ Paddle Boarding	☐ Tennis	☐ _____
☐ Geocaching	☐ Photography	☐ Walking	☐ _____

Traveling by: ☐ ☐ ☐ ☐ ☐ ☐ ☐ ☐ ☐ ☐ ☐ ☐

Reservation Information:

_____

Places we discovered along the way

_____
_____

Places to stop and see along the way

_____
_____

Add your favorite ticket stub, postcard, photo, stamp or drawing here

LET NEW ADVENTURES ≫ BEGIN →

Port Orford Heads State Park

Region: South Coast - **Close to:** Port Orford

State Park

Star Rating
☆☆☆☆☆

My favorite thing about this place is...

Why I went ...

Who I went with ...

When I went ...

What I did...

What I saw...

What I learned...

An unforgettable moment...

A laughable moment...

A surprising moment...

An unforeseeable moment...

Wildlife spotted...

Snapped a selfie | Location...

Took a park sign photo? - ☐ y ☐ n

My List
☐ _____
☐ _____
☐ _____
☐ _____
☐ _____
☐ _____
☐ _____
☐ _____
☐ _____
☐ _____
☐ _____
☐ _____
☐ _____
☐ _____
☐ _____
☐ _____
☐ _____
☐ _____

And so the Adventure begins

The weather was ...

www.mynaturebookadventures.com

Plan Your Trip:

☐ Day Trip ☐ Overnight Stay
Reservations required: ☐ y ☐ n
Date reservations made: _____
Refund Policy: ☐ y ☐ n Site #: _____
Confirmation #: _____
Miles to travel: _____
Time traveling: _____
Dog friendly?: ☐ y ☐ n

Activities Accomplished:

- ☐ Archery
- ☐ Biking
- ☐ Birding
- ☐ Boating
- ☐ Camping
- ☐ Caving
- ☐ Geocaching
- ☐ Fishing
- ☐ Hiking
- ☐ Horseback Riding
- ☐ Hunting
- ☐ Off-Roading
- ☐ Paddle Boarding
- ☐ Photography
- ☐ Picnicking
- ☐ Rock Climbing
- ☐ Shooting Range
- ☐ Stargazing
- ☐ Swimming
- ☐ Tennis
- ☐ Walking
- ☐ Wildlife Watching
- ☐ _____
- ☐ _____
- ☐ _____
- ☐ _____
- ☐ _____
- ☐ _____

Traveling by:

Reservation Information:

Places we discovered along the way

Places to stop and see along the way

Add your favorite ticket stub, postcard, photo, stamp or drawing here

LET NEW ADVENTURES
»» BEGIN →

Samuel H. Boardman State Scenic Corridor

Region: South Coast - *Close to:* Brookings
Scenic Corridor

Star Rating ☆☆☆☆☆

My favorite thing about this place is... _____
Why I went ... _____
Who I went with ... _____
When I went ... _____
What I did... _____
What I saw... _____

What I learned... _____

An unforgettable moment... _____

A laughable moment... _____

A surprising moment... _____

An unforeseeable moment... _____

Wildlife spotted... _____

Snapped a selfie | Location... _____
Took a park sign photo? - ☐ y ☐ n

The weather was ...

My List
☐ _____
☐ _____
☐ _____
☐ _____
☐ _____
☐ _____
☐ _____
☐ _____
☐ _____
☐ _____
☐ _____
☐ _____
☐ _____
☐ _____
☐ _____
☐ _____

And so the Adventure begins

Plan Your Trip:

☐ Day Trip ☐ Overnight Stay

Reservations required: ☐ y ☐ n

Date reservations made: _____

Refund Policy: ☐ y ☐ n Site #: _____

Confirmation #: _____

Miles to travel: _____

Time traveling: _____

Dog friendly?: ☐ y ☐ n

Activities Accomplished:

- ☐ Archery
- ☐ Biking
- ☐ Birding
- ☐ Boating
- ☐ Camping
- ☐ Caving
- ☐ Geocaching
- ☐ Fishing
- ☐ Hiking
- ☐ Horseback Riding
- ☐ Hunting
- ☐ Off-Roading
- ☐ Paddle Boarding
- ☐ Photography
- ☐ Picnicking
- ☐ Rock Climbing
- ☐ Shooting Range
- ☐ Stargazing
- ☐ Swimming
- ☐ Tennis
- ☐ Walking
- ☐ Wildlife Watching
- ☐ _____
- ☐ _____
- ☐ _____
- ☐ _____
- ☐ _____
- ☐ _____

Traveling by: ☐ ☐ ☐ ☐ ☐ ☐ ☐ ☐ ☐ ☐ ☐ ☐

Reservation information:

Places we discovered along the way

Places to stop and see along the way

Add your favorite ticket stub, postcard, photo, stamp or drawing here

LET NEW ADVENTURES ≫ BEGIN →

www.mynaturebookadventures.com

Seven Devils State Recreation Site

Region: South Coast - **Close to:** Bandon

Recreation Site

Star Rating
☆☆☆☆☆

My favorite thing about this place is... _____

Why I went ... _____

Who I went with ... _____

When I went ... _____

What I did... _____

What I saw... _____

What I learned... _____

An unforgettable moment... _____

A laughable moment... _____

A surprising moment... _____

An unforeseeable moment... _____

Wildlife spotted... _____

Snapped a selfie | Location... _____

Took a park sign photo? - ☐ y ☐ n

The weather was ...

My List
☐ _____
☐ _____
☐ _____
☐ _____
☐ _____
☐ _____
☐ _____
☐ _____
☐ _____
☐ _____
☐ _____
☐ _____
☐ _____
☐ _____
☐ _____
☐ _____
☐ _____
☐ _____

And so the Adventure begins

Plan Your Trip:

☐ Day Trip ☐ Overnight Stay

Reservations required: ☐ y ☐ n

Date reservations made: _____

Refund Policy: ☐ y ☐ n Site #: _____

Confirmation #: _____

Miles to travel: _____

Time traveling: _____

Dog friendly?: ☐ y ☐ n

Activities Accomplished:

- ☐ Archery
- ☐ Biking
- ☐ Birding
- ☐ Boating
- ☐ Camping
- ☐ Caving
- ☐ Geocaching
- ☐ Fishing
- ☐ Hiking
- ☐ Horseback Riding
- ☐ Hunting
- ☐ Off-Roading
- ☐ Paddle Boarding
- ☐ Photography
- ☐ Picnicking
- ☐ Rock Climbing
- ☐ Shooting Range
- ☐ Stargazing
- ☐ Swimming
- ☐ Tennis
- ☐ Walking
- ☐ Wildlife Watching
- ☐ _____
- ☐ _____
- ☐ _____
- ☐ _____
- ☐ _____
- ☐ _____

Traveling by: ☐ ☐ ☐ ☐ ☐ ☐ ☐ ☐ ☐ ☐ ☐ ☐

Reservation Information:

Places we discovered along the way

Places to stop and see along the way

Add your favorite ticket stub, postcard, photo, stamp or drawing here

LET NEW ADVENTURES
»› BEGIN →

Shore Acres State Park

Region: South Coast - **Close to:** Coos Bay

State Park

Star Rating

My favorite thing about this place is...

Why I went ...

Who I went with ...

When I went ...

What I did...

What I saw...

What I learned...

An unforgettable moment...

A laughable moment...

A surprising moment...

An unforeseeable moment...

Wildlife spotted...

Snapped a selfie | Location...

Took a park sign photo? - ☐ y ☐ n

The weather was ...

My List

And so the Adventure begins

www.mynaturebookadventures.com

329

Plan Your Trip:

☐ Day Trip ☐ Overnight Stay

Reservations required: ☐ y ☐ n

Date reservations made: _____

Refund Policy: ☐ y ☐ n Site #: _____

Confirmation #: _____

Miles to travel: _____

Time traveling: _____

Dog friendly?: ☐ y ☐ n

Activities Accomplished:

- ☐ Archery
- ☐ Biking
- ☐ Birding
- ☐ Boating
- ☐ Camping
- ☐ Caving
- ☐ Geocaching
- ☐ Fishing
- ☐ Hiking
- ☐ Horseback Riding
- ☐ Hunting
- ☐ Off-Roading
- ☐ Paddle Boarding
- ☐ Photography
- ☐ Picnicking
- ☐ Rock Climbing
- ☐ Shooting Range
- ☐ Stargazing
- ☐ Swimming
- ☐ Tennis
- ☐ Walking
- ☐ Wildlife Watching
- ☐ _____
- ☐ _____
- ☐ _____
- ☐ _____
- ☐ _____
- ☐ _____

Traveling by:

Reservation Information:

Places we discovered along the way

Places to stop and see along the way

Add your favorite ticket stub, postcard, photo, stamp or drawing here

LET NEW ADVENTURES »› BEGIN →

Sunset Bay State Park

Region: South Coast - **Close to:** Coos Bay
State Park

Star Rating
☆☆☆☆☆

My favorite thing about this place is... _____

Why I went ... _____

Who I went with ... _____

When I went ... _____

What I did... _____

What I saw... _____

What I learned... _____

An unforgettable moment... _____

A laughable moment... _____

A surprising moment... _____

An unforeseeable moment... _____

Wildlife spotted... _____

Snapped a selfie | Location... _____

Took a park sign photo? - ☐ y ☐ n

The weather was ...

My List
☐ _____
☐ _____
☐ _____
☐ _____
☐ _____
☐ _____
☐ _____
☐ _____
☐ _____
☐ _____
☐ _____
☐ _____
☐ _____
☐ _____
☐ _____
☐ _____
☐ _____

And so the Adventure begins

www.mynaturebookadventures.com

331

Plan Your Trip:

☐ Day Trip   ☐ Overnight Stay

Reservations required: ☐ y ☐ n

Date reservations made: _____

Refund Policy: ☐ y ☐ n Site #: _____

Confirmation #: _____

Miles to travel: _____

Time traveling: _____

Dog friendly?: ☐ y ☐ n

Activities Accomplished:

- ☐ Archery
- ☐ Biking
- ☐ Birding
- ☐ Boating
- ☐ Camping
- ☐ Caving
- ☐ Geocaching
- ☐ Fishing
- ☐ Hiking
- ☐ Horseback Riding
- ☐ Hunting
- ☐ Off-Roading
- ☐ Paddle Boarding
- ☐ Photography
- ☐ Picnicking
- ☐ Rock Climbing
- ☐ Shooting Range
- ☐ Stargazing
- ☐ Swimming
- ☐ Tennis
- ☐ Walking
- ☐ Wildlife Watching
- ☐ _____
- ☐ _____
- ☐ _____
- ☐ _____
- ☐ _____
- ☐ _____

Traveling by:

Reservation Information:

Places we discovered along the way

Places to stop and see along the way

Add your favorite ticket stub, postcard, photo, stamp or drawing here

LET NEW ADVENTURES
»» BEGIN →

www.mynaturebookadventures.com

Umpqua State Scenic Corridor

Region: South Coast - **Close to:** Reedsport

Scenic Corridor

Star Rating

My favorite thing about this place is...

Why I went ...

Who I went with ...

When I went ...

What I did...

What I saw...

What I learned...

An unforgettable moment...

A laughable moment...

A surprising moment...

An unforeseeable moment...

Wildlife spotted...

Snapped a selfie | Location...

Took a park sign photo? - ☐ y ☐ n

The weather was ...

My List

And so the Adventure begins

Plan Your Trip:

☐ Day Trip   ☐ Overnight Stay

Reservations required: ☐ y ☐ n

Date reservations made: _____

Refund Policy: ☐ y ☐ n Site #: _____

Confirmation #: _____

Miles to travel: _____

Time traveling: _____

Dog friendly?: ☐ y ☐ n

Activities Accomplished:

- ☐ Archery
- ☐ Biking
- ☐ Birding
- ☐ Boating
- ☐ Camping
- ☐ Caving
- ☐ Geocaching

- ☐ Fishing
- ☐ Hiking
- ☐ Horseback Riding
- ☐ Hunting
- ☐ Off-Roading
- ☐ Paddle Boarding
- ☐ Photography

- ☐ Picnicking
- ☐ Rock Climbing
- ☐ Shooting Range
- ☐ Stargazing
- ☐ Swimming
- ☐ Tennis
- ☐ Walking

- ☐ Wildlife Watching
- ☐ _____
- ☐ _____
- ☐ _____
- ☐ _____
- ☐ _____
- ☐ _____

Traveling by:

Reservation Information:

Places we discovered along the way

Places to stop and see along the way

Add your favorite ticket stub, postcard, photo, stamp or drawing here

LET NEW ADVENTURES ≫ BEGIN →

334 www.mynaturebookadventures.com

William M. Tugman State Park

Region: South Coast - **Close to:** Reedsport
State Park

Star Rating
☆☆☆☆☆

My favorite thing about this place is...
Why I went ...
Who I went with ...
When I went ...
What I did...
What I saw...

What I learned...

An unforgettable moment...

A laughable moment...

A surprising moment...

An unforeseeable moment...

Wildlife spotted...
Snapped a selfie | Location...
Took a park sign photo? - ☐ y ☐ n

The weather was ...

My List

And so the Adventure begins

www.mynaturebookadventures.com
335

Plan Your Trip:

☐ Day Trip   ☐ Overnight Stay

Reservations required: ☐ y ☐ n
Date reservations made: _____
Refund Policy: ☐ y ☐ n Site #: _____
Confirmation #: _____
Miles to travel: _____
Time traveling: _____
Dog friendly?: ☐ y ☐ n

Activities Accomplished:

- ☐ Archery
- ☐ Biking
- ☐ Birding
- ☐ Boating
- ☐ Camping
- ☐ Caving
- ☐ Geocaching
- ☐ Fishing
- ☐ Hiking
- ☐ Horseback Riding
- ☐ Hunting
- ☐ Off-Roading
- ☐ Paddle Boarding
- ☐ Photography
- ☐ Picnicking
- ☐ Rock Climbing
- ☐ Shooting Range
- ☐ Stargazing
- ☐ Swimming
- ☐ Tennis
- ☐ Walking
- ☐ Wildlife Watching
- ☐ _____
- ☐ _____
- ☐ _____
- ☐ _____
- ☐ _____
- ☐ _____

Traveling by:

☐ ☐ ☐ ☐ ☐ ☐ ☐ ☐ ☐ ☐ ☐ ☐

Reservation Information:

Places we discovered along the way

Places to stop and see along the way

Add your favorite ticket stub, postcard, photo, stamp or drawing here

LET NEW ADVENTURES ≫ BEGIN →

336 www.mynaturebookadventures.com

Winchuck State Recreation Site

Region: South Coast - **Close to:** Brookings

Recreation Site

Star Rating
☆☆☆☆☆

My favorite thing about this place is...

Why I went ...

Who I went with ...

When I went ...

What I did...

What I saw...

What I learned...

An unforgettable moment...

A laughable moment...

A surprising moment...

An unforeseeable moment...

Wildlife spotted...

Snapped a selfie | Location...

Took a park sign photo? - ☐ y ☐ n

My List

And so the Adventure begins

The weather was ...

www.mynaturebookadventures.com

337

Plan Your Trip:

☐ Day Trip ☐ Overnight Stay

Reservations required: ☐y ☐n

Date reservations made: _____

Refund Policy: ☐y ☐n Site #: _____

Confirmation #: _____

Miles to travel: _____

Time traveling: _____

Dog friendly?: ☐y ☐n

Activities Accomplished:

☐ Archery
☐ Biking
☐ Birding
☐ Boating
☐ Camping
☐ Caving
☐ Geocaching

☐ Fishing
☐ Hiking
☐ Horseback Riding
☐ Hunting
☐ Off-Roading
☐ Paddle Boarding
☐ Photography

☐ Picnicking
☐ Rock Climbing
☐ Shooting Range
☐ Stargazing
☐ Swimming
☐ Tennis
☐ Walking

☐ Wildlife Watching
☐ _____
☐ _____
☐ _____
☐ _____
☐ _____
☐ _____

Traveling by:

Reservation Information:

Places we discovered along the way

Places to stop and see along the way

Add your favorite ticket stub, postcard, photo, stamp or drawing here

LET NEW ADVENTURES BEGIN →

Booth State Scenic Corridor

Region: Southern Oregon - *Close to:* Lakeview

Scenic Corridor

Star Rating

My favorite thing about this place is…

Why I went …

Who I went with …

When I went …

What I did…

What I saw…

What I learned…

An unforgettable moment…

A laughable moment…

A surprising moment…

An unforeseeable moment…

Wildlife spotted…

Snapped a selfie | Location…

Took a park sign photo? - ☐ y ☐ n

The weather was …

My List

And so the Adventure begins

www.mynaturebookadventures.com

339

Plan Your Trip:

☐ Day Trip ☐ Overnight Stay

Reservations required: ☐ y ☐ n

Date reservations made: _____

Refund Policy: ☐ y ☐ n Site #: _____

Confirmation #: _____

Miles to travel: _____

Time traveling: _____

Dog friendly?: ☐ y ☐ n

Activities Accomplished:

- ☐ Archery
- ☐ Biking
- ☐ Birding
- ☐ Boating
- ☐ Camping
- ☐ Caving
- ☐ Geocaching
- ☐ Fishing
- ☐ Hiking
- ☐ Horseback Riding
- ☐ Hunting
- ☐ Off-Roading
- ☐ Paddle Boarding
- ☐ Photography
- ☐ Picnicking
- ☐ Rock Climbing
- ☐ Shooting Range
- ☐ Stargazing
- ☐ Swimming
- ☐ Tennis
- ☐ Walking
- ☐ Wildlife Watching
- ☐ _____
- ☐ _____
- ☐ _____
- ☐ _____
- ☐ _____
- ☐ _____

Traveling by: ☐ ☐ ☐ ☐ ☐ ☐ ☐ ☐ ☐ ☐ ☐ ☐

Reservation Information:

Places we discovered along the way

Places to stop and see along the way

Add your favorite ticket stub, postcard, photo, stamp or drawing here

LET NEW ADVENTURES ›› BEGIN →

Casey State Recreation Site

Region: Southern Oregon - **Close to:** Medford
Recreation Site

Star Rating
☆☆☆☆☆

My favorite thing about this place is... _____

Why I went ... _____

Who I went with ... _____

When I went ... _____

What I did... _____

What I saw... _____

What I learned... _____

An unforgettable moment... _____

A laughable moment... _____

A surprising moment... _____

An unforeseeable moment... _____

Wildlife spotted... _____

Snapped a selfie | Location... _____

Took a park sign photo? - ☐ y ☐ n

The weather was ...

My List
☐ _____
☐ _____
☐ _____
☐ _____
☐ _____
☐ _____
☐ _____
☐ _____
☐ _____
☐ _____
☐ _____
☐ _____
☐ _____
☐ _____
☐ _____
☐ _____

And so the Adventure begins

www.mynaturebookadventures.com

Plan Your Trip:

☐ Day Trip ☐ Overnight Stay

Reservations required: ☐ y ☐ n
Date reservations made: _____
Refund Policy: ☐ y ☐ n Site #: _____
Confirmation #: _____
Miles to travel: _____
Time traveling: _____
Dog friendly?: ☐ y ☐ n

Activities Accomplished:

☐ Archery	☐ Fishing	☐ Picnicking	☐ Wildlife Watching
☐ Biking	☐ Hiking	☐ Rock Climbing	☐ _____
☐ Birding	☐ Horseback Riding	☐ Shooting Range	☐ _____
☐ Boating	☐ Hunting	☐ Stargazing	☐ _____
☐ Camping	☐ Off-Roading	☐ Swimming	☐ _____
☐ Caving	☐ Paddle Boarding	☐ Tennis	☐ _____
☐ Geocaching	☐ Photography	☐ Walking	☐ _____

Traveling by: ☐ ☐ ☐ ☐ ☐ ☐ ☐ ☐ ☐ ☐ ☐ ☐

Reservation Information:

Places we discovered along the way

Places to stop and see along the way

Add your favorite ticket stub, postcard, photo, stamp or drawing here

LET NEW ADVENTURES
»» BEGIN →

Chandler State Wayside

Region: Southern Oregon - **Close to:** Lakeview

Wayside

Star Rating
☆☆☆☆☆

My favorite thing about this place is...

Why I went ...

Who I went with ...

When I went ...

What I did...

What I saw...

What I learned...

An unforgettable moment...

A laughable moment...

A surprising moment...

An unforeseeable moment...

Wildlife spotted...

Snapped a selfie | Location...

Took a park sign photo? - ☐ y ☐ n

The weather was ...

My List

And so the Adventure begins

www.mynaturebookadventures.com

343

Plan Your Trip:

☐ Day Trip ☐ Overnight Stay

Reservations required: ☐ y ☐ n

Date reservations made: _____

Refund Policy: ☐ y ☐ n Site #: _____

Confirmation #: _____

Miles to travel: _____

Time traveling: _____

Dog friendly?: ☐ y ☐ n

Activities Accomplished:

☐ Archery	☐ Fishing	☐ Picnicking	☐ Wildlife Watching
☐ Biking	☐ Hiking	☐ Rock Climbing	☐ _____
☐ Birding	☐ Horseback Riding	☐ Shooting Range	☐ _____
☐ Boating	☐ Hunting	☐ Stargazing	☐ _____
☐ Camping	☐ Off-Roading	☐ Swimming	☐ _____
☐ Caving	☐ Paddle Boarding	☐ Tennis	☐ _____
☐ Geocaching	☐ Photography	☐ Walking	☐ _____

Traveling by:

☐ ☐ ☐ ☐ ☐ ☐ ☐ ☐ ☐ ☐ ☐ ☐

Reservation Information:

Places we discovered along the way

Places to stop and see along the way

Add your favorite ticket stub, postcard, photo, stamp or drawing here

LET NEW ADVENTURES ≫ BEGIN →

344

www.mynaturebookadventures.com

Collier Memorial State Park

Region: Southern Oregon - ***Close to:*** Klamath Falls

State Park

Star Rating ☆☆☆☆☆

My favorite thing about this place is... _____

Why I went ... _____

Who I went with ... _____

When I went ... _____

What I did... _____

What I saw... _____

What I learned... _____

An unforgettable moment... _____

A laughable moment... _____

A surprising moment... _____

An unforeseeable moment... _____

Wildlife spotted... _____

Snapped a selfie | Location... _____

Took a park sign photo? - ☐ y ☐ n

The weather was ...

My List
☐ _____
☐ _____
☐ _____
☐ _____
☐ _____
☐ _____
☐ _____
☐ _____
☐ _____
☐ _____
☐ _____
☐ _____
☐ _____
☐ _____
☐ _____
☐ _____
☐ _____
☐ _____

And so the Adventure begins

www.mynaturebookadventures.com

Plan Your Trip:

☐ Day Trip   ☐ Overnight Stay

Reservations required: ☐ y ☐ n

Date reservations made: _____

Refund Policy: ☐ y ☐ n   Site #: _____

Confirmation #: _____

Miles to travel: _____

Time traveling: _____

Dog friendly?: ☐ y ☐ n

Activities Accomplished:

- ☐ Archery
- ☐ Biking
- ☐ Birding
- ☐ Boating
- ☐ Camping
- ☐ Caving
- ☐ Geocaching
- ☐ Fishing
- ☐ Hiking
- ☐ Horseback Riding
- ☐ Hunting
- ☐ Off-Roading
- ☐ Paddle Boarding
- ☐ Photography
- ☐ Picnicking
- ☐ Rock Climbing
- ☐ Shooting Range
- ☐ Stargazing
- ☐ Swimming
- ☐ Tennis
- ☐ Walking
- ☐ Wildlife Watching
- ☐ _____
- ☐ _____
- ☐ _____
- ☐ _____
- ☐ _____
- ☐ _____
- ☐ _____

Traveling by: ☐ ☐ ☐ ☐ ☐ ☐ ☐ ☐ ☐ ☐ ☐ ☐

Reservation Information:

Places we discovered along the way

Places to stop and see along the way

Add your favorite ticket stub, postcard, photo, stamp or drawing here

LET NEW ADVENTURES BEGIN →

Golden State Heritage Site

Region: Southern Oregon - **Close to:** Grants Pass

Heritage Site

Star Rating
☆☆☆☆☆

My favorite thing about this place is... _____

Why I went ... _____

Who I went with ... _____

When I went ... _____

What I did... _____

What I saw... _____

What I learned... _____

An unforgettable moment... _____

A laughable moment... _____

A surprising moment... _____

An unforeseeable moment... _____

Wildlife spotted... _____

Snapped a selfie | Location... _____

Took a park sign photo? - ☐ y ☐ n

The weather was ...

My List
☐ _____
☐ _____
☐ _____
☐ _____
☐ _____
☐ _____
☐ _____
☐ _____
☐ _____
☐ _____
☐ _____
☐ _____
☐ _____
☐ _____
☐ _____
☐ _____

And so the Adventure begins

Plan Your Trip:

☐ Day Trip ☐ Overnight Stay

Reservations required: ☐ y ☐ n
Date reservations made: _____
Refund Policy: ☐ y ☐ n Site #: _____
Confirmation #: _____
Miles to travel: _____
Time traveling: _____
Dog friendly?: ☐ y ☐ n

Activities Accomplished:

☐ Archery	☐ Fishing	☐ Picnicking	☐ Wildlife Watching
☐ Biking	☐ Hiking	☐ Rock Climbing	☐ _____
☐ Birding	☐ Horseback Riding	☐ Shooting Range	☐ _____
☐ Boating	☐ Hunting	☐ Stargazing	☐ _____
☐ Camping	☐ Off-Roading	☐ Swimming	☐ _____
☐ Caving	☐ Paddle Boarding	☐ Tennis	☐ _____
☐ Geocaching	☐ Photography	☐ Walking	☐ _____

Traveling by:

☐ ☐ ☐ ☐ ☐ ☐ ☐ ☐ ☐ ☐ ☐ ☐

Reservation Information:

Places we discovered along the way

Places to stop and see along the way

Add your favorite ticket stub, postcard, photo, stamp or drawing here

LET NEW ADVENTURES ≫ BEGIN →

Goose Lake State Recreation Area

Region: Southern Oregon - **Close to:** Lakeview

Recreation Area

Star Rating ☆☆☆☆☆

My favorite thing about this place is...

Why I went ...

Who I went with ...

When I went ...

What I did...

What I saw...

What I learned...

An unforgettable moment...

A laughable moment...

A surprising moment...

An unforeseeable moment...

Wildlife spotted...

Snapped a selfie | Location...

Took a park sign photo? - ☐ y ☐ n

The weather was ...

My List

And so the Adventure begins

Plan Your Trip:

☐ Day Trip ☐ Overnight Stay

Reservations required: ☐ y ☐ n

Date reservations made: _____

Refund Policy: ☐ y ☐ n Site #: _____

Confirmation #: _____

Miles to travel: _____

Time traveling: _____

Dog friendly?: ☐ y ☐ n

Activities Accomplished:

☐ Archery	☐ Fishing	☐ Picnicking	☐ Wildlife Watching
☐ Biking	☐ Hiking	☐ Rock Climbing	☐ _____
☐ Birding	☐ Horseback Riding	☐ Shooting Range	☐ _____
☐ Boating	☐ Hunting	☐ Stargazing	☐ _____
☐ Camping	☐ Off-Roading	☐ Swimming	☐ _____
☐ Caving	☐ Paddle Boarding	☐ Tennis	☐ _____
☐ Geocaching	☐ Photography	☐ Walking	☐ _____

Traveling by:
☐ ☐ ☐ ☐ ☐ ☐ ☐ ☐ ☐ ☐ ☐ ☐

Reservation Information:

Places we discovered along the way

_____
_____
_____

Places to stop and see along the way

_____
_____
_____

Add your favorite ticket stub, postcard, photo, stamp or drawing here

LET NEW ADVENTURES ≫ BEGIN →

Illinois River Forks State Park
Region: Southern Oregon - **Close to:** Cave Junction
State Park

Star Rating

My favorite thing about this place is...

Why I went ...

Who I went with ...

When I went ...

What I did...

What I saw...

What I learned...

An unforgettable moment...

A laughable moment...

A surprising moment...

An unforeseeable moment...

Wildlife spotted...

Snapped a selfie | Location...

Took a park sign photo? - ☐y ☐n

The weather was ...

My List

And so the Adventure begins

www.mynaturebookadventures.com

351

Plan Your Trip:

☐ Day Trip ☐ Overnight Stay
Reservations required: ☐ y ☐ n
Date reservations made: _____
Refund Policy: ☐ y ☐ n Site #: _____
Confirmation #: _____
Miles to travel: _____
Time traveling: _____
Dog friendly?: ☐ y ☐ n

Activities Accomplished:

- ☐ Archery
- ☐ Biking
- ☐ Birding
- ☐ Boating
- ☐ Camping
- ☐ Caving
- ☐ Geocaching
- ☐ Fishing
- ☐ Hiking
- ☐ Horseback Riding
- ☐ Hunting
- ☐ Off-Roading
- ☐ Paddle Boarding
- ☐ Photography
- ☐ Picnicking
- ☐ Rock Climbing
- ☐ Shooting Range
- ☐ Stargazing
- ☐ Swimming
- ☐ Tennis
- ☐ Walking
- ☐ Wildlife Watching
- ☐ _____
- ☐ _____
- ☐ _____
- ☐ _____
- ☐ _____
- ☐ _____

Traveling by: ☐ car ☐ truck ☐ SUV ☐ van ☐ airplane ☐ RV ☐ bicycle ☐ bus ☐ train ☐ helicopter ☐ motorcycle ☐ boat

Reservation Information:

_____

Places we discovered along the way
_____
_____
_____

Places to stop and see along the way
_____
_____
_____

Add your favorite ticket stub, postcard, photo, stamp or drawing here

LET NEW ADVENTURES
»> BEGIN →

Jackson F. Kimball State Recreation Site

Region: Southern Oregon - **Close to:** Fort Klamath
Recreation Site

Star Rating ☆☆☆☆☆

My favorite thing about this place is… _____

Why I went … _____

Who I went with … _____

When I went … _____

What I did… _____

What I saw… _____

What I learned… _____

An unforgettable moment… _____

A laughable moment… _____

A surprising moment… _____

An unforeseeable moment… _____

Wildlife spotted… _____

Snapped a selfie | Location… _____

Took a park sign photo? - ☐ y ☐ n

The weather was …

My List
☐ _____
☐ _____
☐ _____
☐ _____
☐ _____
☐ _____
☐ _____
☐ _____
☐ _____
☐ _____
☐ _____
☐ _____
☐ _____
☐ _____
☐ _____
☐ _____
☐ _____

And so the Adventure begins

Plan Your Trip:

☐ Day Trip ☐ Overnight Stay

Reservations required: ☐ y ☐ n
Date reservations made: _____
Refund Policy: ☐ y ☐ n Site #: _____
Confirmation #: _____
Miles to travel: _____
Time traveling: _____
Dog friendly?: ☐ y ☐ n

Activities Accomplished:

☐ Archery
☐ Biking
☐ Birding
☐ Boating
☐ Camping
☐ Caving
☐ Geocaching

☐ Fishing
☐ Hiking
☐ Horseback Riding
☐ Hunting
☐ Off-Roading
☐ Paddle Boarding
☐ Photography

☐ Picnicking
☐ Rock Climbing
☐ Shooting Range
☐ Stargazing
☐ Swimming
☐ Tennis
☐ Walking

☐ Wildlife Watching
☐ _____
☐ _____
☐ _____
☐ _____
☐ _____
☐ _____

Traveling by:

Reservation information:

Places we discovered along the way
_____
_____
_____

Places to stop and see along the way
_____
_____
_____

Add your favorite ticket stub, postcard, photo, stamp or drawing here

LET NEW ADVENTURES ≫ BEGIN →

354
www.mynaturebookadventures.com

Joseph H. Stewart State Recreation Area

Region: Southern Oregon - ***Close to:*** Medford

Recreation Area

Star Rating
☆☆☆☆☆

My favorite thing about this place is...

Why I went ...

Who I went with ...

When I went ...

What I did...

What I saw...

What I learned...

An unforgettable moment...

A laughable moment...

A surprising moment...

An unforeseeable moment...

Wildlife spotted...

Snapped a selfie | Location...

Took a park sign photo? - ☐ y ☐ n

The weather was ...

My List

And so the Adventure begins

www.mynaturebookadventures.com

355

Plan Your Trip:

☐ Day Trip ☐ Overnight Stay

Reservations required: ☐ y ☐ n

Date reservations made: _____

Refund Policy: ☐ y ☐ n Site #: _____

Confirmation #: _____

Miles to travel: _____

Time traveling: _____

Dog friendly?: ☐ y ☐ n

Activities Accomplished:

☐ Archery	☐ Fishing	☐ Picnicking	☐ Wildlife Watching
☐ Biking	☐ Hiking	☐ Rock Climbing	☐ _____
☐ Birding	☐ Horseback Riding	☐ Shooting Range	☐ _____
☐ Boating	☐ Hunting	☐ Stargazing	☐ _____
☐ Camping	☐ Off-Roading	☐ Swimming	☐ _____
☐ Caving	☐ Paddle Boarding	☐ Tennis	☐ _____
☐ Geocaching	☐ Photography	☐ Walking	☐ _____

Traveling by:

☐ ☐ ☐ ☐ ☐ ☐ ☐ ☐ ☐ ☐ ☐ ☐ ☐

Reservation Information:

Places we discovered along the way

Places to stop and see along the way

Add your favorite ticket stub, postcard, photo, stamp or drawing here

LET NEW ADVENTURES ≫ BEGIN →

OC&E Woods Line State Trail

Region: Southern Oregon - **Close to:** Klamath Falls

State Trail

Star Rating ☆☆☆☆☆

My favorite thing about this place is... _____

Why I went ... _____

Who I went with ... _____

When I went ... _____

What I did... _____

What I saw... _____

What I learned... _____

An unforgettable moment... _____

A laughable moment... _____

A surprising moment... _____

An unforeseeable moment... _____

Wildlife spotted... _____

Snapped a selfie | Location... _____

Took a park sign photo? - ☐ y ☐ n

The weather was ...

My List
☐ _____
☐ _____
☐ _____
☐ _____
☐ _____
☐ _____
☐ _____
☐ _____
☐ _____
☐ _____
☐ _____
☐ _____
☐ _____
☐ _____
☐ _____
☐ _____
☐ _____

And so the Adventure begins

www.mynaturebookadventures.com

Plan Your Trip:

☐ Day Trip ☐ Overnight Stay

Reservations required: ☐ y ☐ n

Date reservations made: _____

Refund Policy: ☐ y ☐ n Site #: _____

Confirmation #: _____

Miles to travel: _____

Time traveling: _____

Dog friendly?: ☐ y ☐ n

Activities Accomplished:

☐ Archery	☐ Fishing	☐ Picnicking	☐ Wildlife Watching
☐ Biking	☐ Hiking	☐ Rock Climbing	☐ _____
☐ Birding	☐ Horseback Riding	☐ Shooting Range	☐ _____
☐ Boating	☐ Hunting	☐ Stargazing	☐ _____
☐ Camping	☐ Off-Roading	☐ Swimming	☐ _____
☐ Caving	☐ Paddle Boarding	☐ Tennis	☐ _____
☐ Geocaching	☐ Photography	☐ Walking	☐ _____

Traveling by:

Reservation Information:

Places we discovered along the way

Places to stop and see along the way

Add your favorite ticket stub, postcard, photo, stamp or drawing here

LET NEW ADVENTURES ≫ BEGIN →

Prospect State Scenic Viewpoint

Region: Southern Oregon - **Close to:** Prospect
Scenic Viewpoint

Star Rating
☆☆☆☆☆

My favorite thing about this place is... _____

Why I went ... _____

Who I went with ... _____

When I went ... _____

What I did... _____

What I saw... _____

What I learned... _____

An unforgettable moment... _____

A laughable moment... _____

A surprising moment... _____

An unforeseeable moment... _____

Wildlife spotted... _____

Snapped a selfie | Location... _____

Took a park sign photo? - ☐ y ☐ n

The weather was ...

My List
☐ _____
☐ _____
☐ _____
☐ _____
☐ _____
☐ _____
☐ _____
☐ _____
☐ _____
☐ _____
☐ _____
☐ _____
☐ _____
☐ _____
☐ _____

And so the Adventure begins

Plan Your Trip:

☐ Day Trip ☐ Overnight Stay

Reservations required: ☐ y ☐ n

Date reservations made: _____

Refund Policy: ☐ y ☐ n Site #: _____

Confirmation #: _____

Miles to travel: _____

Time traveling: _____

Dog friendly?: ☐ y ☐ n

Activities Accomplished:

- ☐ Archery
- ☐ Biking
- ☐ Birding
- ☐ Boating
- ☐ Camping
- ☐ Caving
- ☐ Geocaching
- ☐ Fishing
- ☐ Hiking
- ☐ Horseback Riding
- ☐ Hunting
- ☐ Off-Roading
- ☐ Paddle Boarding
- ☐ Photography
- ☐ Picnicking
- ☐ Rock Climbing
- ☐ Shooting Range
- ☐ Stargazing
- ☐ Swimming
- ☐ Tennis
- ☐ Walking
- ☐ Wildlife Watching
- ☐ _____
- ☐ _____
- ☐ _____
- ☐ _____
- ☐ _____
- ☐ _____

Traveling by: ☐ ☐ ☐ ☐ ☐ ☐ ☐ ☐ ☐ ☐ ☐ ☐

Reservation Information:

Places we discovered along the way

Places to stop and see along the way

Add your favorite ticket stub, postcard, photo, stamp or drawing here

LET NEW ADVENTURES ≫ BEGIN →

TouVelle State Recreation Site

Region: Southern Oregon - **Close to:** Medford

Recreation Site

Star Rating
☆☆☆☆☆

My favorite thing about this place is... _____

Why I went ... _____

Who I went with ... _____

When I went ... _____

What I did... _____

What I saw... _____

What I learned... _____

An unforgettable moment... _____

A laughable moment... _____

A surprising moment... _____

An unforeseeable moment... _____

Wildlife spotted... _____

Snapped a selfie | Location... _____

Took a park sign photo? - ☐ y ☐ n

The weather was ...

My List
☐ _____
☐ _____
☐ _____
☐ _____
☐ _____
☐ _____
☐ _____
☐ _____
☐ _____
☐ _____
☐ _____
☐ _____
☐ _____
☐ _____
☐ _____
☐ _____

And so the Adventure begins

www.mynaturebookadventures.com

Plan Your Trip:

☐ Day Trip   ☐ Overnight Stay

Reservations required: ☐ y ☐ n

Date reservations made: _____

Refund Policy: ☐ y ☐ n Site #: _____

Confirmation #: _____

Miles to travel: _____

Time traveling: _____

Dog friendly?: ☐ y ☐ n

Activities Accomplished:

☐ Archery	☐ Fishing	☐ Picnicking	☐ Wildlife Watching
☐ Biking	☐ Hiking	☐ Rock Climbing	☐ _____
☐ Birding	☐ Horseback Riding	☐ Shooting Range	☐ _____
☐ Boating	☐ Hunting	☐ Stargazing	☐ _____
☐ Camping	☐ Off-Roading	☐ Swimming	☐ _____
☐ Caving	☐ Paddle Boarding	☐ Tennis	☐ _____
☐ Geocaching	☐ Photography	☐ Walking	☐ _____

Traveling by:

Reservation Information:

_____

Places we discovered along the way

_____
_____
_____

Places to stop and see along the way

_____
_____
_____

Add your favorite ticket stub, postcard, photo, stamp or drawing here

LET NEW ADVENTURES
»» BEGIN →

www.mynaturebookadventures.com

Tub Springs State Wayside

Region: Southern Oregon - **Close to:** Ashland

Wayside

Star Rating ☆☆☆☆☆

My favorite thing about this place is... _____

Why I went ... _____

Who I went with ... _____

When I went ... _____

What I did... _____

What I saw... _____

What I learned... _____

An unforgettable moment... _____

A laughable moment... _____

A surprising moment... _____

An unforeseeable moment... _____

Wildlife spotted... _____

Snapped a selfie | Location... _____

Took a park sign photo? - ☐ y ☐ n

The weather was ...

My List
☐ _____
☐ _____
☐ _____
☐ _____
☐ _____
☐ _____
☐ _____
☐ _____
☐ _____
☐ _____
☐ _____
☐ _____
☐ _____
☐ _____
☐ _____
☐ _____
☐ _____

And so the Adventure begins

Plan Your Trip:

☐ Day Trip ☐ Overnight Stay

Reservations required: ☐ y ☐ n
Date reservations made: _____
Refund Policy: ☐ y ☐ n Site #: _____
Confirmation #: _____
Miles to travel: _____
Time traveling: _____
Dog friendly?: ☐ y ☐ n

Activities Accomplished:

☐ Archery
☐ Biking
☐ Birding
☐ Boating
☐ Camping
☐ Caving
☐ Geocaching

☐ Fishing
☐ Hiking
☐ Horseback Riding
☐ Hunting
☐ Off-Roading
☐ Paddle Boarding
☐ Photography

☐ Picnicking
☐ Rock Climbing
☐ Shooting Range
☐ Stargazing
☐ Swimming
☐ Tennis
☐ Walking

☐ Wildlife Watching
☐ _____
☐ _____
☐ _____
☐ _____
☐ _____
☐ _____

Traveling by:

Reservation Information:

Places we discovered along the way

Places to stop and see along the way

Add your favorite ticket stub, postcard, photo, stamp or drawing here

LET NEW ADVENTURES ≫ BEGIN →

364

www.mynaturebookadventures.com

Valley of the Rogue State Recreation Area

Region: Southern Oregon - **Close to:** Grants Pass

Recreation Area

Star Rating

My favorite thing about this place is... _____

Why I went ... _____

Who I went with ... _____

When I went ... _____

What I did... _____

What I saw... _____

What I learned... _____

An unforgettable moment... _____

A laughable moment... _____

A surprising moment... _____

An unforeseeable moment... _____

Wildlife spotted... _____

Snapped a selfie | Location... _____

Took a park sign photo? - ☐ y ☐ n

The weather was ...

My List

And so the Adventure begins

www.mynaturebookadventures.com

365

Plan Your Trip:

☐ Day Trip ☐ Overnight Stay

Reservations required: ☐ y ☐ n

Date reservations made: _____

Refund Policy: ☐ y ☐ n   Site #: _____

Confirmation #: _____

Miles to travel: _____

Time traveling: _____

Dog friendly?: ☐ y ☐ n

Activities Accomplished:

- ☐ Archery
- ☐ Biking
- ☐ Birding
- ☐ Boating
- ☐ Camping
- ☐ Caving
- ☐ Geocaching

- ☐ Fishing
- ☐ Hiking
- ☐ Horseback Riding
- ☐ Hunting
- ☐ Off-Roading
- ☐ Paddle Boarding
- ☐ Photography

- ☐ Picnicking
- ☐ Rock Climbing
- ☐ Shooting Range
- ☐ Stargazing
- ☐ Swimming
- ☐ Tennis
- ☐ Walking

- ☐ Wildlife Watching
- ☐ _____
- ☐ _____
- ☐ _____
- ☐ _____
- ☐ _____
- ☐ _____

Traveling by:

Reservation information:

Places we discovered along the way

Places to stop and see along the way

Add your favorite ticket stub, postcard, photo, stamp or drawing here

LET NEW ADVENTURES BEGIN →

Wolf Creek Inn State Heritage Site

Region: Southern Oregon - **Close to:** Grants Pass

Heritage Site

Star Rating ☆☆☆☆☆

My favorite thing about this place is... _____

Why I went ... _____

Who I went with ... _____

When I went ... _____

What I did... _____

What I saw... _____

What I learned... _____

An unforgettable moment... _____

A laughable moment... _____

A surprising moment... _____

An unforeseeable moment... _____

Wildlife spotted... _____

Snapped a selfie | Location... _____

Took a park sign photo? - ☐ y ☐ n

The weather was ...

My List
☐ _____
☐ _____
☐ _____
☐ _____
☐ _____
☐ _____
☐ _____
☐ _____
☐ _____
☐ _____
☐ _____
☐ _____
☐ _____
☐ _____
☐ _____

And so the Adventure begins

Plan Your Trip:

☐ Day Trip ☐ Overnight Stay
Reservations required: ☐ y ☐ n
Date reservations made: _____
Refund Policy: ☐ y ☐ n Site #: _____
Confirmation #: _____
Miles to travel: _____
Time traveling: _____
Dog friendly?: ☐ y ☐ n

Activities Accomplished:

☐ Archery	☐ Fishing	☐ Picnicking	☐ Wildlife Watching
☐ Biking	☐ Hiking	☐ Rock Climbing	☐ _____
☐ Birding	☐ Horseback Riding	☐ Shooting Range	☐ _____
☐ Boating	☐ Hunting	☐ Stargazing	☐ _____
☐ Camping	☐ Off-Roading	☐ Swimming	☐ _____
☐ Caving	☐ Paddle Boarding	☐ Tennis	☐ _____
☐ Geocaching	☐ Photography	☐ Walking	☐ _____

Traveling by: ☐ ☐ ☐ ☐ ☐ ☐ ☐ ☐ ☐ ☐ ☐ ☐

Reservation Information:

Places we discovered along the way

Places to stop and see along the way

Add your favorite ticket stub, postcard, photo, stamp or drawing here

LET NEW ADVENTURES BEGIN →

Alderwood State Wayside

Region: Willamette Valley - **Close to:** Junction City

Wayside

Star Rating ☆☆☆☆☆

My favorite thing about this place is...

Why I went ...

Who I went with ...

When I went ...

What I did...

What I saw...

What I learned...

An unforgettable moment...

A laughable moment...

A surprising moment...

An unforeseeable moment...

Wildlife spotted...

Snapped a selfie | Location...

Took a park sign photo? - ☐ y ☐ n

The weather was ...

My List

And so the Adventure begins

www.mynaturebookadventures.com

Plan Your Trip:

☐ Day Trip ☐ Overnight Stay

Reservations required: ☐ y ☐ n

Date reservations made: _____

Refund Policy: ☐ y ☐ n   Site #: _____

Confirmation #: _____

Miles to travel: _____

Time traveling: _____

Dog friendly?: ☐ y ☐ n

Activities Accomplished:

- ☐ Archery
- ☐ Biking
- ☐ Birding
- ☐ Boating
- ☐ Camping
- ☐ Caving
- ☐ Geocaching
- ☐ Fishing
- ☐ Hiking
- ☐ Horseback Riding
- ☐ Hunting
- ☐ Off-Roading
- ☐ Paddle Boarding
- ☐ Photography
- ☐ Picnicking
- ☐ Rock Climbing
- ☐ Shooting Range
- ☐ Stargazing
- ☐ Swimming
- ☐ Tennis
- ☐ Walking
- ☐ Wildlife Watching
- ☐ _____
- ☐ _____
- ☐ _____
- ☐ _____
- ☐ _____
- ☐ _____

Traveling by: ☐ ☐ ☐ ☐ ☐ ☐ ☐ ☐ ☐ ☐ ☐ ☐

Reservation Information:

Places we discovered along the way

Places to stop and see along the way

Add your favorite ticket stub, postcard, photo, stamp or drawing here

LET NEW ADVENTURES BEGIN →

Cascadia State Park

Region: Willamette Valley - **Close to:** Sweet Home
State Park

Star Rating
☆☆☆☆☆

My favorite thing about this place is...
Why I went ...
Who I went with ...
When I went ...
What I did...
What I saw...

What I learned...

An unforgettable moment...

A laughable moment...

A surprising moment...

An unforeseeable moment...

Wildlife spotted...

Snapped a selfie | Location...
Took a park sign photo? - ☐ y ☐ n

The weather was ...

My List
☐ _____
☐ _____
☐ _____
☐ _____
☐ _____
☐ _____
☐ _____
☐ _____
☐ _____
☐ _____
☐ _____
☐ _____
☐ _____
☐ _____
☐ _____
☐ _____
☐ _____

And so the Adventure begins

Plan Your Trip:

☐ Day Trip   ☐ Overnight Stay

Reservations required: ☐ y ☐ n

Date reservations made: _____

Refund Policy: ☐ y ☐ n   Site #: _____

Confirmation #: _____

Miles to travel: _____

Time traveling: _____

Dog friendly?: ☐ y ☐ n

Reservation Information:

_____

Places we discovered along the way
_____
_____
_____

Places to stop and see along the way
_____
_____
_____

Activities Accomplished:

- ☐ Archery
- ☐ Biking
- ☐ Birding
- ☐ Boating
- ☐ Camping
- ☐ Caving
- ☐ Geocaching

- ☐ Fishing
- ☐ Hiking
- ☐ Horseback Riding
- ☐ Hunting
- ☐ Off-Roading
- ☐ Paddle Boarding
- ☐ Photography

- ☐ Picnicking
- ☐ Rock Climbing
- ☐ Shooting Range
- ☐ Stargazing
- ☐ Swimming
- ☐ Tennis
- ☐ Walking

- ☐ Wildlife Watching
- ☐ _____
- ☐ _____
- ☐ _____
- ☐ _____
- ☐ _____
- ☐ _____

Traveling by: 🚗 🛻 🚙 🚐 ✈️ 🚆 🚴 🚌 🚂 🚁 🏍️ 🛥️

Add your favorite ticket stub, postcard, photo, stamp or drawing here

LET NEW ADVENTURES ≫ BEGIN →

372   www.mynaturebookadventures.com

Champoeg State Heritage Area

Region: Willamette Valley - **Close to:** Newberg

Heritage Area

Star Rating
☆☆☆☆☆

My favorite thing about this place is... _____

Why I went ... _____

Who I went with ... _____

When I went ... _____

What I did... _____

What I saw... _____

What I learned... _____

An unforgettable moment... _____

A laughable moment... _____

A surprising moment... _____

An unforeseeable moment... _____

Wildlife spotted... _____

Snapped a selfie | Location... _____

Took a park sign photo? - ☐ y ☐ n

The weather was ...

My List
☐ _____
☐ _____
☐ _____
☐ _____
☐ _____
☐ _____
☐ _____
☐ _____
☐ _____
☐ _____
☐ _____
☐ _____
☐ _____
☐ _____
☐ _____
☐ _____
☐ _____
☐ _____

And so the Adventure begins

www.mynaturebookadventures.com

Plan Your Trip:

☐ Day Trip ☐ Overnight Stay

Reservations required: ☐ y ☐ n

Date reservations made: _____

Refund Policy: ☐ y ☐ n Site #: _____

Confirmation #: _____

Miles to travel: _____

Time traveling: _____

Dog friendly?: ☐ y ☐ n

Activities Accomplished:

- ☐ Archery
- ☐ Biking
- ☐ Birding
- ☐ Boating
- ☐ Camping
- ☐ Caving
- ☐ Geocaching
- ☐ Fishing
- ☐ Hiking
- ☐ Horseback Riding
- ☐ Hunting
- ☐ Off-Roading
- ☐ Paddle Boarding
- ☐ Photography
- ☐ Picnicking
- ☐ Rock Climbing
- ☐ Shooting Range
- ☐ Stargazing
- ☐ Swimming
- ☐ Tennis
- ☐ Walking
- ☐ Wildlife Watching
- ☐ _____
- ☐ _____
- ☐ _____
- ☐ _____
- ☐ _____
- ☐ _____

Traveling by:

☐ ☐ ☐ ☐ ☐ ☐ ☐ ☐ ☐ ☐ ☐ ☐

Reservation Information:

Places we discovered along the way

Places to stop and see along the way

Add your favorite ticket stub, postcard, photo, stamp or drawing here

LET NEW ADVENTURES
»› BEGIN →

Detroit Lake State Recreation Area

Region: Willamette Valley - ***Close to:*** Detroit
Recreation Area

Star Rating ☆☆☆☆☆

My favorite thing about this place is... _____

Why I went ... _____

Who I went with ... _____

When I went ... _____

What I did... _____

What I saw... _____

What I learned... _____

An unforgettable moment... _____

A laughable moment... _____

A surprising moment... _____

An unforeseeable moment... _____

Wildlife spotted... _____

Snapped a selfie | Location... _____

Took a park sign photo? - ☐ y ☐ n

The weather was ...

My List
☐ _____
☐ _____
☐ _____
☐ _____
☐ _____
☐ _____
☐ _____
☐ _____
☐ _____
☐ _____
☐ _____
☐ _____
☐ _____
☐ _____
☐ _____
☐ _____

And so the Adventure begins

Plan Your Trip:

☐ Day Trip ☐ Overnight Stay

Reservations required: ☐ y ☐ n

Date reservations made: _____

Refund Policy: ☐ y ☐ n Site #: _____

Confirmation #: _____

Miles to travel: _____

Time traveling: _____

Dog friendly?: ☐ y ☐ n

Activities Accomplished:

☐ Archery	☐ Fishing	☐ Picnicking	☐ Wildlife Watching
☐ Biking	☐ Hiking	☐ Rock Climbing	☐ _____
☐ Birding	☐ Horseback Riding	☐ Shooting Range	☐ _____
☐ Boating	☐ Hunting	☐ Stargazing	☐ _____
☐ Camping	☐ Off-Roading	☐ Swimming	☐ _____
☐ Caving	☐ Paddle Boarding	☐ Tennis	☐ _____
☐ Geocaching	☐ Photography	☐ Walking	☐ _____

Traveling by: ☐ ☐ ☐ ☐ ☐ ☐ ☐ ☐ ☐ ☐ ☐ ☐

Reservation Information:

_____

Places we discovered along the way

_____

Places to stop and see along the way

_____

Add your favorite ticket stub, postcard, photo, stamp or drawing here

LET NEW ADVENTURES ≫ BEGIN →

Dexter State Recreation Site

Region: Willamette Valley - **Close to:** Springfield
Recreation Site

Star Rating
☆☆☆☆☆

My favorite thing about this place is...

Why I went ...

Who I went with ...

When I went ...

What I did...

What I saw...

What I learned...

An unforgettable moment...

A laughable moment...

A surprising moment...

An unforeseeable moment...

Wildlife spotted...

Snapped a selfie | Location...

Took a park sign photo? - ☐ y ☐ n

The weather was ...

My List

And so the Adventure begins

Plan Your Trip:

☐ Day Trip ☐ Overnight Stay

Reservations required: ☐ y ☐ n

Date reservations made: _____

Refund Policy: ☐ y ☐ n Site #: _____

Confirmation #: _____

Miles to travel: _____

Time traveling: _____

Dog friendly?: ☐ y ☐ n

Activities Accomplished:

☐ Archery	☐ Fishing	☐ Picnicking	☐ Wildlife Watching
☐ Biking	☐ Hiking	☐ Rock Climbing	☐ _____
☐ Birding	☐ Horseback Riding	☐ Shooting Range	☐ _____
☐ Boating	☐ Hunting	☐ Stargazing	☐ _____
☐ Camping	☐ Off-Roading	☐ Swimming	☐ _____
☐ Caving	☐ Paddle Boarding	☐ Tennis	☐ _____
☐ Geocaching	☐ Photography	☐ Walking	☐ _____

Traveling by:

☐ ☐ ☐ ☐ ☐ ☐ ☐ ☐ ☐ ☐ ☐ ☐

Add your favorite ticket stub, postcard, photo, stamp or drawing here

LET NEW ADVENTURES ›› BEGIN →

Reservation Information:

Places we discovered along the way

_____
_____
_____

Places to stop and see along the way

_____
_____
_____

www.mynaturebookadventures.com

Elijah Bristow State Park

Region: Willamette Valley - **Close to:** Eugene

State Park

Star Rating
☆☆☆☆☆

My favorite thing about this place is... _____

Why I went ... _____

Who I went with ... _____

When I went ... _____

What I did... _____

What I saw... _____

What I learned... _____

An unforgettable moment... _____

A laughable moment... _____

A surprising moment... _____

An unforeseeable moment... _____

Wildlife spotted... _____

Snapped a selfie | Location... _____

Took a park sign photo? - ☐ y ☐ n

The weather was ...

My List
☐ _____
☐ _____
☐ _____
☐ _____
☐ _____
☐ _____
☐ _____
☐ _____
☐ _____
☐ _____
☐ _____
☐ _____
☐ _____
☐ _____
☐ _____
☐ _____
☐ _____

And so the Adventure begins

Plan Your Trip:

☐ Day Trip   ☐ Overnight Stay

Reservations required: ☐ y ☐ n

Date reservations made: _____

Refund Policy: ☐ y ☐ n Site #: _____

Confirmation #: _____

Miles to travel: _____

Time traveling: _____

Dog friendly?: ☐ y ☐ n

Activities Accomplished:

- ☐ Archery
- ☐ Biking
- ☐ Birding
- ☐ Boating
- ☐ Camping
- ☐ Caving
- ☐ Geocaching
- ☐ Fishing
- ☐ Hiking
- ☐ Horseback Riding
- ☐ Hunting
- ☐ Off-Roading
- ☐ Paddle Boarding
- ☐ Photography
- ☐ Picnicking
- ☐ Rock Climbing
- ☐ Shooting Range
- ☐ Stargazing
- ☐ Swimming
- ☐ Tennis
- ☐ Walking
- ☐ Wildlife Watching
- ☐ _____
- ☐ _____
- ☐ _____
- ☐ _____
- ☐ _____
- ☐ _____

Traveling by: ☐ car ☐ truck ☐ SUV ☐ van ☐ plane ☐ trolley ☐ bike ☐ bus ☐ train ☐ helicopter ☐ motorcycle ☐ boat

Reservation Information:

Places we discovered along the way

_____
_____
_____

Places to stop and see along the way

_____
_____
_____

Add your favorite ticket stub, postcard, photo, stamp or drawing here

LET NEW ADVENTURES ≫ BEGIN →

Erratic Rock State Natural Site

Region: Willamette Valley - **Close to:** Sheridan
Natural Site

Star Rating
☆☆☆☆☆

My favorite thing about this place is... _____

Why I went ... _____

Who I went with ... _____

When I went ... _____

What I did... _____

What I saw... _____

What I learned... _____

An unforgettable moment... _____

A laughable moment... _____

A surprising moment... _____

An unforeseeable moment... _____

Wildlife spotted... _____

Snapped a selfie | Location... _____

Took a park sign photo? - ☐ y ☐ n

The weather was ...

My List
☐ _____
☐ _____
☐ _____
☐ _____
☐ _____
☐ _____
☐ _____
☐ _____
☐ _____
☐ _____
☐ _____
☐ _____
☐ _____
☐ _____
☐ _____
☐ _____
☐ _____
☐ _____
☐ _____

And so the Adventure begins

Plan Your Trip:

☐ Day Trip ☐ Overnight Stay

Reservations required: ☐y ☐n

Date reservations made: _____

Refund Policy: ☐y ☐n Site #: _____

Confirmation #: _____

Miles to travel: _____

Time traveling: _____

Dog friendly?: ☐y ☐n

Activities Accomplished:

☐ Archery	☐ Fishing	☐ Picnicking	☐ Wildlife Watching
☐ Biking	☐ Hiking	☐ Rock Climbing	☐ _____
☐ Birding	☐ Horseback Riding	☐ Shooting Range	☐ _____
☐ Boating	☐ Hunting	☐ Stargazing	☐ _____
☐ Camping	☐ Off-Roading	☐ Swimming	☐ _____
☐ Caving	☐ Paddle Boarding	☐ Tennis	☐ _____
☐ Geocaching	☐ Photography	☐ Walking	☐ _____

Traveling by:

☐ ☐ ☐ ☐ ☐ ☐ ☐ ☐ ☐ ☐ ☐ ☐

Reservation Information:

Places we discovered along the way

Places to stop and see along the way

Add your favorite ticket stub, postcard, photo, stamp or drawing here

LET NEW ADVENTURES
»› BEGIN →

Fall Creek State Recreation Site

Region: Willamette Valley - **Close to:** Springfield
Recreation Site

Star Rating ☆☆☆☆☆

My favorite thing about this place is... _____
Why I went ... _____
Who I went with ... _____
When I went ... _____
What I did... _____
What I saw... _____

What I learned... _____

An unforgettable moment... _____

A laughable moment... _____

A surprising moment... _____

An unforeseeable moment... _____

Wildlife spotted... _____

Snapped a selfie | Location... _____

Took a park sign photo? - ☐ y ☐ n

The weather was ...

My List

And so the Adventure begins

www.mynaturebookadventures.com
383

Plan Your Trip:

_____

☐ Day Trip   ☐ Overnight Stay

Reservations required: ☐ y ☐ n

Date reservations made: _____

Refund Policy: ☐ y ☐ n Site #: _____

Confirmation #: _____

Miles to travel: _____

Time traveling: _____

Dog friendly?: ☐ y ☐ n

Activities Accomplished:

☐ Archery
☐ Biking
☐ Birding
☐ Boating
☐ Camping
☐ Caving
☐ Geocaching

☐ Fishing
☐ Hiking
☐ Horseback Riding
☐ Hunting
☐ Off-Roading
☐ Paddle Boarding
☐ Photography

☐ Picnicking
☐ Rock Climbing
☐ Shooting Range
☐ Stargazing
☐ Swimming
☐ Tennis
☐ Walking

☐ Wildlife Watching
☐ _____
☐ _____
☐ _____
☐ _____
☐ _____
☐ _____

Traveling by:

☐ ☐ ☐ ☐ ☐ ☐ ☐ ☐ ☐ ☐ ☐ ☐

Add your favorite ticket stub, postcard, photo, stamp or drawing here

LET NEW ADVENTURES ≫ BEGIN →

Reservation Information:

_____

Places we discovered along the way

_____

Places to stop and see along the way

_____

www.mynaturebookadventures.com

Fort Yamhill State Heritage Area

Region: Willamette Valley - **Close to:** Grand Ronde

Heritage Area

Star Rating
☆☆☆☆☆

My favorite thing about this place is... _____

Why I went ... _____

Who I went with ... _____

When I went ... _____

What I did... _____

What I saw... _____

What I learned... _____

An unforgettable moment... _____

A laughable moment... _____

A surprising moment... _____

An unforeseeable moment... _____

Wildlife spotted... _____

📷 Snapped a selfie | Location... _____

📷 Took a park sign photo? - ☐ y ☐ n

The weather was ... ☐ ☐ ☐ ☐ ☐ ☐ ☐

My List
☐ _____
☐ _____
☐ _____
☐ _____
☐ _____
☐ _____
☐ _____
☐ _____
☐ _____
☐ _____
☐ _____
☐ _____
☐ _____
☐ _____
☐ _____
☐ _____
☐ _____
☐ _____

And so the Adventure begins

www.mynaturebookadventures.com

Plan Your Trip:

☐ Day Trip   ☐ Overnight Stay

Reservations required: ☐ y ☐ n

Date reservations made: _____

Refund Policy: ☐ y ☐ n Site #: _____

Confirmation #: _____

Miles to travel: _____

Time traveling: _____

Dog friendly?: ☐ y ☐ n

Activities Accomplished:

☐ Archery	☐ Fishing	☐ Picnicking	☐ Wildlife Watching
☐ Biking	☐ Hiking	☐ Rock Climbing	☐ _____
☐ Birding	☐ Horseback Riding	☐ Shooting Range	☐ _____
☐ Boating	☐ Hunting	☐ Stargazing	☐ _____
☐ Camping	☐ Off-Roading	☐ Swimming	☐ _____
☐ Caving	☐ Paddle Boarding	☐ Tennis	☐ _____
☐ Geocaching	☐ Photography	☐ Walking	☐ _____

Traveling by:

☐ ☐ ☐ ☐ ☐ ☐ ☐ ☐ ☐ ☐ ☐ ☐

Reservation Information:

Places we discovered along the way

Places to stop and see along the way

Add your favorite ticket stub, postcard, photo, stamp or drawing here

LET NEW ADVENTURES ≫ BEGIN →

Holman State Wayside

Region: Willamette Valley - **Close to:** Salem
Wayside

Star Rating
☆☆☆☆☆

My favorite thing about this place is... _____

Why I went ... _____

Who I went with ... _____

When I went ... _____

What I did... _____

What I saw... _____

What I learned... _____

An unforgettable moment... _____

A laughable moment... _____

A surprising moment... _____

An unforeseeable moment... _____

Wildlife spotted... _____

Snapped a selfie | Location... _____

Took a park sign photo? - ☐ y ☐ n

The weather was ...

My List

And so the Adventure begins

www.mynaturebookadventures.com

387

Plan Your Trip:

☐ Day Trip   ☐ Overnight Stay

Reservations required: ☐y ☐n
Date reservations made: _____
Refund Policy: ☐y ☐n Site #: _____
Confirmation #: _____
Miles to travel: _____
Time traveling: _____
Dog friendly?: ☐y ☐n

Activities Accomplished:

- ☐ Archery
- ☐ Biking
- ☐ Birding
- ☐ Boating
- ☐ Camping
- ☐ Caving
- ☐ Geocaching
- ☐ Fishing
- ☐ Hiking
- ☐ Horseback Riding
- ☐ Hunting
- ☐ Off-Roading
- ☐ Paddle Boarding
- ☐ Photography
- ☐ Picnicking
- ☐ Rock Climbing
- ☐ Shooting Range
- ☐ Stargazing
- ☐ Swimming
- ☐ Tennis
- ☐ Walking
- ☐ Wildlife Watching
- ☐ _____
- ☐ _____
- ☐ _____
- ☐ _____
- ☐ _____
- ☐ _____

Traveling by:

Reservation Information:

Places we discovered along the way

Places to stop and see along the way

Add your favorite ticket stub, postcard, photo, stamp or drawing here

LET NEW ADVENTURES BEGIN →

www.mynaturebookadventures.com

Jasper State Recreation Site

Region: Willamette Valley - **Close to:** Springfield
Recreation Site

Star Rating
☆☆☆☆☆

My favorite thing about this place is...
Why I went ...
Who I went with ...
When I went ...
What I did...
What I saw...

What I learned...

An unforgettable moment...

A laughable moment...

A surprising moment...

An unforeseeable moment...

Wildlife spotted...

Snapped a selfie | Location...

Took a park sign photo? - ☐ y ☐ n

The weather was ...

My List

And so the Adventure begins

www.mynaturebookadventures.com

389

Plan Your Trip:

☐ Day Trip   ☐ Overnight Stay

Reservations required: ☐ y ☐ n

Date reservations made: _____

Refund Policy: ☐ y ☐ n Site #: _____

Confirmation #: _____

Miles to travel: _____

Time traveling: _____

Dog friendly?: ☐ y ☐ n

Activities Accomplished:

- ☐ Archery
- ☐ Biking
- ☐ Birding
- ☐ Boating
- ☐ Camping
- ☐ Caving
- ☐ Geocaching

- ☐ Fishing
- ☐ Hiking
- ☐ Horseback Riding
- ☐ Hunting
- ☐ Off-Roading
- ☐ Paddle Boarding
- ☐ Photography

- ☐ Picnicking
- ☐ Rock Climbing
- ☐ Shooting Range
- ☐ Stargazing
- ☐ Swimming
- ☐ Tennis
- ☐ Walking

- ☐ Wildlife Watching
- ☐ _____
- ☐ _____
- ☐ _____
- ☐ _____
- ☐ _____
- ☐ _____

Traveling by:

Reservation Information:

Places we discovered along the way

Places to stop and see along the way

Add your favorite ticket stub, postcard, photo, stamp or drawing here

LET NEW ADVENTURES ›› BEGIN →

www.mynaturebookadventures.com

Lowell State Recreation Site

Region: Willamette Valley - **Close to:** Springfield

Recreation Site

Star Rating
☆☆☆☆☆

My favorite thing about this place is... _____

Why I went ... _____

Who I went with ... _____

When I went ... _____

What I did... _____

What I saw... _____

What I learned... _____

An unforgettable moment... _____

A laughable moment... _____

A surprising moment... _____

An unforeseeable moment... _____

Wildlife spotted... _____

Snapped a selfie | Location... _____

Took a park sign photo? - ☐ y ☐ n

The weather was ...

My List
☐ _____
☐ _____
☐ _____
☐ _____
☐ _____
☐ _____
☐ _____
☐ _____
☐ _____
☐ _____
☐ _____
☐ _____
☐ _____
☐ _____
☐ _____

And so the Adventure begins

www.mynaturebookadventures.com

391

Plan Your Trip:

☐ Day Trip ☐ Overnight Stay
Reservations required: ☐ y ☐ n
Date reservations made: _____
Refund Policy: ☐ y ☐ n Site #: _____
Confirmation #: _____
Miles to travel: _____
Time traveling: _____
Dog friendly?: ☐ y ☐ n

Activities Accomplished:

- ☐ Archery
- ☐ Biking
- ☐ Birding
- ☐ Boating
- ☐ Camping
- ☐ Caving
- ☐ Geocaching
- ☐ Fishing
- ☐ Hiking
- ☐ Horseback Riding
- ☐ Hunting
- ☐ Off-Roading
- ☐ Paddle Boarding
- ☐ Photography
- ☐ Picnicking
- ☐ Rock Climbing
- ☐ Shooting Range
- ☐ Stargazing
- ☐ Swimming
- ☐ Tennis
- ☐ Walking
- ☐ Wildlife Watching
- ☐ _____
- ☐ _____
- ☐ _____
- ☐ _____
- ☐ _____
- ☐ _____

Traveling by:

Reservation Information:

Places we discovered along the way

Places to stop and see along the way

Add your favorite ticket stub, postcard, photo, stamp or drawing here

LET NEW ADVENTURES BEGIN →

www.mynaturebookadventures.com

Maples Rest Area

Region: Willamette Valley - **Close to:** Mill City

Rest Area

Star Rating
☆☆☆☆☆

My favorite thing about this place is...

Why I went ...

Who I went with ...

When I went ...

What I did...

What I saw...

What I learned...

An unforgettable moment...

A laughable moment...

A surprising moment...

An unforeseeable moment...

Wildlife spotted...

Snapped a selfie | Location...

Took a park sign photo? - ☐ y ☐ n

My List
☐ ___
☐ ___
☐ ___
☐ ___
☐ ___
☐ ___
☐ ___
☐ ___
☐ ___
☐ ___
☐ ___
☐ ___
☐ ___
☐ ___
☐ ___
☐ ___
☐ ___

And so the Adventure begins

The weather was ...

www.mynaturebookadventures.com

Plan Your Trip:

☐ Day Trip   ☐ Overnight Stay

Reservations required: ☐ y ☐ n
Date reservations made: _____
Refund Policy: ☐ y ☐ n Site #: _____
Confirmation #: _____
Miles to travel: _____
Time traveling: _____
Dog friendly?: ☐ y ☐ n

Activities Accomplished:

☐ Archery	☐ Fishing	☐ Picnicking	☐ Wildlife Watching
☐ Biking	☐ Hiking	☐ Rock Climbing	☐ _____
☐ Birding	☐ Horseback Riding	☐ Shooting Range	☐ _____
☐ Boating	☐ Hunting	☐ Stargazing	☐ _____
☐ Camping	☐ Off-Roading	☐ Swimming	☐ _____
☐ Caving	☐ Paddle Boarding	☐ Tennis	☐ _____
☐ Geocaching	☐ Photography	☐ Walking	☐ _____

Traveling by:

☐ ☐ ☐ ☐ ☐ ☐ ☐ ☐ ☐ ☐ ☐ ☐

Reservation Information:

_____

Places we discovered along the way

_____
_____
_____

Places to stop and see along the way

_____
_____
_____

Add your favorite ticket stub, postcard, photo, stamp or drawing here

LET NEW ADVENTURES ≫ BEGIN →

Maud Williamson State Recreation Site

Region: Willamette Valley - ***Close to:*** Salem
Recreation Site

Star Rating
☆☆☆☆☆

My favorite thing about this place is... _____

Why I went ... _____

Who I went with ... _____

When I went ... _____

What I did... _____

What I saw... _____

What I learned... _____

An unforgettable moment... _____

A laughable moment... _____

A surprising moment... _____

An unforeseeable moment... _____

Wildlife spotted... _____

Snapped a selfie | Location... _____

Took a park sign photo? - ☐ y ☐ n

The weather was ...

My List
☐ _____
☐ _____
☐ _____
☐ _____
☐ _____
☐ _____
☐ _____
☐ _____
☐ _____
☐ _____
☐ _____
☐ _____
☐ _____
☐ _____
☐ _____
☐ _____

And so the Adventure begins

Plan Your Trip:

☐ Day Trip ☐ Overnight Stay

Reservations required: ☐ y ☐ n

Date reservations made: _____

Refund Policy: ☐ y ☐ n Site #: _____

Confirmation #: _____

Miles to travel: _____

Time traveling: _____

Dog friendly?: ☐ y ☐ n

Activities Accomplished:

☐ Archery
☐ Biking
☐ Birding
☐ Boating
☐ Camping
☐ Caving
☐ Geocaching

☐ Fishing
☐ Hiking
☐ Horseback Riding
☐ Hunting
☐ Off-Roading
☐ Paddle Boarding
☐ Photography

☐ Picnicking
☐ Rock Climbing
☐ Shooting Range
☐ Stargazing
☐ Swimming
☐ Tennis
☐ Walking

☐ Wildlife Watching
☐ _____
☐ _____
☐ _____
☐ _____
☐ _____
☐ _____

Traveling by:

☐ ☐ ☐ ☐ ☐ ☐ ☐ ☐ ☐ ☐ ☐ ☐

Reservation Information:

Places we discovered along the way

Places to stop and see along the way

Add your favorite ticket stub, postcard, photo, stamp or drawing here

LET NEW ADVENTURES
»» BEGIN →

396 www.mynaturebookadventures.com

Mongold Day-Use Area

Region: Willamette Valley - **Close to:** Detroit
Boat launch (part of Detroit Lake SRA)

Star Rating ☆☆☆☆☆

My favorite thing about this place is... _____

Why I went ... _____

Who I went with ... _____

When I went ... _____

What I did... _____

What I saw... _____

What I learned... _____

An unforgettable moment... _____

A laughable moment... _____

A surprising moment... _____

An unforeseeable moment... _____

Wildlife spotted... _____

Snapped a selfie | Location... _____

Took a park sign photo? - ☐ y ☐ n

The weather was ...

My List
☐ _____

And so the Adventure begins

www.mynaturebookadventures.com

397

Plan Your Trip:

_____

☐ Day Trip ☐ Overnight Stay

Reservations required: ☐ y ☐ n

Date reservations made: _____

Refund Policy: ☐ y ☐ n Site #: _____

Confirmation #: _____

Miles to travel: _____

Time traveling: _____

Dog friendly?: ☐ y ☐ n

Activities Accomplished:

☐ Archery	☐ Fishing	☐ Picnicking	☐ Wildlife Watching
☐ Biking	☐ Hiking	☐ Rock Climbing	☐ _____
☐ Birding	☐ Horseback Riding	☐ Shooting Range	☐ _____
☐ Boating	☐ Hunting	☐ Stargazing	☐ _____
☐ Camping	☐ Off-Roading	☐ Swimming	☐ _____
☐ Caving	☐ Paddle Boarding	☐ Tennis	☐ _____
☐ Geocaching	☐ Photography	☐ Walking	☐ _____

Traveling by:

☐ car ☐ truck ☐ SUV ☐ van ☐ plane ☐ trolley ☐ bike ☐ bus ☐ train ☐ helicopter ☐ motorcycle ☐ boat

Reservation Information:

_____
_____

Places we discovered along the way

_____
_____
_____

Places to stop and see along the way

_____
_____
_____

Add your favorite ticket stub, postcard, photo, stamp or drawing here

LET NEW ADVENTURES ≫ BEGIN →

North Santiam State Recreation Area

Region: Willamette Valley - **Close to:** Mill City

Recreation Area

Star Rating

My favorite thing about this place is... _____

Why I went ... _____

Who I went with ... _____

When I went ... _____

What I did... _____

What I saw... _____

What I learned... _____

An unforgettable moment... _____

A laughable moment... _____

A surprising moment... _____

An unforeseeable moment... _____

Wildlife spotted... _____

Snapped a selfie | Location... _____

Took a park sign photo? - ☐ y ☐ n

The weather was ...

My List

And so the Adventure begins

Plan Your Trip:

☐ Day Trip   ☐ Overnight Stay

Reservations required: ☐ y ☐ n

Date reservations made: _____

Refund Policy: ☐ y ☐ n Site #: _____

Confirmation #: _____

Miles to travel: _____

Time traveling: _____

Dog friendly?: ☐ y ☐ n

Activities Accomplished:

☐ Archery	☐ Fishing	☐ Picnicking	☐ Wildlife Watching
☐ Biking	☐ Hiking	☐ Rock Climbing	☐ _____
☐ Birding	☐ Horseback Riding	☐ Shooting Range	☐ _____
☐ Boating	☐ Hunting	☐ Stargazing	☐ _____
☐ Camping	☐ Off-Roading	☐ Swimming	☐ _____
☐ Caving	☐ Paddle Boarding	☐ Tennis	☐ _____
☐ Geocaching	☐ Photography	☐ Walking	☐ _____

Traveling by:

Reservation Information:

Places we discovered along the way

Places to stop and see along the way

Add your favorite ticket stub, postcard, photo, stamp or drawing here

LET NEW ADVENTURES BEGIN →

Sarah Helmick State Recreation Site

Region: Willamette Valley - **Close to:** Monmouth
Recreation Site

Star Rating ☆☆☆☆☆

My favorite thing about this place is... _____
Why I went ... _____
Who I went with ... _____
When I went ... _____
What I did... _____
What I saw... _____

What I learned... _____

An unforgettable moment... _____

A laughable moment... _____

A surprising moment... _____

An unforeseeable moment... _____

Wildlife spotted... _____
Snapped a selfie | Location... _____
Took a park sign photo? - ☐ y ☐ n

The weather was ...

My List
☐ _____
☐ _____
☐ _____
☐ _____
☐ _____
☐ _____
☐ _____
☐ _____
☐ _____
☐ _____
☐ _____
☐ _____
☐ _____
☐ _____
☐ _____
☐ _____

And so the Adventure begins

Plan Your Trip:

☐ Day Trip ☐ Overnight Stay

Reservations required: ☐ y ☐ n

Date reservations made: _____

Refund Policy: ☐ y ☐ n Site #: _____

Confirmation #: _____

Miles to travel: _____

Time traveling: _____

Dog friendly?: ☐ y ☐ n

Activities Accomplished:

- ☐ Archery
- ☐ Biking
- ☐ Birding
- ☐ Boating
- ☐ Camping
- ☐ Caving
- ☐ Geocaching

- ☐ Fishing
- ☐ Hiking
- ☐ Horseback Riding
- ☐ Hunting
- ☐ Off-Roading
- ☐ Paddle Boarding
- ☐ Photography

- ☐ Picnicking
- ☐ Rock Climbing
- ☐ Shooting Range
- ☐ Stargazing
- ☐ Swimming
- ☐ Tennis
- ☐ Walking

- ☐ Wildlife Watching
- ☐ _____
- ☐ _____
- ☐ _____
- ☐ _____
- ☐ _____
- ☐ _____

Traveling by: ☐ ☐ ☐ ☐ ☐ ☐ ☐ ☐ ☐ ☐ ☐ ☐

Reservation Information:

Places we discovered along the way

Places to stop and see along the way

Add your favorite ticket stub, postcard, photo, stamp or drawing here

LET NEW ADVENTURES ≫ BEGIN →

www.mynaturebookadventures.com

Silver Falls State Park

Region: Willamette Valley - **Close to:** Silverton

State Park

Star Rating

My favorite thing about this place is... _____

Why I went ... _____

Who I went with ... _____

When I went ... _____

What I did... _____

What I saw... _____

What I learned... _____

An unforgettable moment... _____

A laughable moment... _____

A surprising moment... _____

An unforeseeable moment... _____

Wildlife spotted... _____

Snapped a selfie | Location... _____

Took a park sign photo? - ☐ y ☐ n

My List

And so the Adventure begins

The weather was ...

www.mynaturebookadventures.com

403

Plan Your Trip:

☐ Day Trip ☐ Overnight Stay

Reservations required: ☐ y ☐ n

Date reservations made: _____

Refund Policy: ☐ y ☐ n Site #: _____

Confirmation #: _____

Miles to travel: _____

Time traveling: _____

Dog friendly?: ☐ y ☐ n

Activities Accomplished:

- ☐ Archery
- ☐ Biking
- ☐ Birding
- ☐ Boating
- ☐ Camping
- ☐ Caving
- ☐ Geocaching
- ☐ Fishing
- ☐ Hiking
- ☐ Horseback Riding
- ☐ Hunting
- ☐ Off-Roading
- ☐ Paddle Boarding
- ☐ Photography
- ☐ Picnicking
- ☐ Rock Climbing
- ☐ Shooting Range
- ☐ Stargazing
- ☐ Swimming
- ☐ Tennis
- ☐ Walking
- ☐ Wildlife Watching
- ☐ _____
- ☐ _____
- ☐ _____
- ☐ _____
- ☐ _____
- ☐ _____

Traveling by: ☐ ☐ ☐ ☐ ☐ ☐ ☐ ☐ ☐ ☐ ☐ ☐

Reservation Information:

Places we discovered along the way

Places to stop and see along the way

Add your favorite ticket stub, postcard, photo, stamp or drawing here

LET NEW ADVENTURES ≫ BEGIN →

State Capitol State Park

Region: Willamette Valley - *Close to:* Salem

State Park

Star Rating
☆☆☆☆☆

My favorite thing about this place is… _____

Why I went … _____

Who I went with … _____

When I went … _____

What I did… _____

What I saw… _____

What I learned… _____

An unforgettable moment… _____

A laughable moment… _____

A surprising moment… _____

An unforeseeable moment… _____

Wildlife spotted… _____

Snapped a selfie | Location… _____

Took a park sign photo? - ☐ y ☐ n

The weather was …

My List
☐ _____
☐ _____
☐ _____
☐ _____
☐ _____
☐ _____
☐ _____
☐ _____
☐ _____
☐ _____
☐ _____
☐ _____
☐ _____
☐ _____
☐ _____
☐ _____
☐ _____

And so the Adventure begins

www.mynaturebookadventures.com

405

Plan Your Trip:

☐ Day Trip   ☐ Overnight Stay

Reservations required: ☐ y ☐ n

Date reservations made: _____

Refund Policy: ☐ y ☐ n   Site #: _____

Confirmation #: _____

Miles to travel: _____

Time traveling: _____

Dog friendly?: ☐ y ☐ n

Activities Accomplished:

☐ Archery	☐ Fishing	☐ Picnicking	☐ Wildlife Watching
☐ Biking	☐ Hiking	☐ Rock Climbing	☐ _____
☐ Birding	☐ Horseback Riding	☐ Shooting Range	☐ _____
☐ Boating	☐ Hunting	☐ Stargazing	☐ _____
☐ Camping	☐ Off-Roading	☐ Swimming	☐ _____
☐ Caving	☐ Paddle Boarding	☐ Tennis	☐ _____
☐ Geocaching	☐ Photography	☐ Walking	☐ _____

Traveling by: ☐ ☐ ☐ ☐ ☐ ☐ ☐ ☐ ☐ ☐ ☐ ☐

Reservation Information:

_____

Places we discovered along the way

_____
_____
_____

Places to stop and see along the way

_____
_____
_____

Add your favorite ticket stub, postcard, photo, stamp or drawing here

LET NEW ADVENTURES
»› BEGIN →

Thompson's Mills State Heritage Site

Region: Willamette Valley - **Close to:** Shedd
Heritage Site

Star Rating
☆☆☆☆☆

My favorite thing about this place is...

Why I went ...

Who I went with ...

When I went ...

What I did...

What I saw...

What I learned...

An unforgettable moment...

A laughable moment...

A surprising moment...

An unforeseeable moment...

Wildlife spotted...

Snapped a selfie | Location...

Took a park sign photo? - ☐ y ☐ n

The weather was ...

My List

And so the Adventure begins

www.mynaturebookadventures.com

407

Plan Your Trip:

☐ Day Trip ☐ Overnight Stay

Reservations required: ☐ y ☐ n

Date reservations made: _____

Refund Policy: ☐ y ☐ n Site #: _____

Confirmation #: _____

Miles to travel: _____

Time traveling: _____

Dog friendly?: ☐ y ☐ n

Activities Accomplished:

☐ Archery	☐ Fishing	☐ Picnicking	☐ Wildlife Watching
☐ Biking	☐ Hiking	☐ Rock Climbing	☐ _____
☐ Birding	☐ Horseback Riding	☐ Shooting Range	☐ _____
☐ Boating	☐ Hunting	☐ Stargazing	☐ _____
☐ Camping	☐ Off-Roading	☐ Swimming	☐ _____
☐ Caving	☐ Paddle Boarding	☐ Tennis	☐ _____
☐ Geocaching	☐ Photography	☐ Walking	☐ _____

Traveling by:

☐ ☐ ☐ ☐ ☐ ☐ ☐ ☐ ☐ ☐ ☐ ☐

Reservation Information:

Places we discovered along the way

Places to stop and see along the way

Add your favorite ticket stub, postcard, photo, stamp or drawing here

LET NEW ADVENTURES ›› BEGIN →

Washburne State Wayside

Region: Willamette Valley - **Close to:** Junction City

Wayside

Star Rating
☆☆☆☆☆

My favorite thing about this place is… _____

Why I went … _____

Who I went with … _____

When I went … _____

What I did… _____

What I saw… _____

What I learned… _____

An unforgettable moment… _____

A laughable moment… _____

A surprising moment… _____

An unforeseeable moment… _____

Wildlife spotted… _____

Snapped a selfie | Location… _____

Took a park sign photo? - ☐ y ☐ n

The weather was …

My List
☐ _____
☐ _____
☐ _____
☐ _____
☐ _____
☐ _____
☐ _____
☐ _____
☐ _____
☐ _____
☐ _____
☐ _____
☐ _____
☐ _____
☐ _____
☐ _____
☐ _____

And so the Adventure begins

Plan Your Trip:

☐ Day Trip   ☐ Overnight Stay

Reservations required: ☐y ☐n

Date reservations made: _____

Refund Policy: ☐y ☐n Site #: _____

Confirmation #: _____

Miles to travel: _____

Time traveling: _____

Dog friendly?: ☐y ☐n

Activities Accomplished:

- ☐ Archery
- ☐ Biking
- ☐ Birding
- ☐ Boating
- ☐ Camping
- ☐ Caving
- ☐ Geocaching
- ☐ Fishing
- ☐ Hiking
- ☐ Horseback Riding
- ☐ Hunting
- ☐ Off-Roading
- ☐ Paddle Boarding
- ☐ Photography
- ☐ Picnicking
- ☐ Rock Climbing
- ☐ Shooting Range
- ☐ Stargazing
- ☐ Swimming
- ☐ Tennis
- ☐ Walking
- ☐ Wildlife Watching
- ☐ _____
- ☐ _____
- ☐ _____
- ☐ _____
- ☐ _____
- ☐ _____

Traveling by: ☐ ☐ ☐ ☐ ☐ ☐ ☐ ☐ ☐ ☐ ☐ ☐

Reservation Information:

Places we discovered along the way

Places to stop and see along the way

Add your favorite ticket stub, postcard, photo, stamp or drawing here

LET NEW ADVENTURES ›› BEGIN →

Willamette Mission State Park

Region: Willamette Valley - **Close to:** Salem

State Park

Star Rating
☆☆☆☆☆

My favorite thing about this place is...

Why I went ...

Who I went with ...

When I went ...

What I did...

What I saw...

What I learned...

An unforgettable moment...

A laughable moment...

A surprising moment...

An unforeseeable moment...

Wildlife spotted...

Snapped a selfie | Location...

Took a park sign photo? - ☐ y ☐ n

The weather was ...

My List

And so the Adventure begins

www.mynaturebookadventures.com

Plan Your Trip:

☐ Day Trip ☐ Overnight Stay

Reservations required: ☐ y ☐ n

Date reservations made: _____

Refund Policy: ☐ y ☐ n Site #: _____

Confirmation #: _____

Miles to travel: _____

Time traveling: _____

Dog friendly?: ☐ y ☐ n

Activities Accomplished:

- ☐ Archery
- ☐ Biking
- ☐ Birding
- ☐ Boating
- ☐ Camping
- ☐ Caving
- ☐ Geocaching
- ☐ Fishing
- ☐ Hiking
- ☐ Horseback Riding
- ☐ Hunting
- ☐ Off-Roading
- ☐ Paddle Boarding
- ☐ Photography
- ☐ Picnicking
- ☐ Rock Climbing
- ☐ Shooting Range
- ☐ Stargazing
- ☐ Swimming
- ☐ Tennis
- ☐ Walking
- ☐ Wildlife Watching
- ☐ _____
- ☐ _____
- ☐ _____
- ☐ _____
- ☐ _____
- ☐ _____
- ☐ _____

Traveling by:

Reservation Information:

Places we discovered along the way

Places to stop and see along the way

Add your favorite ticket stub, postcard, photo, stamp or drawing here

LET NEW ADVENTURES BEGIN →

Pick Your Own Place

Star Rating
☆☆☆☆☆

My favorite thing about this place is... _____

Why I went ... _____

Who I went with ... _____

When I went ... _____

What I did... _____

What I saw... _____

What I learned... _____

An unforgettable moment... _____

A laughable moment... _____

A surprising moment... _____

An unforeseeable moment... _____

Wildlife spotted... _____

📷 Snapped a selfie | Location... _____

📷 Took a park sign photo? - ☐ y ☐ n

The weather was ... ☐ ☐ ☐ ☐ ☐ ☐ ☐

My List
☐ _____
☐ _____
☐ _____
☐ _____
☐ _____
☐ _____
☐ _____
☐ _____
☐ _____
☐ _____
☐ _____
☐ _____
☐ _____
☐ _____
☐ _____
☐ _____
☐ _____

And so the Adventure begins

Plan Your Trip:

☐ Day Trip ☐ Overnight Stay

Reservations required: ☐ y ☐ n

Date reservations made: _____

Refund Policy: ☐ y ☐ n Site #: _____

Confirmation #: _____

Miles to travel: _____

Time traveling: _____

Dog friendly?: ☐ y ☐ n

Activities Accomplished:

☐ Archery	☐ Fishing	☐ Picnicking	☐ Wildlife Watching
☐ Biking	☐ Hiking	☐ Rock Climbing	☐ _____
☐ Birding	☐ Horseback Riding	☐ Shooting Range	☐ _____
☐ Boating	☐ Hunting	☐ Stargazing	☐ _____
☐ Camping	☐ Off-Roading	☐ Swimming	☐ _____
☐ Caving	☐ Paddle Boarding	☐ Tennis	☐ _____
☐ Geocaching	☐ Photography	☐ Walking	☐ _____

Traveling by:

☐ ☐ ☐ ☐ ☐ ☐ ☐ ☐ ☐ ☐ ☐ ☐

Reservation Information:

_____

Places we discovered along the way

_____
_____
_____

Places to stop and see along the way

_____
_____
_____

Add your favorite ticket stub, postcard, photo, stamp or drawing here

LET NEW ADVENTURES ›› BEGIN →

414   www.mynaturebookadventures.com

Pick Your Own Place

Star Rating ☆☆☆☆☆

My favorite thing about this place is... _____

Why I went ... _____

Who I went with ... _____

When I went ... _____

What I did... _____

What I saw... _____

What I learned... _____

An unforgettable moment... _____

A laughable moment... _____

A surprising moment... _____

An unforeseeable moment... _____

Wildlife spotted... _____

Snapped a selfie | Location... _____

Took a park sign photo? - ☐ y ☐ n

The weather was ...

My List
☐ _____
☐ _____
☐ _____
☐ _____
☐ _____
☐ _____
☐ _____
☐ _____
☐ _____
☐ _____
☐ _____
☐ _____
☐ _____
☐ _____
☐ _____
☐ _____
☐ _____

And so the Adventure begins

www.mynaturebookadventures.com

Plan Your Trip:

☐ Day Trip ☐ Overnight Stay

Reservations required: ☐ y ☐ n

Date reservations made: _____

Refund Policy: ☐ y ☐ n Site #: _____

Confirmation #: _____

Miles to travel: _____

Time traveling: _____

Dog friendly?: ☐ y ☐ n

Activities Accomplished:

☐ Archery	☐ Fishing	☐ Picnicking	☐ Wildlife Watching
☐ Biking	☐ Hiking	☐ Rock Climbing	☐ _____
☐ Birding	☐ Horseback Riding	☐ Shooting Range	☐ _____
☐ Boating	☐ Hunting	☐ Stargazing	☐ _____
☐ Camping	☐ Off-Roading	☐ Swimming	☐ _____
☐ Caving	☐ Paddle Boarding	☐ Tennis	☐ _____
☐ Geocaching	☐ Photography	☐ Walking	☐ _____

Traveling by: ☐ ☐ ☐ ☐ ☐ ☐ ☐ ☐ ☐ ☐ ☐ ☐

Reservation Information:

Places we discovered along the way

Places to stop and see along the way

Add your favorite ticket stub, postcard, photo, stamp or drawing here

LET NEW ADVENTURES ≫ BEGIN →

Pick Your Own Place

Star Rating ☆☆☆☆☆

My favorite thing about this place is... _____

Why I went ... _____

Who I went with ... _____

When I went ... _____

What I did... _____

What I saw... _____

What I learned... _____

An unforgettable moment... _____

A laughable moment... _____

A surprising moment... _____

An unforeseeable moment... _____

Wildlife spotted... _____

Snapped a selfie | Location... _____

Took a park sign photo? - ☐ y ☐ n

The weather was ...

My List
☐ _____
☐ _____
☐ _____
☐ _____
☐ _____
☐ _____
☐ _____
☐ _____
☐ _____
☐ _____
☐ _____
☐ _____
☐ _____
☐ _____
☐ _____
☐ _____
☐ _____

And so the Adventure begins

www.mynaturebookadventures.com

Plan Your Trip:

☐ Day Trip   ☐ Overnight Stay

Reservations required: ☐ y ☐ n

Date reservations made: _____

Refund Policy: ☐ y ☐ n Site #: _____

Confirmation #: _____

Miles to travel: _____

Time traveling: _____

Dog friendly?: ☐ y ☐ n

Activities Accomplished:

☐ Archery
☐ Biking
☐ Birding
☐ Boating
☐ Camping
☐ Caving
☐ Geocaching

☐ Fishing
☐ Hiking
☐ Horseback Riding
☐ Hunting
☐ Off-Roading
☐ Paddle Boarding
☐ Photography

☐ Picnicking
☐ Rock Climbing
☐ Shooting Range
☐ Stargazing
☐ Swimming
☐ Tennis
☐ Walking

☐ Wildlife Watching
☐ _____
☐ _____
☐ _____
☐ _____
☐ _____
☐ _____

Traveling by:

☐ ☐ ☐ ☐ ☐ ☐ ☐ ☐ ☐ ☐ ☐ ☐

Reservation information:

Places we discovered along the way

Places to stop and see along the way

Add your favorite ticket stub, postcard, photo, stamp or drawing here

LET NEW ADVENTURES ≫ BEGIN →

www.mynaturebookadventures.com

Pick Your Own Place

Star Rating ☆☆☆☆☆

My favorite thing about this place is... _____

Why I went ... _____

Who I went with ... _____

When I went ... _____

What I did... _____

What I saw... _____

What I learned... _____

An unforgettable moment... _____

A laughable moment... _____

A surprising moment... _____

An unforeseeable moment... _____

Wildlife spotted... _____

Snapped a selfie | Location... _____

Took a park sign photo? - ☐ y ☐ n

The weather was ...

My List
☐ _____
☐ _____
☐ _____
☐ _____
☐ _____
☐ _____
☐ _____
☐ _____
☐ _____
☐ _____
☐ _____
☐ _____
☐ _____
☐ _____
☐ _____
☐ _____
☐ _____
☐ _____

And so the Adventure begins

www.mynaturebookadventures.com

Plan Your Trip:

☐ Day Trip ☐ Overnight Stay

Reservations required: ☐ y ☐ n

Date reservations made: _____

Refund Policy: ☐ y ☐ n Site #: _____

Confirmation #: _____

Miles to travel: _____

Time traveling: _____

Dog friendly?: ☐ y ☐ n

Activities Accomplished:

- ☐ Archery
- ☐ Biking
- ☐ Birding
- ☐ Boating
- ☐ Camping
- ☐ Caving
- ☐ Geocaching

- ☐ Fishing
- ☐ Hiking
- ☐ Horseback Riding
- ☐ Hunting
- ☐ Off-Roading
- ☐ Paddle Boarding
- ☐ Photography

- ☐ Picnicking
- ☐ Rock Climbing
- ☐ Shooting Range
- ☐ Stargazing
- ☐ Swimming
- ☐ Tennis
- ☐ Walking

- ☐ Wildlife Watching
- ☐ _____
- ☐ _____
- ☐ _____
- ☐ _____
- ☐ _____
- ☐ _____

Traveling by: ☐ ☐ ☐ ☐ ☐ ☐ ☐ ☐ ☐ ☐ ☐ ☐

Reservation Information:

Places we discovered along the way

Places to stop and see along the way

Add your favorite ticket stub, postcard, photo, stamp or drawing here

LET NEW ADVENTURES BEGIN →

Pick Your Own Place

Star Rating ☆☆☆☆☆

My favorite thing about this place is... _____
Why I went ... _____
Who I went with ... _____
When I went ... _____
What I did... _____
What I saw... _____

What I learned... _____

An unforgettable moment... _____

A laughable moment... _____

A surprising moment... _____

An unforeseeable moment... _____

Wildlife spotted... _____

My List
- _____
- _____
- _____
- _____
- _____
- _____
- _____
- _____
- _____
- _____
- _____
- _____
- _____
- _____
- _____
- _____

And so the Adventure begins

Snapped a selfie | Location... _____
Took a park sign photo? - ☐ y ☐ n
The weather was ...

www.mynaturebookadventures.com

Notes:

Notes:

Notes:

Notes:

ADVENTURE

Like our books?
Check out some of these favorites in our National Parks Collections

National Parks Adventure Book
www.mynaturebookadventures.com

National Historic Sites Adventure Book
www.mynaturebookadventures.com